FLEET AIR ARM
at war

FLEET AIR ARM
at war

Ray Sturtivant

LONDON
IAN ALLAN LTD

First published 1982

ISBN 0 7110 1084 6

Design by Robert C. Wilcockson

© Ray Sturtivant 1982

Published by Ian Allan Ltd, Shepperton, Surrey;
and printed by Ian Allan Printing Ltd at their
works at Coombelands in Runnymede,
England

Contents

Acknowledgements

At the height of World War 2 the Fleet Air Arm had about 200 squadrons in existence, including second line units. These were engaged in a variety of duties, but little or no account of the invaluable work performed has ever appeared in the majority of cases. This book sets out to help remedy this a little, with the assistance of a considerable number of former wartime members of that service. Of the many others who have an interest in its history, I am especially indebted to Mick Burrow for his constant support and help with research into this difficult subject, for which many of the contemporary official records no longer exist.

Enthusiastic assistance was given in searching out material and photographs by members of both the Fleet Air Arm Officers' Association and the Telegraphist Air Gunners Association. Jack Waterman, editor of the FAAOA journal *Fly Navy* and author of the privately produced book *The Fleet Air Arm History* has been of considerable help including finding Association members able to fill gaps in the material or photographic coverage. Equally helpful were Jack Bryant, editor of the journal of the TAG Association, and Ken Sims, the membership secretary of that Association, who generously allowed me to make free use of extracts from his own unpublished work on the wartime experiences of himself and other TAGs. The assistance is also acknowledged of the British Aviation Research Group, many of whose members are keenly interested in Fleet Air Arm history.

The extracts from squadron diaries appear by permission of the Controller of HM Stationery Office. These Crown Copyright documents are held in the Public Record Office under reference numbers ADM 207/1 to ADM 207/53 inclusive, and similarly held is the original of the combat report by Victor Lowden, who has generously agreed to its use, this latter being deposited under reference number ADM 199/838. Cdr Barry Nation's account of his capture of Blida aerodrome, which he has kindly allowed me to reproduce, has previously appeared in *Invasion North Africa* by the late Capt S. W. C. Pack, published in 1978 by Ian Allan Ltd.

It is not possible to list by name all those who have assisted in some way during my many years of research, but the following are among those who have helped with this particular book, many by providing personal recollections, which in some instances have corrected previously published accounts:

Bob Allerton; Peter R. Arnold; Hubert Beardshaw; R. V. (Joe) Beckett; John E. Blain; Dorothy Branwell; Malcolm J. Brown; Rear-Adm Dennis R. F. Cambell CB, DSC; Neville K. Cambell; Ken Chambers; J. R. S. Chisham; Bill Chorley; A. Glyn Clayton; Capt J. C. Cockburn DSC, RN (Rtd); Lt Cdr L. A. Cox, RN (Rtd), Curator of the FAA Museum; Cdr Robert N. Everett OBE, RN (Rtd); Ivor Faulconer; Cdr M. B. Philip Francklin DSC, RN (Rtd); Dennis Gardiner; Len Greenham; Cdr R. C. Hay DSO, DSC, RN (Rtd); Cdr H. M. A. Hayes RN (Rtd); Cdr H. Maurice Humphreys VRD, RNR; Jack Issaverdens; Capt Charles L. Keighly-Peach RN (Rtd); W. Gordon Lambert; John Lees-Jones; Capt E. D. G. Lewin CB, CBE, DSO, DSC, RN (Rtd); Ray Little; S. W. (Jan) Lock; L. Lovell, Librarian of the FAA Museum; Victor S. Lowden; Fred C. Lynn; Cdr Brian A. MacCaw DSC, RN (Rtd); Capt W. Robert MacWhirter DSC, RN (Rtd); Lt C. F. Motley (RN); Dennis Mudd; Eric Myall; Cdr S. G. Orr DSC, AFC, RN (Rtd); Ron Pankhurst; Lt-Cdr Harry Phillips RN (Rtd); Cdr J. P. D. Rafferty VRD, RNR; John D. R. Rawlings; Lt-Cdr F. C. (Ben) Rice DSM, RN (Rtd); Geoffrey R. N. Riley; Bruce R. Robertson; Douglas A. Rough; Peter Scott; Lt-Cdr Ronald A. Shilcock RN (Rtd); David J. Smith; V. H. Spencer; Gordon L. P. Steer; F. A. Swanton; Dr. A. M. (Tony) Sweeting; Allan H. Thomson; John Tipp; Eric W. Tyler; A. Rohan Wadham; Richard L. Ward; Ray Williams; C. H. Wood; Gordon Wright; R. K. L. (Dick) Yeo.

Glossary

AA	Anti-aircraft (ack-ack)		L/Air	Leading Airman
a/c	Aircraft		Lt	Lieutenant
AI	Airborne Interception radar		Lt-Cdr	Lieutenant-Commander
AMO	Air Ministry Order		MAC-ship	Merchant aircraft carrier
AP	Armour Piercing (bomb)		Mae West	Life jacket
AS	Anti-submarine		MC	Medium calibre
ASV	Air to surface vessel radar		MG	Machine gun
Badgeman	Wearer of good conduct stripes		Mid	Midshipman
Bowser	Petrol tanker		MS	Minesweeper
Buzz	Rumour (slang)		M/T	Motor transport
CAP	Combat Air Patrol		MV	Merchant Vessel
Capt	Captain		N/Air	Naval Airman
Cdr	Commander		Oleo	Undercarriage leg
C-in-C	Commander-in-Chief		Plot	Radar sighting
CPO	Chief Petty Officer		PO	Petty Officer
CVE	Escort carrier (American built)		Range	Position aircraft on carrier prior to flying off
DC	Depth charge		R-boat	Small German minesweeper
DI	Daily inspection		RNSR	RN Special Reserve
DLCO	Deck Landing Control Officer (batsman)		RP	Rocket projectile
DLT	Deck landing training		R/T	Radio telephone (VHF radio equipment)
e/a	Enemy aircraft		Sandra	Beacon guiding system
E-boat	Small offensive German motor torpedo boat		Senior Pilot	Second in command of FAA squadron
ETA	Estimated time of arrival		Sponson	Projecting gun platform
FAA	Fleet Air Arm		Stooge	Fly unobjectively (slang)
FDO	Fighter Direction Officer		Sub-Lt	Sub-Lieutenant
Flak	Enemy anti-aircraft fire		TacR	Tactical Reconnaissance
G/force	Force of gravity		2nd TAF	Second Tactical Air Force
GGS	Gyro gun sight		TAG	Telegraphist air gunner
Goofer	Spectator (slang)		TTA	Large offensive German torpedo boat
GP	General Purpose (bomb)		Tiffy	Artificer (slang)
HA	High Angle anti-aircraft gun		Tomcat	Visual identification of friendly aircraft by standing patrol over Fleet
Hoggin (or Hogwash)	Sea (slang)		TSR	Torpedo Spotter Reconnaissance
HO	Hostilities only rating		u/s	Unserviceable
Hosepipe	Spray gunfire (slang)		V/S	Visual signalling (by Aldis lamp in the case of aircraft)
Jack Dusty	Stores clerk (slang)		Window	Anti-radar metal strips
Jink	Corkscrew movement		W/T	Wireless telegraphy
Killick	Leading rating (slang)		YG Beacon	Homing beacon

Hostilities Commence

When war was declared on 3 September 1939 the Royal Navy possessed seven carriers, of which only the *Ark Royal* was of modern construction, having commissioned eight months earlier. She carried six Fleet Air Arm squadrons and was attached to the Home Fleet. *Courageous* carried only two Swordfish squadrons and was attached to the Channel Force, as was *Hermes* which had just recommissioned at Plymouth after a refit and was about to embark the Swordfish of No 814 Squadron from Worthy Down. *Argus* was in reserve at Portsmouth, whilst *Furious* was due for an extended refit, but in the circumstances this had to be postponed, and instead she undertook deck landing training in the Firth of Forth. *Glorious* was with the Mediterranean Fleet and had four squadrons aboard, whilst *Eagle* had two squadrons and was with the Far East Fleet. In addition to these, the seaplane carrier *Albatross* was on its way to Freetown, Sierra Leone, for anti-submarine patrols off the West African coast by her eight Walruses of No 710 Squadron.

The main danger was seen to be the U-boat, and accordingly *Courageous* and *Hermes* were despatched to the South-West Approaches, for anti-submarine patrols, and *Ark Royal* to the North-West Approaches. Before the lessons of inadequate preparation and tactics could be learned, the *U-39* very nearly succeeded in striking *Ark Royal* with a torpedo on 14 September. Then three days later *Courageous* was struck by three torpedoes fired by *U-29*, and sank with the

Right: HMS *Ark Royal* viewed from one of her Swordfish as it circles around her whilst she sails in the South Atlantic during the early months of the war.
Cdr R. N. Everett

loss of 17 officers and 464 ratings. Shortly before the sinking she had been landing on Swordfish of Nos 811 and 822 Squadrons returning from an attack on a U-boat.

On 26 September *Ark Royal* was lucky to survive unscathed from a bombing attack. Lt-Cdr D. R. F. Cambell RN (now Rear-Adm Dennis Cambell) was the CO of No 803 Squadron of Skuas aboard her at that time, and recollects:

'A British submarine patrolling off Heligoland had been damaged in some way, and she was having trouble getting home. The Home Fleet was therefore ordered down to the Heligoland Bight to escort her back. Ahead of the Fleet as it sailed south were two large cruisers, followed by the battleships *Nelson* and *Rodney* with the *Ark Royal* third in line, and escorting destroyers all the way around.

'It was a perfectly clear day in the North Sea, and we had not been going long when we were picked up by three Dornier Do18 flying boats, which circled around the Fleet on the horizon. Nine Skuas of Nos 800 and 803 Squadrons were immediately launched in a free take-off, each sub-flight of three aircraft attacking a different shadower. We rushed to the attack with great delight thinking this was our big chance, blazing away with the only ammunition we had, which was .303 ball. This was unlikely to do much damage unless we hit something vital, but one of our sub-flights was successful, due to one bullet going through the radiator of their Dornier, which had to come down in the water due to the loss of its coolant.'

The crew of four were picked up by the destroyer *Somali*, and the distinction of being credited with the first air success of the war went to Lt B. S. McEwen RN of No 803 Squadron, his air gunner being PO B. M. Seymour. The shadowers had meanwhile signalled the position of the Fleet, and a small force of Heinkels was promptly despatched. Rear-Adm Cambell continues: 'After returning to the ship, the Fleet started to return to Scapa Flow. At about 14.00hrs, I was having a late lunch when suddenly there was an almighty bang and the ship shook like a jelly. It appeared that one of the German bombers had dropped a bomb just ahead of the ship, but Capt Power managed to swing her clear and she had ridden through the explosion, shaken herself, but suffered no substantial damage.

'On returning, the bomber pilot, Adolphe Francke, reported that he thought he had hit the *Ark Royal* — he had obviously looked back and seen an enormous splash enveloping the ship. Reconnaissance aircraft were sent out, but these evidently came upon the two cruisers, mistook them for the two battleships, noticed there was no carrier astern of them and obviously returned and reported the *Ark Royal* had indeed been sunk. Francke was awarded the Iron Cross and promoted to Oberleutnant. That evening we heard on the radio for the first time "Lord Haw-Haw" asking "Where is the *Ark Royal*? Britons, ask your Admiralty", and this went on for weeks until she was finally proved to be going strong.'

Shortly after this, *Furious* relieved *Ark Royal* in the Home Fleet, and the latter then engaged in patrols in the South Atlantic with Force K. Similar duties were undertaken by the aircraft of *Hermes* operating mainly from Dakar and covering the West Indies, whilst *Glorious* carried out patrols in the Aden area and *Eagle* in the East Indies.

The main task of these carriers was to search for German commerce raiders. It was known that a surface raider, possibly the pocket battleship *Admiral Scheer*, was operating in the South Atlantic, where it was attacking merchant shipping. The Swordfish and Skuas of *Ark Royal* searched a large area without success, but patrols were not without incident. Two lives were lost when two Swordfish crashed on 25 November, and in another incident on 8 December. Sub-Lt P. T. Bethell RN, pilot of Skua L2880 of No 800 Squadron was killed when his

Left: Vice-Adm L. V. Wells, CB, DSO, the Vice-Adm Aircraft Carriers, who commanded Force K in the South Atlantic from the beginning of October 1939 during its search for the German raider, which turned out to be the ill-fated *Graf Spee*. *Cdr R. N. Everett*

Below: Officers relaxing on the quarter deck of HMS *Ark Royal*. The two on the right are sitting on a rubber dinghy which is inflated ready to be dropped over the side if any of the crew should fall overboard, a task which these days would probably fall to the ship's search and rescue helicopter. *Cdr R. N. Everett*

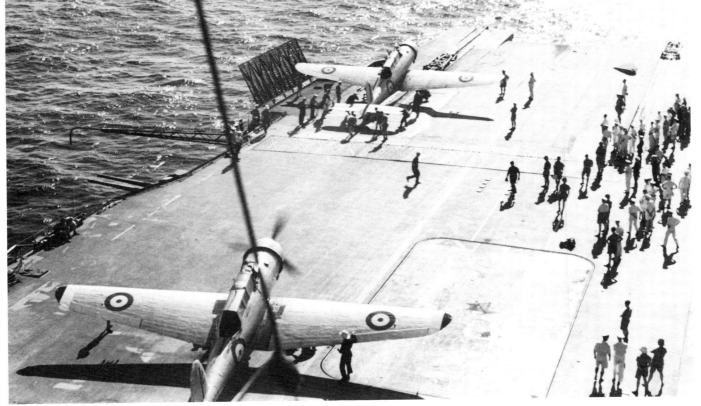

Above: Two Skuas of No 800 Squadron being prepared for catapulting from HMS *Ark Royal*, somewhere in the South Atlantic during November 1939. The machine in the foreground is L2877 'C', which later forced landed in the sea on 24 April 1940, being one of several aircraft from the ship which ran out of fuel when returning from a raid on Trondheim. Most of the crews of these aircraft were picked up, including that of L2877, piloted then by Lt C. P. Campbell-Horsfall RN who later commanded No 808 Squadron (Fulmars).
Cdr R. N. Everett

Right: A Skua of No 800 Squadron about to be catapulted from HMS *Ark Royal* during November 1939. As it stands ready on the hydraulic catapult, watched by a crowd of 'goofers', the battle-cruiser HMS *Renown* can be seen plodding along to port. The two ships were at that time the main elements in Force K, searching the South Atlantic for the German pocket battleship.
Cdr R. N. Everett

machine went over the port bow, having missed all arrester wires landing on. Happily his air gunner, PO (A) G. L. Taylor, was rescued.

The South Atlantic raider was eventually chased into the mouth of the River Plate by the cruisers *Ajax*, *Achilles* and *Exeter*, having been identified by then as the *Admiral Graf Spee*, a sister ship of the *Admiral Scheer*. She was sighted at dawn on 13 December, and immediately opened fire at a range of 10 miles. Despite this, preparations were made to fly off the catapult aircraft of No 718 Squadron, but the two *Exeter* Walruses, K8341 and K8343 were soon damaged by shell splinters and were consequently jettisoned. *Achilles* was without an aircraft at the time, its No 720 Squadron Walrus being overhauled ashore, but No 718 Squadron had two Seafox seaplanes aboard

Ajax, and one of these was fuelled and ready for take-off. The pilot, Lt E. D. G. Lewin RN and his observer, Lt R. E. N. Kearney RN climbed into the cockpit, although their machine was now whipping badly from the blast of the ship's turret, which had already damaged the second aircraft. They were catapulted off at 06.37hrs and climbed to 3,000ft, just under the cloud base into which they could climb if necessary.

Exeter fell behind after receiving hits, but the other two cruisers continued the chase with the Seafox signalling the results of their fire to both ships. At one point Lt Lewin closed in to ascertain the extent of the damage, and estimated that at least 30 hits had been made, but he then had to withdraw as he was being hit by anti-aircraft fire. Eventually he skilfully landed alongside *Ajax* despite some swell, and his Seafox was quickly re-embarked and prepared for another flight.

The *Graf Spee* now made for Montevideo, where she sought refuge, the British ships remaining about 40-50 miles away from the harbour. Lt Lewin made reconnaissance flights every day, being careful to keep outside territorial waters. At about 17.30hrs on 17 December it was learned that the enemy ship had weighed anchor, and the Seafox took-off once more, Lt Lewin positioning himself outside the mouth of the harbour. Whilst at a height of 3,000ft about two miles from the *Graf Spee*, he suddenly saw a number of spots of light around her upper deck, followed soon afterwards by a large explosion forward of her battle tower and a pillar of smoke. He quickly realised that in fact she was being scuttled, and at 20.54hrs his observer signalled '*Spee* has blown herself up'. Lt Lewin was awarded the DSC for the vital part he had played in this action, and Lt Kearney was mentioned in despatches, these being the first honours gained by the Fleet Air Arm during World War 2.

Not all the Fleet Air Arm's operational activities during this first winter of the war were undertaken from ships. Towards the end of 1939, No 804 Squadron formed at Hatston for the defence of Scapa Flow, equipped with Sea Gladiators. Commanded by Lt-Cdr J. C. Cockburn RN, they operated under the control of 13 Group, RAF Fighter Command and were very active at times, especially during the early months of 1940, as can be seen from these squadron diary entries for 10 April 1940:

'A tremendous day for HMS *Sparrowhawk*, the first and we hope by no means the last. No 804 began their fun at 16.05hrs when Yellow Section flew off to Copinsay. There were a great many plots on the board, the weather fine with layers of cloud varying in density up to about 10,000ft. About 16.40hrs Yellow 3 (PO Sabey) saw a Do17 and the Section gave chase. Sub-Lt Fell (Yellow 1) got in a burst at about 500yd as the Do17 disappeared into the cloud, but followed him in. Yellow 2 (PO Peacock) went in above the cloud as he came out so did the Do17 400yd away. Peacock got in a burst before the e/a

Below: Sunday morning parade aboard HMS *Ark Royal* somewhere in the tropics. Several RAF uniforms can be seen amongst the ship's company, a not uncommon sight aboard a carrier early in the war, since the Fleet Air Arm had only recently gained its independence from the RAF. In the left foreground is the ship's tannoy, whilst two of the hinged wireless masts can be seen extended horizontally over the side in the lowered 'flying' position. *Cdr R. N. Everett*

Bottom: Swordfish K8867 of No 812 Squadron ashore at RN Air Station Dekheila near Alexandria in April 1940. Code 'G3P' underneath the upper wing surfaces and on the fin denotes the parent carrier as being HMS *Glorious*, then operating in the Mediterranean but soon to be transferred to colder waters, with tragic results. *Cdr R. N. Everett*

dived away back into the clouds. We were later informed that Do17 was crying SOS with a leaking petrol tank and did not reach his base.

'At 16.45hrs Red (1 Carver, 2 Gibson, 3 Ogilvy) were sent to patrol between Copinsay and Burray. As soon as they got there Red 1 saw a Heinkel 111K about 10 miles east going north-east. Hot pursuit was begun and as the Section followed, Hurricanes could be seen gathering on the cloud-dodging Heinkel's tail. After a few minutes the e/a began climbing, twisting and diving. By the time Red Section arrived and got within range No 43 Squadron had done their job. The e/a's motors were idling and he dived down to 20ft over the sea. For two or three miles he held at 20ft with a dark oil streak trailing behind him on the sea and finally flopped port wing first. Six Hurricanes and Red Section flew around the wreck as 'Nifty' got the position and saw the fuselage break in half, the port wing come off and the remainder sink as three of the crew swam for it.

'At 20.45hrs the evening blitzkreig began. Red were scrambled to Copinsay and 15-20 e/as were reported approaching from the east at 20,000ft so Red patrolled at 18,000ft between Copinsay and Burray. By 21.00hrs all Sections were in the sky and the party had started, the guns putting up an ugly barrage. Yellow had the first chase (1 CO, 2 Fell, 3 Sabey) after an e/a which was in a long dive towards Kirkwall and which peppered Kirkwall and Hatston with front guns.

Right: Swordfish of No 820 Squadron disembarked from HMS *Ark Royal* to RNAS Dekheila early in April 1940. The two machines in the foreground are believed to be L9729 '4A' and P4137 '4K'. P4137 survived until 15 April 1941 when it was lost in a night torpedo attack on the Albanian port of Valona, being at that time with No 815 Squadron and operating from a base in Greece. *Cdr R. N. Everett*

Below: Two Swordfish of No 820 Squadron with wings folded, parked near the squadron tents at RNAS Dekheila in April 1940. Most of the squadron disembarked on 2 April, but only a week later they were re-embarked hastily when HMS *Ark Royal* and HMS *Glorious* were ordered to make for Gibraltar at high speed due to the German invasion of Norway. *Cdr R. N. Everett*

Yellow Section unfortunately could not keep pace though the optimistic Yellow 3 gave the e/a a burst at a very long range in order to ease his repressed fighting spirit.

'At 21.10hrs Red (1 Carver, 2 Gibson, 3 Ogilvy) dived down to 11,000ft about four miles east of Burray. Unfortunately Red 2 was left behind in the dive. As soon as they flattened out a bomber crossed 200yd ahead from port to starboard, Red 1 and Red 3 turned and pursued and loosed off nearly all ammunition, gradually closing in from 300-200yd. The enemy fired back narrowly and finally turned and dived away to the SE with smoke coming from his starboard motor.

'During this party Blue Section (1 Smeeton, 2 Stockwell, 3 Theobald) were lurking further west and came galloping up on seeing the shooting. Plenty of e/a were coming in and so Smee chose a back one and stuffed himself under its tail. He and his section rattled away with such good effect that the e/a was last seen in a flat right hand spiral going down towards South Ronaldsay. Unfortunately no wreckage was found and so the very probable result could not be confirmed. By 21.50hrs the party was over and 11 Gladiators had returned. The 12th was Blue who shortly afterwards could be heard calling "Where am I?". "Nifty" told him and led him back to Wick where he spent the night.'

It is interesting to note that in these northern climes there was sufficient light available for day fighters to be able to operate so late into the night. The 'Nifty' mentioned in this extract was the code name for the RAF Controller at Wick, who directed the squadron whilst in the air. Wick had one of the first RDF (radar) installations, run by a Sqn Ldr Ambler.

Several members of No 804 Squadron had distinguished subsequent careers. Sub-Lt Fell later became Adm Sir Michael Fell KCB,

DSO, DSC, whilst Sub-Lt Smeeton became Vice-Adm Sir Richard Smeeton KCB, MBE, and Lt Gibson became Vice-Adm Sir Donald Gibson KCB, DSC. The Commanding Officer went on to become Capt J. C. Cockburn DSC, RN, whilst Lt Carver became Capt R. H. P. Carver CBE, DSC, RN. The latter gave the squadron a seasonal present on Christmas Day 1940 by shooting down a Ju88 over Orkney, soon after midday. He was flying one of the squadron's first Martlet Is, and had the satisfaction of seeing the enemy machine execute a wheels up landing not far from Hatston.

On 9 April 1940, the Germans invaded Norway, and the so-called 'Phoney War' was over. *Ark Royal* and *Glorious* were both exercising in the warm sun and fine weather of the Mediterranean, but the next day were ordered to make for Gibraltar at best possible speed in order to rejoin the Home Fleet. Hostilities were now to commence in earnest.

The Tide Recedes

Events now began to shape in Europe from which a vastly different pattern of war was to emerge by the summer of 1940. The Fleet Air Arm was to be highly involved, and many and varied were the experiences of its members.

Gordon ('Shiner') Wright was a ships writer aboard HMS *Furious*:

'I joined her in Plymouth sound on 1 March 1940, together with another RNSR scribe; we two were the only HO ratings of the Accountant Branch then on board, and for the first few months we had to rough it plenty, the killick of the Mess seeing to it that it was us who did most of the scrubbing out and preparing for Rounds. As time went by we settled into the scheme of things, although sleeping on a bare table with only an overcoat and one blanket for warmth during the Norwegian campaign was no picnic! The mess was so overcrowded that hammock-slinging space became the perks of the badgemen — the "jack-dusties" invariably slept in their store-rooms and offices.

'Whenever we returned to the UK from our ferrying trips with Hurricane aircraft — this was from the autumn of 1940 onwards — we would return to the Tail o' the Bank at Greenock. These trips were firstly to Takoradi, on the Gold Coast, where the planes would make the overland journey to Cairo in long hops, and later to Gibraltar where we would be joined by *Ark Royal* and sail as far as we dared into the Mediterranean.

'After participating in the Norwegian campaign, during which we operated around Tromso, Trondheim, Narvik and Bergen with two squadrons of Swordfish and a flight of Gladiators, we took a cargo of £20million gold bullion across to Halifax, Nova Scotia, in June 1940. We stayed there for 10 carefree days, then returned to Liverpool, loaded to the gunnels with nylon stockings and sugar bags, just in time for a large-scale air raid. We then went up to Scapa for 16 long dreary weeks during which time the monotony of our existence was only relieved by the occasional "hit and run" raids with units of the Home Fleet on the German-occupied Norwegian coast defences. On one of these raids, on Trondheim, several of our Gladiators failed to return, having been shot up either by the shore batteries or Messerschmitts.'

Also aboard *Furious* was N/Air John Blain, a TAG serving with No 818 Squadron, which took part in what came to be known as the second Battle of Narvik. He recalls:

'We were ordered to carry out another attack to coincide with the attack by the *Warspite* and her destroyer escort. Four of No 818's aircraft were left, and with No 816 Squadron we took-off for the attack. As usual it was snowing. Visibility was often zero, and the mountain slopes crowded us in on either side. Our only maps were blow-ups of local road maps.

'Our first glimpse of the carnage to come

Below: HMS *Furious* at anchor in Scapa Flow during 1940, protected by barrage balloons. During the Norwegian campaign she embarked the Swordfish of Nos 816 and 818 Squadrons, which were actively engaged from 11 April 1940. *IWM*

Above: Tromsofjord viewed from a Swordfish of either No 816 or No 818 Squadron from HMS *Furious* on 20 April 1940, during the Norwegian campaign. *Gordon Wright*

was the burning hulk of a German destroyer on our starboard side as we flew up the fjord. Suddenly the visibility cleared and stretched out below us was the *Warspite*, all battle ensigns flying, surrounded by ensign-bedecked destroyer escorts. Her great guns were firing like a giant heavyweight throwing hard sharp punches. Coming out of Narvik Harbour were the German Maas class destroyers, line ahead with the German battle ensign flying from their mastheads.

'At that moment No 818 Squadron was flying in line astern as we dived to drop our bombs on the German destroyers. Flak began to climb lazily up to us and the period of time became very personal. Tracer bullets whipped through the tail, and I let off a few bursts at the destroyer below. Bombs were away and a few moments later, or years, my aircraft was circling on its own, awaiting the rest of the squadron. One aircraft came to join us. Hours later it seemed the remainder of No 816 rendezvoused with us and we turned to fly through a pass to rejoin the *Furious*.

'After the Battle of Narvik the movements of the *Furious* are a little hazy in my memory, but from Narvik we proceeded north to Tromso, and here the cold was intense. My next assignment was a flight back over to the Narvik area, where again we were received with a flak attack from the mountains. Suddenly, we noticed a group of German aircraft lined up on a frozen lake

below us. We dived down to examine them, and flak came up, followed by a Dornier aircraft. I fired at the Dornier, but with the diving and twisting of the Swordfish I am quite sure that my efforts were purely token. We decided to return to the carrier, and I sent a radio message giving the position of the lake.

'On reaching the carrier we found that the radio operators had not received the signal, and my maintenance was suspect. However, the remainder of the two squadrons took off to bomb the lake. They had not returned when darkness fell, so the Captain decided to light up the flight deck for the returning aircraft to land on. They had had no practice in night landings and the number of operational aircraft was now becoming critical, but they all landed safely.

'Later, when N/Air Tappin returned on board, after being rescued by a destroyer when his aircraft was lost at Narvik a few days earlier, he asked who had sent out the signal of the enemy planes on the lake. Apparently to help out the destroyer he had been keeping a W/T watch. That cleared me of faulty maintenance of my radio set!'

When *Warspite* entered Ofot Fjord on 13 April, she had aboard her two Swordfish seaplanes of No 700 Squadron. At 11.52hrs, machine L9767 was catapulted off for observation duties, piloted by PO F. C. Rice, his observer being Lt-Cdr W. L. M. Brown

Above: A scene aboard HMS *Ark Royal* during the Norwegian campaign. Fleet Air Arm squadron members are clothed in such warm apparel as they had available, including a type of Balaclava helmet. Behind them can be seen the ship's pom-pom guns, known as 'Chicago pianos', which expended a considerable amount of ammunition when the ship was under attack, but brought very little result. *Cdr R. N. Everett*

Right: A near miss on HMS *Ark Royal* during the afternoon of 1 May 1940. A stick of bombs dropped by three high level German bombers sends up a wall of water and spray, through which the ship sailed immediately afterwards. *via Cdr R. N. Everett*

RN and his telegraphist air gunner L/Air M. G. Pacey. The aircraft flew between steep cliffs as it headed towards Narvik and Bjerkvik, with low clouds roofing over the fjord. A German destroyer was sighted, but a British destroyer opened fire and she quickly withdrew. Soon afterwards the *U-64* was sighted by Ben Rice, as he flew up the narrow Herjangsfjord to Bjerkvik, anchored near the jetty. He dived down to drop two 100lb anti-submarine and two 250lb anti-submarine bombs from 300ft, and Maurice Pacey fired his guns at the conning tower. The first bomb hit the bows of the submarine and the deadly attack resulted in it sinking within half a minute, though not before it had opened fire on the Swordfish, damaging the tailplane. The remainder of this patrol was not without incident, several enemy destroyers being

sighted and torpedo attacks being reported. In an action in mid-afternoon one enemy destroyer ran aground, and the Swordfish dropped the remainder of her bombs on her, leaving the British force to finish her off. The same crew later took part in an anti-submarine and observation patrol in P4192 during a bombardment of Narvik on 24 April.

Narvik was captured by the Allies, the Royal Navy playing a prominent part by landing crack French regiments for the assault. However, by the middle of May the German offensive on the Western Front had developed, and the French High Command decided that their troops were urgently required for the defence of France. It therefore came as something of a shock to the British forces in Norway when the

evacuation of that country was decided on after control of Narvik and the north had been firmly established.

On 22 May Admiral of the Fleet Lord Cork and Orrery, the Allied Commander, whose flagship *Effingham* had been sunk after stranding on an unchartered rock, flew from his base at Harstad in the ship's Walrus, P5663 piloted by Lt P. Francklin RN, to *Devonshire* at Tromso to confer with Vice-Adm John Cunningham. On 23 May he flew to a deep fjord near Tennes to meet the King of Norway and arrange for the King's evacuation in *Devonshire*, then flying on to meet Adm Cunningham a second time. This coincided with an air attack by German aircraft, but fortunately neither *Devonshire* nor the Walrus were damaged. There was considerable German air activity at this time, and the *Devonshire's* Walrus (P5647) had shortly before been shot down, Lt R. W. Benson-Dare RN and his crew all being killed.

There were many other examples of the value of the Walrus amphibian flying boats operating in the Norwegian campaign, another being that of Lt John Ievers who located and then organised with Norwegian labour the construction of an airfield at Bardufoss.

The Allied evacuation of Norway was completed early in June, the naval forces being covered by *Ark Royal* and *Glorious*. On 7 June the RAF Hurricanes based in Norway were successfully landed on *Glorious*, and *Effingham's* Walrus which had

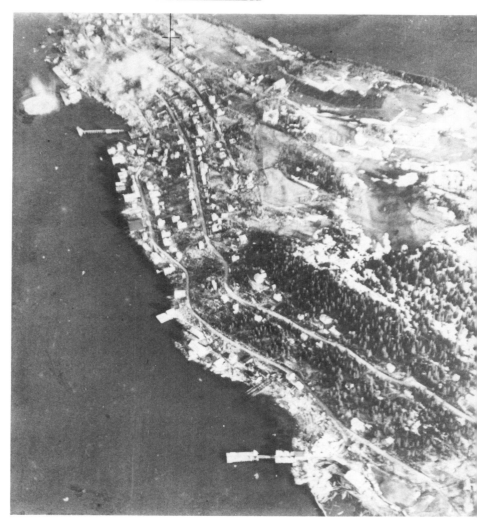

Top: Skua 'L6G' of No 806 Squadron (probably L3011) during the spring of 1940. The squadron was based at Worthy Down during the evacuation of Dunkirk, flying each day to RAF Detling to give fighter cover over the English Channel. *via P. H. T. Green*

Above: Sub-Lt S. G. Orr standing in front of a Roc of No 806 Squadron whilst they were based at RNAS Worthy Down. The squadron had four of these machines, including L3075 and L3105, but they were not a success in this role, and soon afterwards the type was relegated to target towing duties with the Fleet Requirements Units. *Cdr S. G. Orr*

also been ordered to land on *Glorious* was diverted to *Ark Royal*. *Glorious* was sunk with only a few survivors early on 8 June.

Furious was now out of the reckoning so far as Norway was concerned, being about to escort an Atlantic convoy, but on 13 June *Ark Royal* sent off 15 Skuas of Nos 800 and 803 Squadrons to attack *Scharnhorst* and other enemy warships in Trondheim Fjord, each machine being armed with a 500lb bomb. Surprise was lost owing to an attack by RAF Beauforts on Vaernes airfield being made early, and only seven aircraft returned after the squadrons had flown through heavy flak to reach their target. Amongst those who failed to return were Lt E. G. D. Finch-Noyes RN and Lt-Cdr J. Cason RN the respective squadron commanders.

This was the last involvement of carriers in the Norwegian campaign, but six Swordfish

of Nos 821 and 823 Squadrons took-off from Hatston on 21 June for a torpedo attack on *Scharnhorst*, which was then on her way back to Kiel for repairs. No hits were made, perhaps not surprisingly since the crews were short of torpedo practice, and as they turned away after the attack, two of them were shot down.

Shore based squadrons of the Fleet Air Arm were also active over France during the evacuation of Dunkirk, operating mainly from Detling. Sub-Lt (A) S. G. Orr RNVR (now Cdr S. G. Orr DSC, AFC, RN, Rtd), who was then serving with No 806 Squadron, recalls:

'In April 1940 the squadron was working up at West Freugh (in Scotland), and consisted of eight Skuas and three Rocs. I joined it with five other RNVR (A) officers on

22 April, to replace six RN officers who had been sent to Hatston for Nos 800 and 803 Squadrons for Norwegian operations. On 1 May the squadron moved to Hatston and took part in bombing raids on Bergen, then on 26 May we flew to Worthy Down in order to give fighter cover for the evacuation of Dunkirk.

'We flew to Detling each day, and operated all day from there. As a point of interest, the very first flight of three Skuas, flown by Lt Campbell-Horsfall and Mids Marshall and Hogg, were all shot down by RAF Spitfires, who mistook them for German aircraft. All three managed to ditch their aircraft, and were picked up by boats returning from Dunkirk. The only injury suffered was that Campbell-Horsfall had a finger shot off. Mid Marshall was later killed in the Stuka dive bombing attack on HMS *Illustrious* in January 1941, and Mid Hogg was killed in an aircraft accident later in the war.

'After Dunkirk we remained at Worthy Down to reform with Mk 1 Fulmars, prior to embarking in HMS *Illustrious* for a work up period, and then sailed for the Mediterranean in August.'

The last troops to be pulled out left the Dunkirk beaches on 4 June, but Swordfish and Skuas continued to operate against enemy targets. The last FAA unit to leave Detling was No 801 Squadron, whose Skuas and Rocs were withdrawn to Hatston on 23 June.

Below and bottom: Two views of a partially burnt out Swordfish near Ekne, on the south side of Trondheimfjord. The crew of three had forced landed at about 04.00hrs on 22 September 1940, probably after becoming lost. They removed one of the instruments, which they dropped in a nearby fjord, and set fire to their aircraft. After surrendering to the Sheriff of Skogn, they were handed over to the Germans, who took away the remains of their aircraft.
G. Vodahl via Vinje/B. Olsen

In Memory

Below: Lt Walker instructs a group of Telegraphist Air Gunners of No 12 Course (RNVR) at RNAS Worthy Down, otherwise HMS *Kestrel*, early in the war. The Lewis gun is fitted with a Norman Vane foresight, but both gun and sight quickly became outdated. The two TAGs in the centre of the picture have been identified as Freddy Brock and Jim Taylor. The anonymous author of the account in this chapter was trained on a following course.
via TAG Association

Each spring, on a Sunday morning, the Telegraphist Air Gunners Association holds a memorial service by the FAA Memorial on the seafront at Lee-on-Solent. One of those who attend has written this poignant account as a tribute to the memory of just one of his many comrades remembered at that time, not all of whom gave their lives in the air, and few so close to the setting of the service.

On 16 August 1940 the writer of this account, then a young TAG, was posted to RN Air Station Lee-on-Solent, better known in naval parlance as HMS *Daedalus*. At that time the Luftwaffe were carrying out a series of attacks on aerodromes in southern England, and *Daedalus* had the misfortune to be amongst its targets that day, this being the only raid made during the war on a RN Barracks.

'One hour after arriving at *Daedalus* on this fateful August day, the sirens sounded. We took little notice, until we suddenly heard an unfamiliar aircraft engine noise which I was to hear many times in years to come — the dreaded "Stuka". It became obvious that we were their target, and we made a mad dash

for shelter, the one I entered being half underground near the sick bay. The first aircraft commenced his maddening dive and the bombs came rushing and screaming down. Our only defence, one Bofors gun which stopped firing very quickly, and a twin Lewis which had a stoppage and therefore also remained silent. So 15 Stukas did as they pleased, with no opposition. The noise cannot be described. One bomb which seemed destined for our shelter exploded outside the sick bay; the shelter rocked, blast and dust came rushing in and made us choke — we were very frightened.

'When the noise quietened a little, I ventured outside. The sight appalled me, flames and smoke were belching from the hangars, and men were apparently struggling to pull aircraft out of one of them. Outside the sick bay was a huge crater, the Surgeon Commander's car destroyed and sitting on top of a tree. I became too curious and was spotted by the Chief Sick Berth "Tiffy". "You", he yelled, "any more ratings in that shelter?" I said "Yes". "Right, I want you and five others to collect dead bodies." I froze on the spot — I had never seen a dead person. I went back to the shelter, but nobody wanted to know — they told me what the Chief could do. Before I could turn round, Chief was behind me and pointing — "Nearest five out. Follow me," he said. "There is a body by the main gate opposite the Guardroom." A thoughtful person had laid the victim on the biggest and heaviest door they could find, rested his head on a sandbag and covered him with a blanket. We gathered round, but had difficulty getting our fingers under the door. Whilst I struggled at one corner, a sick berth "tiffy" pulled back the blanket, and the mutilation I witnessed nearly made me sick. I said "Why the bloody hell did you do that?" he replied "You've got to get used to it some time". Somehow we lifted the door, and Chief wanted it taken to a garage near the sick bay. Halfway there it got so heavy we asked Chief for a rest — he moaned but agreed. We eventually arrived at the garage, and laid the body next to another one.

"Right", said Chief, "the next one is by the Control Tower". Dragging our feet behind him we followed , only to find a huge crater and a lot of blood splattered against a wall, but no body. Chief seemed very upset about this, and whilst he was making enquiries all six of us sidled off slowly.

'Twelve or fifteen people were killed that day, including a milkman on the seafront on the perimeter of the aerodrome, a Royal Marine and a TAG. Chaos reigned for several hours — everyone appeared dazed and wandered about aimlessly. The damage was extensive — a large chunk of concrete had fallen through the roof of the dining room, but somehow the cooks managed to rustle up a meal. A strong rumour went around that Jerry had begun his invasion, and we were then issued with "pikes", a long pole with a bayonet fixed on the end. This made us jittery, but slowly order was restored and life continued.

'A few days later, six pallbearers were selected from the particular branch of the service to which the deceased belonged, and I and five other TAGs were detailed. We were instructed to report to the Guardroom at 10.00hrs only to be told that due to air raids the funeral had been delayed one hour. Three hours later we were on our way to a cemetery, I believe at Cosham.

'On arrival we were ushered into a Chapel. Inside was racking with several coffins. We were given a White Ensign, and our coffin was pointed out to us. Nobody told us what to do, but somehow we muddled through. We draped the ensign over the coffin, and the attendant told the two tallest to take the head. We withdrew the coffin from the rack, but then realised that the other four TAGs were shorter, and consequently the coffin did not touch the shoulders of the middle two. Once outside the Chapel we slid the coffin on to an open sided wagon, and the cortege then set off at a slow march down the long gravel drive; several other ratings were being buried at the same time. Half way along the drive the air raid siren sounded. I thought "This is all we want". The wagon finally stopped and we withdrew the coffin on to our shoulders. It was heavy and the edge dug into my collarbone becoming unbearable, and there was also a strong odour emitting from it. On arriving at the graveside, we somehow managed to lower the coffin to the ground, and across the three webbings. Three TAGs went to the other side of the grave. The women were in deep mourning and crying — it was a very sad sight.

'We lowered the coffin into the grave, but no sooner had it touched the bottom than the ack-ack opened up with a vengeance. Several Me109s were overhead firing at barrage balloons, and a couple of these were hit and fell to the ground in flames. I remember the Padre saying "Ashes to ashes and dust to dust", when I heard some shrapnel whistling down. The women were crying and one started to scream, they were very frightened. As I stood there bareheaded, I said a little prayer — "Please God, don't let anything touch us." The Padre's voice drowned by gunfire mumbled on, volleys were fired and bugles sounded as I stood there numbed with fright. I thought, "Poor sod, I wonder what he looked like? How old was he? Suddenly snatched from this world, and had one helluva struggle to reach his final resting place".'

Mediterranean 1940

As the war in Europe drew to its tragic close, the scene shifted to the Mediterranean when Italy entered the war on 6 June 1940. She had no carriers, but her large fleet, which included six battleships, immediately posed a threat to our forces in that arena.

By this time *Eagle* was back in the Mediterranean, having returned two weeks earlier following a refit at Singapore, with the 18 Swordfish of Nos 813 and 824 Squadrons still aboard her. She sailed from Alexandria with the British Fleet on 8 July, and by the

next day her aircraft were in action. Also aboard was a small flight of Sea Gladiators, which were to successfully defend the Fleet against a series of attacks, achieving seven successes and damaging three other enemy aircraft before being withdrawn the following March.

Amongst the TAGs serving in *Eagle* was L/Air Eric Tyler, who had joined No 813 Squadron in April 1939, and was to remain with that unit until November 1941. He has clear recollections of that time:

Below right: Sea Gladiator '6H' of No 813 Squadron's Fighter Flight landing on HMS *Eagle*, its twin hooks being clearly visible beneath the fuselage. Aircraft of this flight were responsible for shooting down several enemy aircraft soon after being added to the strength of the squadron in June 1940. Machines flown included N5513, N5517 and N5567, the flight being withdrawn in March 1941.
Capt C. L. Keighly-Peach, via FAA Museum

Below: HMS *Ark Royal* during an attack on Force H by 40 Savoia SM79 bombers on 9 July 1940. The enemy aircraft attacked in three waves to drop over 100 bombs, one being shot down by the ship's Skuas who also damaged two others. The ship's anti-aircraft guns can be seen firing as bombs fall astern of her. *IWM*

'Compared to other, more modern carriers, the old *Eagle* had practically none of the amenities which made life bearable. She had been laid down during World War 1, and by the time we went to war in 1939 she was nearly a quarter of a century old, and she looked it. Her ventilation system was, to say the least, very antiquated, and in the tropics life below decks was something of a trial.

'Until May 1940 we were engaged in searching the Indian Ocean for enemy raiders, and convoying the first Australian and New Zealand forces to Aden. We had none of the refinements which I later found in the *Illustrious*. The main one being that we had no rest room for aircrews, no briefing room — nothing. The long tedious patrols over thousands of miles of empty ocean became very wearing. We had two squadrons on board, Nos 813 and 824, and one squadron was on stand-by for strike every day, whilst the other carried out all the patrols from dawn to dusk. On the following day the duties were reversed.

'It annoyed me intensely when after

landing after a long four-hour dawn patrol we air gunners had nowhere to smoke. We usually landed well after the ship's company had breakfasted and turned to with the usual ship's routine. The first thing we looked for was a well earned smoke then breakfast. We used the sponson just outside our mess as a smoking area, but as sure as hell the Chief Bosun's mate would be after us with his usual "Put those cigarettes out, it ain't stand easy yet". He conveniently ignored the fact that we had been in the air since probably about five o'clock that morning. The usual routine then was to go down to the galley to collect breakfast, to be greeted with "What the 'ell time do you think this is to come for your breakfast". But we got by despite the difficulties, and all in all the aircrews were a happy bunch of lads.

'Then we had rats — rats as big as cats. Wherever you went there were rats. In the hangar, in the messdecks, in the pipes and electrical channelling which went through the messes, in lockers, under lockers, everywhere. On one occasion the Commander declared war on them, promising a canteen supper to the mess which turned in the largest number of rat's tails. Well over a hundred were killed in a week, but still they persisted. They even managed to get into the bin in the galley which provided hot cocoa for the night watchman. Result, a few very queasy stomachs.

'*Eagle* joined the Fleet at Alexandria on 28 May 1940, and immediately settled in to join in intensive training with the Fleet. After the French Fleet in Alexandria had been immobilised we were free to go after the Italians, and on 7 July we did just that, steaming off blithely to the north towards what was later to be called "Bomb Alley", to the south-west of Crete.

'Nothing much happened until the forenoon of the 8th, when an enemy snooper dropped a small stick of bombs near the Fleet and scooted hastily away. They were only very small bombs and we laughed them off, but by the end of the day we were laughing on the other side of our faces. From about 14.00hrs to 20.00hrs on that day we had five very heavy attacks on the Fleet. The *Eagle* being the only carrier, naturally became the main target for the bombers, and an estimated 200 large bombs were rained down and burst up and down along each side of the ship. The evil crump of scores of high explosive bombs, the crashes of our own high angle AA guns firing at the enemy formations, the stink of cordite and bomb fumes, and the general noise and apparent pandemonium in a ship under heavy air attack is well nigh indescribable.

'During all this hectic activity, we managed to send off aircraft on anti-

Below: A 'cucumber' mine ready for loading underneath a Swordfish of No 818 Squadron aboard HMS *Ark Royal.* This was similar in shape to a torpedo, but had a fixed head and when dropped it fluttered down into the water.
Cdr R. N. Everett

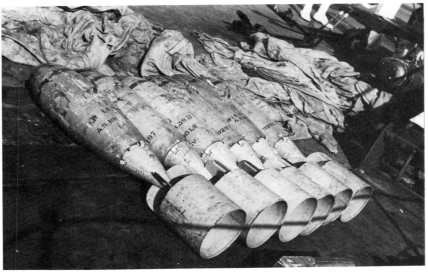

Bottom: 100lb anti-submarine bombs on the deck of HMS *Ark Royal,* awaiting loading on to Swordfish aircraft. This type of bomb was very effective if a stick could be dropped so as to straddle a U-boat, as the detonation would be sufficient to crack open its hull.
Cdr R. N. Everett

submarine patrol. I was in the air during one of these attacks, and an awesome sight it was to see the *Eagle* almost enveloped by dirty black water thrown up by the bomb bursts, but she sailed serenely on through it all without any apparent damage.

'Next morning the Fleet sailed westwards towards the position where it was rumoured some Italian naval units were at sea. My log shows that I was on a dawn search near Taranto in P4159 "E4G", with Lt Leatham as pilot and Lt Grieve as observer, but after nearly 2hr we had sighted nothing and returned to the ship. Later that day the enemy Fleet was definitely sighted, and both fleets were steaming on a closing course. No 824 Squadron was armed with torpedoes

and flown off to attack. My aircraft, with the same pilot and observer were sent off for action-observation duties at about 12.30hrs.

'To me this was a very exciting prospect — to see the approach of two battlefleets and the consequent engagement of capital ships in what might have been the decisive naval action of the war in the Mediterranean, but it was not to be. From our perch at about 10,000ft we watched and reported the movements of the Italian units, course alterations, smoke screens, and watched with great delight as the three British battlers opened up with their 15in main armament. This spectacle lasted about 3hr and then the Italian Fleet lifted up their skirts and ran for safety.

Below: HMS *Furious* and HMS *Argus* in choppy seas in the Mediterranean. *IWM*

Bottom: A dockside scene at Gibraltar in July 1940 around the time of the Oran operation, viewed from HMS *Ark Royal*. The furthest of the two Swordfish is 'T4W' of No 767 Squadron, which had just been evacuated from Hyeres near Toulon, after spending the previous six months giving pupils deck landing training on HMS *Argus*. On the fall of France, the squadron aircraft were dispersed to Gibraltar and Malta. *Cdr R. N. Everett*

'On 11 July, to the south, we picked up a convoy from Gibraltar, but the enemy air forces found us again, and we were subjected to another 15 attacks. Hundreds of bombs were rained down on the fleet and the convoy without any result. Commander Keighly-Peach and Lt Keith managed to shoot down three enemy bombers during these attacks — so we had started to hit back.

'12 July was comparatively quiet with only one air attack, but on the following day I was up on the dawn patrol. We climbed above the clouds just as it was getting light in the east, and there smack in front of us was a beautiful fat Cant reconnaissance seaplane. My pilot turned towards the enemy as if to attack, but I had immediately radioed the necessary signal to the ship, and it seemed within seconds that one of our Gladiators was on the spot and the Cant was on her way down trailing a great plume of black smoke. After another 10 air attacks on the 13th, without any effect, we arrived back in Alexandria. We had been well and truly blooded.'

Two months later the Mediterranean Fleet, now joined by the recently commissioned *Illustrious*, left Alexandria to carry out an attack on the island of Rhodes. Eric Tyler continues his story:
'At 04.00hrs on 4 September, Nos 813 and 824 Squadrons took off from the dark windy flight deck of *Eagle*, and after forming up, we winged our way towards Rhodes. We were to attack Maritza on the west coast, whilst the *Illustrious* squadrons were to attack Calato on the east coast in a sychronised attack.

'It was an eerie feeling flying up the east coast of the island, which we could faintly make out in the distance. To reach our target we had to turn westwards and fly over the hills, then dive down and make our attack. Unfortunately, something had gone wrong with the timing arrangements, and we had a grandstand view of the attack by *Illustrious* aircraft before we reached the position where we were to turn westwards. Naturally the attack on Calato had awakened the island, and the ground defences at Maritza and their fighter defences were waiting to welcome us with open arms.

'I think it must have been with some trepidation that our pilots dived down into the heavy fire from the aerodrome at Maritza, but down they went into the attack. Bomb bursts patterned the target, and we hastily pulled out and flew out to sea. My aircraft carried containers of incendiary bombs, and I noticed when we had got clear that we still had our load on the bomb racks. That was one time when I really should have kept my big mouth shut, but I informed the observer and the pilot immediately decided to go back to the target and drop his load.

'This move was probably better for our health, as the remainder of the squadron had encountered a swarm of Fiat CR42 fighters

Left: A Walrus amphibian landing on HMS *Illustrious* in the Mediterranean during 1940 to return a Swordfish pilot who had been picked up by a British destroyer after ditching. Parked on the left is a visiting Sea Gladiator of No 813 Squadron from HMS *Eagle*. *Cdr S. G. Orr*

Left: Sports on the flight deck of HMS *Ark Royal* whilst the ship was alongside at Gibraltar when in Force H. RAF uniforms are still in evidence at this period. In the rear can be seen 'Jumbo' the ship's mobile crane, which was used for removing crashed aircraft from the flight deck. *Cdr R. N. Everett*

Below: Viewed from an escorting ship, a Swordfish is seen in the air near HMS *Ark Royal* as another is about to take-off. Further Swordfish are ranged aft. *IWM*

which promptly shot down four of them ("E4C", "E4H", "E4K" and "E4M"). By the time we got out, I think the enemy fighters had run out of fuel and were landing.

'The TAGs' mess was sadly thinned out after this attack, as we had already lost one aircraft a couple of days before, and that made us five TAGs short and five aircraft to replace from the dwindling reserves in the Middle East. We were later informed that of the 12 officers and men lost, four were dead and the remainder captured. The crew of the aircraft lost on patrol were also rescued and made prisoner of war.'

Both carriers then returned with the Fleet to Alexandria, where their squadrons disembarked to spend most of the next month at Dekheila. On 11 October, *Illustrious* sailed again from Alexandria, for a raid by her aircraft on the Dodecanese islands, two nights later. No 819 Squadron diary summarises this:

'Nine aircraft of the squadron with six of No 815 Squadron were ranged on deck at 21.00hrs when the ship was in position roughly 10 miles north of Cape Zuano in Crete. We took off at 22.00hrs, and the sub-

flights were formed up and on their way by 22.20hrs. It was a bright moonlight night with a certain amount of cloud about at 3,000ft and upwards, and we had climbed to 7,000ft by the time we reached our target — the barracks, hangars, naval buildings and ships in the harbour, anything of military importance in Portolargo Bay in the island of Leros in the Dodecanese.

'The leading sub-flight dropped their bombs on the SP Hangars and started rather large fires, so guiding the remaining sub-flights on to their targets. A great deal of erratic AA fire of different coloured lights, flaming onions and a certain amount of high explosive was experienced, but 10 tons of bombs in all were dropped in a very short space of time, and within 2min of the start all the aircraft were making their getaway. No aircraft was hit and no personnel injured, and all our aircraft returned safely at 01.00hrs.

'The squadron was led by the CO, Lt-Cdr Hale, with Lt Carline as Senior Observer, and from subsequent reports it appears that the operation was a great success. This was only the second time in history that aircraft have operated from an aircraft carrier entirely by night, the other occasion being

Left: Fulmars, possibly of No 808 Squadron, fly on patrol over a convoy. No 808 Squadron formed at RNAS Worthy Down on 1 July 1940 with 12 Fulmar Is, embarking in HMS *Ark Royal* on 21 October 1940 from RNAS Donibristle. It operated from the carrier in the Mediterranean with great success until the ship was sunk on 14 November 1941, and the squadron then ceased to exist. *IWM*

Below: Swordfish P4123 '2F' of No 810 Squadron bombed up and ranged aboard HMS *Ark Royal.* This machine was subsequently lost when it failed to return from a bombing attack on warships in Dakar harbour on 24 September 1940. *Cdr R. N. Everett*

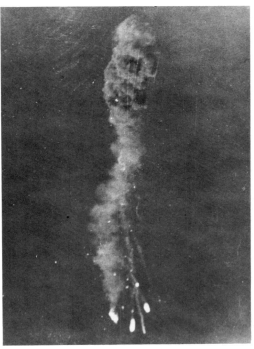

Above: Walrus L2228 about to be catapulted from HMS *Sheffield.* The inscription *Spotter of Spartivento* painted on the nose indicates that this machine had been used for spotting duties during the bombardment of Genoa and Spartivento on 25 November 1940. Piloted by Sub-Lt J. W. R. Groves, it was shot at by Italian destroyers, but evaded damage by taking refuge in the smoke screen laid by the enemy ships. *IWM*

Right: A shot taken by Sub-Lt S. G. Orr with a hand held camera through the windscreen of Fulmar N1881 of No 806 Squadron from HMS *Illustrious* on 9 November 1940, immediately after he had shot down a Cant Z506 seaplane in the Central Mediterranean. The blazing wreckage is seen falling into the sea. *Cdr S. G. Orr*

our raid on Benghazi, and it was worthy of note that on our return to the ship the aircraft landed on in as quick a time as any other carrier had ever done by day. The following day we were continually attacked by Italian aircraft, presumably they were a little annoyed by our raid of the night before but we were not affected, and we eventually arrived back in Alexandria in the early hours of 16 October.'

Less than a month later, the Italian Fleet was subjected to a catastrophic attack whilst in harbour at Taranto. Flying from *Illustrious,* Swordfish from her own squadrons, augmented by five from *Eagle* which was then temporarily out of action, carried out the now famous attack on the night of 11 November. The Italian Fleet withdrew to Naples after this attack, and the heavy losses it had suffered left Adm Cunningham with greatly increased freedom to operate, allowing him to release two of his battleships to other spheres.

Desert Operations

The desert and coastal operations of the land-based squadrons of the Fleet Air Arm have tended to be overshadowed by the activities of their carrier-based counterparts. They carried out a variety of tasks, often at night, in extremely difficult circumstances, and made a valuable contribution to the eventual victory in the Western Desert. Sleeping in tents in primitive conditions, the men worked alongside the RAF who assisted them in maintaining their aircraft and equipment. Aircraft maintenance was a major problem, and inspections were usually made in the evening, the metal of the aircraft being too hot to touch during the day, and aircraft requiring major attention had to be sent back to Dekheila.

Eric Tyler was amongst a small detachment of No 813 Squadron sent ashore towards the end of 1940:

'On 3 December, amid rumours of a big push in the desert against the Italians, three of our Swordfish were sent up to Fuka, loaded with torpedoes. The ground crews and we TAGs followed with our kit and supplies in an old Vickers Valentia (JR9764), probably the most ancient aircraft used in the war. She staggered into the air with her load of men and equipment, and, at a steady 65-70kts lurched her way to our destination.

'We had to make our own camp in the desert some way from the RAF camp, and we soon had a tent erected and camouflaged with oil and sand. A trench dug on one side of the tent provided us with a bomb shelter, which doubled up as a cooking area. Water was supplied daily by a tanker — one gallon per man per day. Surprisingly, there was always a thin layer of ice on the water when we came to wash in the morning, although we were not much bothered about washing or shaving. We were also pestered with swarms of sand fleas, but being away from the ship's routine was a great tonic, and we loved it — dirt, lice and all.

'Wavell's offensive began on 7 December, and we took part in this by bombing the retreating Italian columns along the coast road at Sollum, bombing attacks on Bardia, and dropping flares for night bombardments by HMS *Terror* and a couple of gunboats on the supply depot at Maktila.

Left: A Fulmar of No 806 Squadron being refuelled by Italian prisoners of war whilst temporarily shore based in the Western Desert. *Cdr S. G. Orr*

Above: A rating poses in front of the tail of a Fulmar of No 806 Squadron whose rudder carries the squadron's unofficial emblem. *H. Phillips*

Above right: Members of No 815 Squadron (mainly TAGs) posed on the tailplane of a wrecked Heinkel He 111 which they had discovered on the airstrip at Mersa Matruh around Christmas 1942. From left to right they are Jock Cameron, Flt-Sgt Burlington-Green, Pete Bromley, Ron Goble, PO Air Mech (unidentified), Jan Holden and Ken Sims. *K. Sims/TAG Association*

'I well remember the second of these flare dropping operations. We took along a Hurricane pilot who wanted a ride. I was in the habit of using a steel helmet to sit on when being shot at by ground defences, and when the Hurricane pilot saw this he patronisingly told me there was nothing to be scared about. He soon changed his tune when we were over the target stooging about for a couple of hours, and couldn't get away fast enough when our job was completed. When we landed back at Fuka, he as good as told me that he had never been so scared in his life, and he envied me my steel helmet.

'But all good things come to an end, and my first desert period ended just before Christmas, when I had to go back to Alexandria.'

A number of other FAA squadrons of various types later served in the Western Desert, amongst them No 815 Squadron, which saw active service in Crete and later served in Cyprus, before returning to Dekheila in December 1941. Amongst the TAGs on the squadron was L/Air Ken Sims, who recalls:
'On arrival back at Dekheila, our mixed aircraft squadron was promptly split into two flights. The Swordfish flight with the radar would carry out anti-submarine patrols along the North African coast, whilst the Albacores would carry out night attacks on the enemy land forces. I was to join the Albacore flight, and travelled up by road to the airstrip at Ma'aten Bagush satellite. It was my first experience of the Western Desert proper.

'The 8th Army advance was moving so fast that we wasted no time, and prepared at once to join in. We were to fly largely at night and act as target finders. The slow manoeuvrable machine with good downward visibility — the observer had a bubble side window — made an excellent spotting platform. Furthermore it was navigated across the desert as though over the sea, and could often arrive with fair accuracy at map reference points that had no ground landmarks. Extra flare racks were fitted, the usual load being 16 flares with 4×250lb bombs. If thought desirable, we could take an entire flare load of 32. The bombs were fitted with a protruding metal rod on the nose some 2ft long, the idea of this being to make them explode at surface level to give maximum blast effect rather than bury themselves in the sand. Unfortunately, to fit this rod meant excluding the nose safety pin, and this could make the bomb live on the plane, so it was desirable not to bump the stick with any force.

'When Rommel pulled his surprise move of turning east instead of retreating west when outflanked, he provided us with the first target, at Sidi Rezegh. Both squadrons were briefed to maintain a continuous illumination of the target area throughout the night. The aircraft took off at 20min intervals. We were quite early in the queue and had no difficulty finding them. The spot was a short flying run in from the easily identifiable port of Bardia. The target, tank divisions with their supporting MT, were camped over an extended area. Our first parachute flare showed them up alright, though I was doubtful that it would do so. In the bright light of a parachute flare, every ground object throws a deep black shadow, and one gets an effect similar to pictures of the moon. This part of the desert is in fact rock to a large extent, and certainly had wide areas of rocky outcrop and loose boulders, so I peered down for tell-tale tank tracks and regularities in the shadows which would identify trucks rather than rocks.

'We were at about 5,000ft to give the flares the best survival times, and from that height the terrain was difficult to assess. We scouted around and dropped two more flares singly, looking for the extent and maximum concentration of vehicles. While I was still in doubt as to what I was seeing, my pilot and observer had decided that this was it, and proceeded to drop three or four flares in a group. Almost immediately the ground beneath erupted in clouds of dust as RAF Wellington bombers released strings of bombs across the site. We picked a cluster of shapes on the edge of the spot, dropped another flare over them, and dived to add our bombs on this particular target. As we pulled

out at about 2,000ft, I could see more clearly that these were indeed vehicles, though many had netting draped across breaking up their outlines.

'Our bombs fell well across the group, but as they were scattered and there was subsequently so much dust cloud it was impossible to say how effective they had been. It had not occurred to me to have the rear gun ready for strafing, and we pulled away before I swung it up. There was seemingly no ground fire, though this may have been misleading as one does not always see small arms fire if it has no tracer. Certainly they had no heavy guns, but we had been warned that a certain amount of medium stuff might be around. But they tended not to use anything which would disclose position, unless it was obvious they had been seen, so the danger was that one might come too low, not sensing trouble, and suddenly run smack into a deluge of small arms fire. We didn't learn about all this until later.

'That night seemed very quiet, though I did spot one stream of tracer lick up, pre-

Left: The remains of an Albacore discovered by No 815 Squadron members at Castel Benito airfield, Tripoli. The machine bore Italian markings, but it is not known whether the Italians ever succeeded in getting it airborne.
K. Sims/TAG Association

Right: Swordfish V4308 'C' loaded with a torpedo for coastal operation. This machine later served with No 775 Squadron, the Fleet Requirements Unit at Dekheila, near Alexandria.
FAA Museum

sumably towards a Wellington. We regained some height and dropped our remaining flares singly, holding position to give the follow-on Albacore something to aim at as he was due to arrive. Then we turned for home, and looking back watched a continuation of the illuminating process.'

The detachment returned to Dekheila for a time, later in the month, but on 19 January 1942, Ken returned to Bagush:

'It was back to anti-submarine patrols in Swordfish, but this time with a difference. We now had our secret weapon — radar — and hoped we could find them at night. The North African coast was always busy with our shipping. First there had been the support of Tobruk under siege, now they could run supplies in there for the Army. There were also the runs across to relieve Malta. They would hug the coast under our own air cover as far as possible, and then run the gauntlet across as best they may. The shipping was a mixed bag with a lot of small stuff, but enough to attract a row of enemy submarines, and we still had some warships that made prime targets.

'We immediately embarked on continuous nightly searches. With radar these were not patrols, but searches, and we were the hunters now. With a squadron effort of about eight aircraft, we were able to keep at least one, and usually two, aircraft searching the coastal area out to 50 miles from Alexandria to Tobruk. With overlapping times, we might have as many as four aircraft in the air.

'On the sixth night, 25 January, we struck lucky about 30 miles off Mersa Matruh, hardly an hour after take-off in V4436 "M". We had the first stint that night with a start at 18.00hrs, and being winter this was a dusk patrol, with still a hint of daylight, though very hazy and dull. The observer got an echo at eight miles, so we homed in on it and the pilot got a sighting during the final mile. The half light was fortunate and very helpful, as without the need to illuminate we did not disclose our presence. It all happened very

quickly, and I saw little of the approach as I was hastily reeling in the trailing aerial. When I got up and looked forward we were right down on the water and coming over the top of the submarine, which was lying stationary and seemed caught completely unawares. Our two depth charges dropped in a perfect straddle along the sub's line, and therefore each was close in. I was watching so closely for these that I didn't even notice whether anyone was in the conning tower, but as we pulled up and turned, the sea erupted with the sub lifted up on top of a volcano of water. When it subsided she was still visible, but now on end, with her bows sticking out of the water like a buoy. We circled round watching, but it was getting darker and becoming difficult to pick out detail. There was no sign of oil, but I was convinced we had made a kill. After some minutes the bows slowly disappeared below the surface. It was only later that I began to have doubts that she was anything other than sunk. The observer gave me a position, and I signalled back on our attack, then follow-up aircraft searched the area, but without finding anything further. We landed feeling very elated. After so many hours of patrols, it was something even to find a submarine.'

Even more positive results were achieved later in the year when:

'On the night of 2 June we took off in V4707 "L" from landing ground LG121, to which we had flown the evening before. We combed the bay from Sidi Barrani across to Bardia, and up to the point where the coast turns for Tobruk. We had been searching for more than 2hr when we got a contact at seven miles off the coast, nearly in the middle of the bay. It was a good positive signal, and again we were lucky with the light. Though about 03.00hrs, there was some moon above low patchy cloud which produced a diffused glow allowing visibility of about half a mile. Thus as we approached at no more than 100ft, a submarine was clearly recognisable.

'Again we apparently achieved complete

Above: Albacore N4319 '4F' of No 826 Squadron bombed up ready for desert operations. On 15 December 1941 this machine failed to return from a night attack by the squadron on Derna aerodrome. *FAA Museum*

Above right: Martlets of No 805 Squadron in the Western Desert around 1941. The large machine in the background appears to be a French transport, possibly an escaped Farman. *P. C. S. Chilton via J. D. R. Rawlings*

Centre right: A Sea Gladiator and a Buffalo of No 805 Squadron pictured around May or June 1941 at Dekheila when for a short time the squadron operated a mixture of aircraft which also included Fulmars and three borrowed RAF Hurricanes. In July they re-equipped with Martlets and became part of the RN Fighter Squadron, which also included Nos 803 and 806 Squadrons. This composite squadron also flew Hurricanes. *P. C. S. Chilton via J. D. R. Rawlings*

Above: Martlets of No 805 Squadron being serviced in the Western Desert during 1942. HK842 in the foreground was taken on strength in the Middle East, and consequently its serial number does not fall into a recognised production batch. Behind the other machine can be seen part of the tail of a Lockheed communications aircraft of an RAF squadron.
P. C. S. Chilton via
J. D. R. Rawlings

'As we orbited at 800ft, the observer indicated that I should use my gun, and I spent half an hour pooping off sporadic bursts without getting a shot back in return. Then in due course I heard the relief Swordfish contacting base. I could tell he was close, so gave him a call and repeated the position, then we sheared off so that he would not be misled by a radar contact on us. We could still see the sub, and considered he would too. He did not want illumination that might light him as well. We were too far off to actually see his attack, but we saw the sub spring to life as a stream of tracer went skyward, and he had a hot run in. We had to leave at this point as we were running short of fuel, and landed after 4½hr which was just about our limit without a long range tank.

'The second aircraft could not report any progress from his attack, so there was some feverish phoning from LG121 to Bagush to get a machine armed with bombs, but the situation was resolved by RAF Blenheims who bombed and claimed a sinking. We were credited with a third of the kill, subsequently confirmed as *U-652*.'

For a time, naval fighter aircraft operated in the desert, the RN Fighter Squadron being set up in July 1941 to afford fighter protection to convoys sailing between Mersa Matruh and Tobruk. This unit was a temporary amalgamation of Nos 803, 805 and 806 Squadrons, whose pilots had just returned from operations in Crete and Syria, and desert headquarters were set up at Sidi Haneish South, near Mersa Matruh, on 17 August. They operated under RAF control, their aircraft consisting of eight Martlet Is of No 805 Squadron, still bearing their US Navy airframe numbers prior to issue of British serials, plus 16 borrowed RAF Hurricanes to be operated by the other two squadrons. In addition to convoy protection, they carried out attacks on German land forces and helped escort RAF bombing raids, until reverting to individual squadron status in February 1942.

surprise, and there was no response from the target. As we crossed and dropped our depth charges, I fired two Very lights. It was a good straddle, and the two charges seemed to explode simultaneously, lifting the sub on the peak of the explosion. This time, however, as the water subsided the submarine retained an even keel and just sat there. By now we had come to expect such results from the attack reports of other crews. It seemed that though we could give them a good shaking, charges under a surfaced sub were not sufficiently devastating. Yet even though they must have known we would call up more effort, they made no attempt to submerge, so perhaps there was enough damage to prevent them doing so. A sighting signal had gone off even as we ran in, and this was now followed by a position and a situation report.

Top: Armourers at work on a desert landing ground. Behind them is an Albacore of No 826 Squadron. *FAA Museum*

Above: Albacore '4H' of No 826 Squadron on a coastal patrol armed with a torpedo. This machine appears to be N4378, which failed to return from a squadron strike on 6 March 1943 whilst based at Blida. *FAA Museum*

Left: Swordfish W5970 of No 815 Squadron, which had the misfortune to tip on its nose in soft ground when the pilot landed to pick up the crew of an Albacore which had forced landed on 6 April 1942. It was repaired, and continued to fly with the squadron until at least March 1943, later being relegated to Fleet Requirements Unit duties with No 775 Squadron at Dekheila. *FAA Museum*

Mediterranean and Malta 1941-1942

The Mediterranean theatre continued to be the scene of considerable and varied activity, as the tide of war ebbed and flowed.

Towards the end of December 1940, *Argus* arrived at Gibraltar, carrying aboard her 821X Flight on its way to Malta. At Gibraltar this half-unit was then transferred to *Ark Royal* for onward passage. Ken Sims, then with this unit, recalls:

'We put to sea and turned east. The bustle aboard such a carrier is quite an eye-opener, and we enjoyed goofing at the deck landings. We went off ourselves, and then landed in comfort on the wide deck with ample wind speed and lots of arrester wires. I never knew where next to find my aircraft. With two hangars, the lifts were doubly tiered, but only one traversed the deck, so an aircraft from the lower hangar would lift one deck, be pushed off and the lift lowered. On again with the aircraft, up one deck with the lift and it had arrived on the flight deck. In fact they would move two aircraft at a time, one on each of the lift levels. The result was a continual movement of aircraft around the two hangars, like a double version of the tin mosaics which were popular prewar puzzles with one square missing to allow movement. I never did learn to recognise the signs which identified the hangars, and would arrive at a ladder not knowing if it went up or down,

'At sea, a hangar can be quite frightening. The aircraft are lashed down, and one has to pick a way very carefully past all the deck bolts and guys. The aircraft themselves strain on their fixing, shrieking and moaning, like some prehistoric monster trying to crush you. But there was one obstacle I didn't bargain for. Going through the hangar one day looking for my aircraft to do a DI, I was attacked on the legs by some stinging reptile which caused me to dance and kick violently. It was an air-gunner's trailing aerial tied by string to another aircraft — and he was transmitting! This was of course quite against the rules — low power contact was all that was permitted, and even that only close to harbour. But I was still very green about ships, so when this AG swore at me for pulling down his aerial, I apologised for not seeing it. At a later date he would not have got such a soft reaction.'

Ken was soon to gain experience, and within a few weeks he was participating in a torpedo attack in Swordfish P4080 'B' whilst serving with No 815 Squadron, which he had now joined in Greece. He gives a graphic account of this raid:

'The moon sank swiftly behind the clouds on the horizon as our aircraft glided down into Valona harbour. What had been a brilliant silver orb lighting the sea a few moments before, dwindled to a diffused glow and left us peering from the Swordfish cockpit into the darkening gloom. We had planned on that moonlight lasting at least 15min longer. It was 05.30hrs on the morning of 13 March 1941, and this Albanian port was the major supply route for Italian forces attacking the Greek frontier. RAF reconnaissance had indicated several ships in the harbour.

'The sing of the wing rigging was clearly audible in the cockpit with the engine throttled back to an eerie hum. It was a memorable moment for a TAG about to

Below: HMS *Illustrious* on fire after her flight deck had been pierced by bombs in a heavy dive bombing attack by Ju87s whilst escorting a convoy west of Malta on 10 January 1941. The stores, stowed in the roof of the hangar below, are ablaze. The nearly red hot deck is turning the water from the fire hoses into steam as smoke from the fire below passes through the jagged metal edges of the bomb hole. The after lift has been blown out and can be seen as a dark shape beyond the bomb hole and to the left of the plume of smoke. Six hours later the carrier reached Malta under her own steam. *IWM*

Top: Fulmars of No 808 Squadron taking off from HMS *Ark Royal* and circling before going on patrol. This photograph was taken in April 1941 whilst the carrier was serving with Force H in the Mediterranean. *IWM*

Above: A Fulmar of No 808 Squadron begins its take-off run from the deck of HMS *Ark Royal* in February 1941. In the foreground can be seen the outline of one of the ship's lifts, and ranged aft are Skuas of No 800 Squadron and another Fulmar of No 808 Squadron. No 800 Squadron also received Fulmars two months later. Steaming astern of the carrier is the battle-cruiser HMS *Renown*. *FAA Museum*

experience his first torpedo attack. We had crossed the isthmus and were down to 1,000ft when the darkness was pierced by a myriad of menacing lights flickering up to and all around us — so much for our hope of surprise. The engine burst into life as we took avoiding action, and I saw and heard some shells come dangerously close. The gunner, looking back, sees this more clearly than the pilot. A fabric-sided cockpit is no protection, and one feels terribly vulnerable, but it doesn't prevent an instinctive crouching at the first shock of being under fire.

'Looking forward for a moment to see where we were heading, I was amazed to see our leading aircraft displaying navigation lights! No wonder we were catching it. They were shooting at him, and with the usual trail we were in the way. Over on our starboard beam I could actually see the pit of a Breda gun with its personnel lit up by the flames. We were close enough to reply with the rear gun, but I didn't wish to offer them a sight of their target with the tracer. As we ploughed steadily towards the main harbour the minutes seemed an eternity. They were hosepiping around now from several points, and further jinking was quite pointless.

'Then as suddenly as it had started the firing stopped. We were down low on the water, and I fancy the Italians had at last learned that to fire across a harbour does a lot of damage to one's friends across the way. At Taranto they did a fair job of bombarding their own merchant shipping. From our point of view, however, it was unfortunately the wrong respite as the night was now as black as ink, and our vision had been impaired by the firework display. We turned towards the jetty area and tried to pick out any shape darker than the rest.

'At this moment I was jolted by the aircraft checking, and a sudden change in the surrounding blackness as two silvery plumes rose on each side of us. The undercarriage had hit the water. With great presence of mind, my pilot dropped our tin-fish and incredibly the aircraft lifted clear. We turned away and watched hopefully. The torpedo was going in the right direction, but there was no visible target. We saw nothing, and after a couple of orbits we made our way to the harbour entrance, keeping low. We expected a hot reception here, but slipped through unchallenged and set course for home.

'This meant flying south down the coast to the island of Corfu, and then finding the right valley to turn up to reach the forward grass airfield of Paramythia, which was nestled between the mountains. Here we found that our only success had been a hit on a large ship by the Second Pilot.'

Throughout 1941 and 1942, strenuous efforts continued to get food, supplies and aircraft through to Malta, with occasional convoys running the gauntlet from Gibraltar. Rear-Adm D. R. F. Cambell, recalls these 'Club Runs', as the aircraft deliveries became known, during the time in 1942 when he was Lt-Cdr (Air) in charge of the Air Department of *Argus*:

'We were in company with the *Eagle*, and we used to make sorties from Gibraltar. On a typical run we would sail before dark, make a

Above: Swordfish '5F' of a carrier-based squadron, with bombs and depth charges under the wings, on anti-submarine patrol over a large convoy on its way to the Middle East towards the end of 1941. Possibly of No 816 Squadron aboard HMS *Ark Royal.* IWM

Centre left: HMS *Ark Royal* listing to starboard after being torpedoed by *U-81* on 13 November 1941. Still steaming, Swordfish aircraft can be seen on the forward end of the flight deck with their wings folded. Efforts to tow the carrier to Gibraltar failed, and she sank at 06.13hrs the next day. A number of aircraft managed to reach North Front aerodrome safely, including the whole of No 825 Squadron which was in the air at the time the torpedo exploded. C. H. Wood

Left: HMS *Argus* sailing near Gibraltar in February 1942 during the 'Club Run' period. At that time she had aboard her the Fulmars of No 807 Squadron, which also flew patrols from North Front aerodrome when ashore. A year later this carrier was withdrawn to undertake deck landing training work in the Firth of Clyde. C. H. Wood

feint as if we were going out into the Atlantic, then turn back in the dark. About half way to Malta we would fly off the aircraft, which were usually Hurricanes at that time, and then turn back to Gibraltar.

'This kind of mission was full of complications. For instance the lifts of the *Argus* were too small to take a spread Hurricane, and their wings could not fold. I remember when we came back to the Clyde to collect a load of Hurricanes, they had to be embarked with their wings separately, and put down below. When we reached Gibraltar they had to be disembarked, their wings put back on and then they were transferred to *Eagle*.

'We had a squadron of Fulmars on board for fighter patrols, and Swordfish for anti-submarine patrols. We were usually picked up by a German shadower off Cape de Gata,

but the amount of interference we had from Italian or German aircraft was pretty small, as far as I remember. We were under night attack once, but nothing very much happened.

'I remember one unhappy episode during an operation in which we were to fly Albacores to Malta, which only had Swordfish until then. Having flown off the aircraft from *Eagle* just before sunset, we turned for home, but two hours later there was the sound of approaching aircraft and back came all the Albacores. Apparently they had all found their engines were overheating, and when they got down on the deck they discovered that the oil cooler setting was in the "winter" position instead of the "summer" position, a point that had been overlooked. They would have come down in

Left: An aerial view of the eastern end of North Front aerodrome, Gibraltar, taken by the observer of Swordfish 'E4M' of No 813 Squadron, piloted by Sub-Lt D. R. Mudd, probably on 16 June 1942. Aircraft of Nos 813 and 824 Squadrons alternated between this aerodrome and HMS *Eagle*, which only accommodated one of them at a time. Every midday the nissen huts at the top of the picture were showered by debris from the cliffs above, which were then being blasted to produce material for extending the runway. At the bottom of the picture is the Spanish border. *D. R. Mudd*

Above right: Three Swordfish of No 824 Squadron from North Front flying above the Mediterranean in mid 1942. V4648, the machine nearest the camera, was later transferred to No 813 Squadron, changing its code from '5K' to '4L'. These aircraft carried out numerous patrols in and around the Straits of Gibraltar, later being active during the invasion of North Africa. *D. R. Mudd*

Below right; Sea Hurricane '6F' about to take off from the flight deck of a carrier in the Mediterranean around August 1942, with other Sea Hurricanes and an Albacore and Swordfish also ranged for take off. The carrier, whose arrester wires can be seen clearly, is believed to be HMS *Indomitable* which then had aboard the Sea Hurricanes of Nos 800 and 880 Squadrons, the Albacores of Nos 827 and 831 Squadron and some No 806 Squadron Martlets. Both the Albacore squadrons had a few Swordfish attached to them. *IWM*

the sea if they had gone any further. I rather think that we took them back to Gibraltar, and for some reason, no second attempt was made at the time.

'Early in June we took part in Operation "Harpoon". We in the *Argus* had returned to the Clyde to fetch some more aircraft, and while there we were briefed on the forthcoming operation. This was ostensibly a convoy exercise to Malta, and Force H, of which we were part, was to be reinforced by extra destroyers, cruisers and the battleship *Malaya* wearing the Admiral's flag. We were being sent towards Malta, as we later learned, as a diversion or decoy in the hope that the main enemy effort would be sent against us, and that a much larger convoy

would get in from Alexandria. Things did not quite work out like that. We certainly got attacked a lot, but so did the party the other end, and they did not get through.

'Of our convoy, which was only about six merchant ships or so, I think, four of them were sunk, one or two of them finally got through. We lost one or two cruisers and destroyers. Why the slow old *Argus* was not sunk I will never know — she was under close attack by Italian torpedo bombers and their torpedoes went slithering down the ship's sides, and she must have had a charmed life because we got away without a scratch. Our Fulmar squadron did very well that day, though they lost a few aircraft; they were commanded by Lt Fraser-Harris, and

Above: Martlet AM968 '8M' pictured just after coming to rest after landing on the deck of a carrier, probably HMS *Indomitable* which had the Martlets of No 806 Squadron aboard in August 1942 around the time this photograph was taken. The arrester wires have evidently done their work, and it was unnecessary to raise the safety barrier in the foreground. The wireless aerials are in the extended position over the side of the ship, as flying is in progress. *IWM*

Right: A formation of three Albacores, armed with torpedoes, takes off from Hal Far aerodrome, Malta, on an operational sortie in the Mediterranean. Between October 1941 and June 1943 the Albacores of No 828 Squadron carried out a large number of sorties in the central Mediterranean, suffering heavy casualties. Other Albacore and Swordfish squadrons assisted them in this work at various times. *IWM*

one of his more successful pilots was Peter Twiss who after the war became the world's air speed record holder in the Fairey FD1.'

By the end of July, Malta was rapidly running out of stores, and in mid-August a large single convoy was despatched under the code-name Operation 'Pedestal'. This was heavily attacked, and of the five carriers involved, *Indomitable* was badly damaged and *Eagle* was sunk. However, the five surviving merchant ships of the 14 which set out, did succeed in entering Grand Harbour. The fighter patrols had been extremely active as can be seen from this extract from the diary of No 880 Squadron, then flying Sea Hurricane IBs aboard *Indomitable*:

'**11 August** The Malta convoy. 06.30hrs Lt Fiddes, Lt Smith, Sub-Lt Popham and Sub-Lt Brownlee, Yellow Section, took off to patrol for 1½hrs. 07.45hrs relieved by Lt-Cdr Judd, Sub-Lt Harris and Lts Forrest and Lowe as Black Section. Neither of these sections reported anything. 09.00hrs Lt Cork and Sub-Lts Cruickshank, Haworth and Cunliffe-Owen as Blue Section took off on patrol. At 15,000ft Lt Cork attacked a Ju88 with the Section and its starboard engine was left burning. Blue Section credited with a probable. 18.20hrs Yellow Section took off again on patrol but nothing sighted. 18.35hrs Black Section took off to patrol at 24,000ft. Lt Lowe returned with low oil pressure. Intercepted by a Ju88 which Lt Forrest attacked securing hits on its port engine, and received a hit in his own, but forced landed in the sea unhurt. Sub-Lt Harris then attacked and finished off the Ju88. Lt Forrest and

Sub-Lt Harris credited with half the aircraft each confirmed. 15.45hrs Blue Section patrolled but nothing sighted. 19.15hrs Yellow Section patrolled at 12,000ft, attacked a Ju88 and credited with a probable to the Section. 19.55hrs Black Section patrolled from 25,000ft to 10,000ft. Nothing sighted. Yellow and Black Sections compelled to make night landings. Lt Smith hit the barrier in Z7055. Sub-Lt Popham landed on HMS *Victorious*.

'12 August 09.00hrs Black Section started patrolling at 25,000ft. When returning to land they sighted a Cant Z1007 at 200ft. Lt-Cdr Judd and Sub-Lt Harris shot down the aircraft and credited with half each. 09.15hrs Blue Section on patrol at 7,000ft attacked a Ju88 and shot it down. This was credited to the Section. Lt Cork attacked and shot down another Ju88 — confirmed. 10.20hrs Lt Fiddes took up Yellow Section but nothing sighted. 12.35hrs Lt Cork took up Blue Section on patrol at 5,000ft. Attacked and destroyed a Ju88 and Me110 with several other possibles. Sub-Lt Cruickshank shot down by two aircraft and was killed on diving into the sea. 13.15hrs Lt-Cdr Judd took Black Section up. Sub-Lt Harris was late taking off. Lt-Cdr Judd dived to attack a squadron of He111s which shot him down and he was killed. Sub-Lt Harris returned with low oil pressure. Nothing further was sighted. 17.30hrs Lt-Cdr Bradbury led Black Section but nothing sighted. 18.35hrs Lt-Cdr Bruen led Yellow Section. Sub-Lt Ritchie of No 800 Squadron shot down a Ju87. Lt Fiddes also shot down a Ju87, and was himself shot down by our own flak. Both Yellow and Black Sections landed on HMS *Victorious* as HMS *Indomitable* had been damaged by bombs, Sub-Lt Cunliffe-Owen being killed on board.'

Left: Choppy seas during a Malta convoy, as seen from the deck of HMS *Victorious* which has two Sea Hurricanes of No 885 Squadron visible. She is followed by HMS *Indomitable*, which has her draught screens erected, then HMS *Eagle* followed by a battle-cruiser. *IWM*

Below: Five Sea Hurricane IBs of No 880 Squadron flying in formation whilst the squadron was working up at Arbroath in the early summer of 1941. The squadron later joined HMS *Indomitable*, and during a Malta convoy in August 1942 they destroyed eight enemy aircraft for the loss of three of their own. W9219, nearest the camera, later went to No 760 Squadron at Yeovilton, this being then the Fighter Pool Squadron.
Cdr R. N. Everett

Madagascar

On 7 December 1941 the Japanese Fleet carried out its historic surprise air attack on the US naval base at Pearl Harbor, and immediately the British bases in the Far East became targets for this new enemy. Singapore could not be properly defended, and consequently Colombo now became the main base of the Eastern Fleet under Adm Sir James Somerville. By the beginning of April 1942 this Fleet included the carriers *Formidable*, *Hermes* and *Indomitable*, carrying between them eight squadrons equipped with 90 aircraft. Ashore in Ceylon were another Swordfish squadron and two Fulmar squadrons.

Indomitable had arrived at Addu Atoll, the Fleet anchorage in the Maldives, on 24 March, and there she had joined up with units of the 3rd Battle Squadron. Five days later she sailed with *Warspite*, *Formidable* and other units to attempt to make contact with Japanese fighters operating in the Bay of Bengal. Contact was eventually made, and on 5 April (Easter Sunday) Albacore '5B' of No 827 Squadron from *Indomitable*, piloted by Sub-Lt (A) Grant-Sturgis RNVR was attacked by a Mitsubishi fighter. L/Air G. Dixon the telegraphist air gunner was wounded, but the aircraft returned safely to its parent ship at 17.45hrs. An ASV-equipped Albacore then took off from *For-

midable*, but failed to re-establish contact with the Japanese Fleet, which meanwhile had bombed Colombo and sunk the cruisers *Dorsetshire* and *Cornwall*. No 827 Squadron lost one of its aircraft, T9206 '5C' piloted by Sub-Lt (A) R. J. F. Streatfield RNVR which failed to return from a reconnaissance.

Neither Fleet had sighted the other, but six Swordfish of No 814 Squadron from *Hermes* were shot down by 'Zeke' fighters whilst en route from China Bay to Kokkolei to rejoin their ship. Four days later the other six squadron aircraft made their way safely to Kokkolei, but before they could embark the carrier was sunk by Val dive bombers from the Japanese carriers *Akagi*, *Hirya* and *Soryu*, operating 70 miles south of Trincomalee.

There was now a fear that the Japanese would attempt a landing in East Africa, and the Vichy French island of Madagascar was an obvious target for them to attempt to establish a base. To forestall this, an invasion was mounted early in May on Diego Suarez, a large harbour at the north end of the island. On 5 May, aircraft from *Illustrious* and *Indomitable* began operations in support of the invasion forces, and spotting duties were also carried out by the Walruses of the cruiser *Devonshire*. At dawn, Albacores of Nos 827 and 831 Squadrons from *Indomit-

able struck at the local airfield, setting fire to the hangar, whilst the carrier's fighters prevented the French fighters from taking off, and also attacked anti-aircraft batteries. Fighters from *Illustrious* covered the invasion, whilst her Swordfish went off in three groups of six to attack selected targets. The first group was armed with torpedoes, with which they attacked the sloop *D'Entrecaseaux* and Armed Merchant Cruiser *Bougainville*, the latter being blown up. The second group attacked with depth charges and succeeded in sinking the submarine *Bevezières*. The third group, after dropping leaflets and an ultimatum, bombed a gun battery and the sloop.

In the latter attack, Swordfish DK788 '2A' of No 810 Squadron was hit by anti-aircraft fire, and the squadron's commanding officer, Lt R. N. Everett RN and his crew, Sub-Lt (A) J. H. G. Tapscott and PO R. J. Groves, were taken prisoner after landing in the sea close to the shore, but were later released after troops occupied the nearby town of Antsirane. A similar fate overtook

Above: HMS *Illustrious*, flagship of the Carrier Squadron, Eastern Fleet, sailing off Mombasa during May 1942. On deck are some of her Swordfish, which carried out a total of 57 bombing attacks on Diego Suarez during the three days of the assault. *via Gordon Wright*

Above: Walrus L2288 can be seen aboard the battleship HMS *Resolution*, pictured here during the Madagascar operations. This machine had joined the Ship's Flight at Donibristle in November 1941, and undertook spotting duties during the assault. *IWM*

Left: Fulmar X8569 of No 806 Squadron being manhandled to the after lift of HMS *Illustrious* during the Madagascar operations. Flying had evidently ceased as the wireless aerials are in the raised position. This squadron had begun to re-equip with Martlets in August 1942, but six Fulmars were retained for about six months and operated as No 806B Squadron. *IWM*

Above: The upturned remains of Swordfish DK788 '2A' of No 810 Squadron lying offshore at Diego Suarez. Piloted by Lt R. N. Everett, the squadron CO, with Sub-Lt J. H. G. Tapscott as observer and PO T. P. Groves as the telegraphist air gunner, the machine had to force land in the water when its petrol leaked away after the engine had been hit by shrapnel on 5 May 1942 during the first day's attack. The crew were taken prisoner, but were later released by the invasion forces and were able to inspect their aircraft which is seen here whilst being stripped of useable parts, the engine having already been removed. *Cdr R. N. Everett*

Centre right: Two Fulmars of No 803 Squadron being serviced aboard HMS *Formidable* in the Indian Ocean around the time of the Madagascar operations. The squadron had joined the carrier from Ceylon on 25 April 1942, the day after she sailed to take part in the assault. This photograph has suffered at the hands of the wartime censor, who caused HMS *Indomitable*, the following ship, to be erased as her existence had not been revealed at that time. *IWM*

Below right: High ranking British officers inspecting the remains of a French Potez 63 bomber in a wrecked hangar at Diego Suarez after the surrender. On the left is Rear-Adm Denis Boyd, ashore from his flagship HMS *Indomitable*. He was later to become the Fifth Sea Lord. *IWM*

the crew of Albacore X8950 '5G' of No 827 Squadron from *Indomitable*, piloted by Sub-Lt (A) H. J. M. Pike, which forced landed with engine trouble whilst carrying out a reconnaissance and anti-submarine patrol off the entrance to the harbour. Cdr Robert Everett, now retired, recalls this episode:

'I was taking my squadron in at first light to dive bomb the battery, while No 829 Squadron went in with depth charges to attack a couple of submarines and the rather elegant coastal sloop *D'Entrecaseaux*. All hell let loose by the time we arrived, and we had done two runs when there was an appalling crump underneath the aircraft, and about two or three minutes later the engine stopped. We forced landed in the water, not far from the shore, and the aircraft overturned. The air gunner was trapped upside down in the wreckage, but we were able to get him out, which was not too difficult in a Stringbag. My observer had been thrown out, but he was only slightly hurt, though covered in mud.

'We were able to break the ASV aerials off the aircraft, and destroy the code books, but by the time we had done this the French came down and started firing at us. As our only weapon was my .32 automatic, which had been in the water, we had no choice but to surrender. We were taken up to the barracks, searched and then locked up. In the middle of the night there was a lot of firing, then suddenly an English voice called out "Come on lads, keep moving". They turned out to be Royal Marine Commandoes, brought in by the destroyer *Anthony*, and they made such a noise with their big boots and firing that the French were unnerved. I called out who we were, and they let us out and took us to the officer in charge. Eventually we got back to the *Illustrious*.'

The diary record of No 829 Squadron for that day gives a detailed account of the activities which took place:

'**Dawn Torpedo Attack** Took-off at 03.50hrs and formed up six aircraft according to plan. Proceeded towards Cape Ambre and a fix disclosed that our departure position had been in error by about six miles to westward. This however made very little difference as the coast was crossed at the correct position at 05.01hrs, one minute after the estimated time. The six aircraft were dispersed and made individual searches round the bay in the harbour looking for possible targets. On arrival at the anchorage most aircraft were engaged by light flak from what in the half light might have been a small cruiser or sloop, a Merchant Vessel and some shore AA positions. All aircraft dropped torpedoes at the sloop but it is thought that four of them missed or ran under without exploding and two hit the AMC *Bougainville* which was anchored close by. When the aircraft left at daylight or soon after the *Bougainville* was on fire and had a list to port, an HA Battery had come into action and further light flak positions appeared to have closed up. The sloop had weighed anchor and had gone around the corner under the protection of the HA Battery on the point.

'**Dawn Depth Charge Attack** Six aircraft took off at 03.45hrs and formed up six miles on starboard beam. Took departure at 04.07hrs for a point seven miles off Cape Ambre. Owing to ship's position being in error, and a stronger wind experienced than anticipated, the two sub flights were slightly late in their ETA at Oranjia Pass. The aircraft crossed the coast just north of the Pass at 05.15hrs, 10min after the Torpedo Striking Force as ordered. The aircraft crossed into Irish Bay in line astern, and over into English Bay. No ships of any kind were seen.

The two sub flights split up over Welsh Pool, the first one to examine the anchorage of Port Nièvre and the second to investigate Friend's Creek and the Torpedo Basin. By this time the AMC *Bougainville* was burning fiercely, and the sloop was getting under way. A submarine, subsequently admitted to be the *Glorieuse*, was seen to move into the anchorage from the direction of the jetty. Three aircraft attacked and the submarine was seen to list to starboard, later catching fire. The submarine opened fire on the aircraft, as did a merchant ship lying nearby. As no further submarines were sighted, all but two of the six aircraft returned to the ship. One of the two remaining aircraft also returned as the air gunner had been wounded; the remaining aircraft patrolled the harbour until 07.00hrs, making a final sweep of the creek before leaving. Light AA flak was experienced from the shore batteries, and particularly from the sloop.'

Attacks continued until late in the afternoon of 7 May, when the cease fire was given. The Allied forces were now firmly in control of the northern part of the island, including their main objective of the large and important harbour at Diego Suarez. Once the town had fallen, shore leave was given, and amongst those who went ashore from *Illustrious* was Gordon Wright who recollects:

'A number of us visited the town to see what the place was like, but after discovering that there were no 'eats' available and none of the natives spoke English, limited ourselves to the one 'run'. The surprising thing about Diego Suarez was the number of sweet stalls in the main street, selling coconut toffee and coconut ice in large and apparently unlimited quantities. I suppose the nearby sugar factory at Majunga was responsible for this. At any rate we all seemed to have a very sweet tooth!'

Below: Two naval ratings enjoying a change of scenery from HMS *Indomitable*, as they pass the contrasting Albacores of No 831 Squadron and a native hut. The landing strip at Mackinnon Road had been cleared out of the brush by native labour, and the squadron disembarked here shortly after the successful attack on Diego Suarez, in which they had taken an active part. They were soon back aboard, carrying out patrols over the Indian Ocean. *IWM*

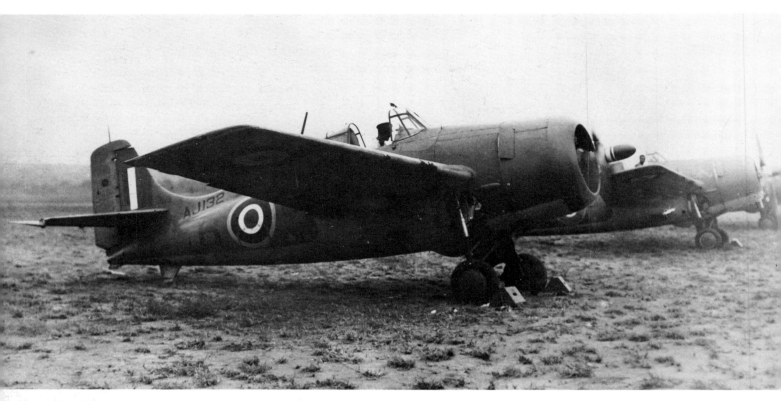

Above: Martlet AJ132 and others of No 881 Squadron ashore in East Africa from HMS *Illustrious*. This machine had previously served with No 806 Squadron, being part of the initial equipment of that squadron when it began to re-equip from Fulmars. After two months ashore at Kilindini and later Mackinnon Road, No 881 Squadron re-embarked on 7 December 1942. *FAA Museum*

Right: Stripping down fire damaged Swordfish of No 829 Squadron after a hangar fire aboard HMS *Illustrious* during the Madagascar operations. Spontaneous combustion had caused the camouflage netting stored in the hangar roof to catch fire, but fortunately the spray extinguished it quickly before it reached the 1,000gal of high octane fuel stored nearby. The Swordfish of No 810 Squadron were also unharmed. *Cdr R. N. Everett*

In September 1942, a final assault was made on the remaining unoccupied territory, in the south of the island. No 829 Squadron was again involved, as its diary briefly records:

Thursday 10 September 1942 Majunga. AM Squadron (nine aircraft) split into four sub flights. One sub flight carrying Mk VII depth charges, remainder carrying 250lb bombs. Orders were to stage demonstration over Majunga at dawn simultaneously with the landing of our troops in the town. No bombing was to be carried out until required by the Army, orders for which would be given by W/T or by flashing from *Albatross* at anchor off Majunga. Dive bombing aircraft were to attack any submarines sighted. Squadron took off at 04.15hrs in pitch darkness and carried out night form. Arrived over Majunga at 05.15hrs, with depth charge aircraft breaking off to sweep over harbour and dived in formation over town. No signs of AA fire and aircraft flew low over town with impunity until 07.00hrs when they returned to ship. No calls were received from Army for bombing, the town having surrendered at 06.30hrs. Sub-Lt Alexander had a bullet hole through lower mainplane, only mark remindful of a rather uneventful sortie for the squadron.

'**Friday 11 September 1942** AM. Ship remained off Majunga for Army reconnaissance purposes. Squadron not required. PM, ship proceeded to Diego Suarez.

'**Friday 18 September 1942** Tamatave. AM.

Two aircraft with No 810 Squadron led by CO take-off before dawn to attack military installations at Tamatave by dive bombing should town not surrender under threat of naval bombarding. Bombing not carried out due to surrender of local military commander. Ship remained in vicinity to fly off aircraft while army carried out occupation of port. PM, ship leave for Durban.'

Right: Sea Hurricane Ib AF966 '7F' of No 880 Squadron taxying towards the forward deck park of HMS *Indomitable* after carrying out patrol duties in the Indian Ocean. These aircraft were actively engaged in the attacks on Diego Suarez, in which they carried out a series of strafing attacks. After standing by for a time at Port Reitz, they re-embarked in July and after rounding the Cape the ship sailed north to Gibraltar and the Mediterranean. *IWM*

Below: Swordfish HS164 '2F' of No 810 Squadron seen over the sea off the East African coast after the Madagascar operations. Radar aerials can be seen on the wing struts, and smoke floats are carried under the wings. The squadrons spent some time ashore at Tanga, after absorbing No 829 Squadron, its sister unit, but rejoined HMS *Illustrious* early in December 1942 and sailed with her to the UK, where re-equipment with Barracudas took place the following spring.
Cdr R. N. Everett

Operations in the Atlantic and Home Waters

Of the many arenas in which the Fleet Air Arm fought, one of the most vital was the Atlantic Ocean. Britain could only continue the war if food and supplies were able to reach her, and most of these had to come from America. The supply lines were subjected to constant attacks from predatory U-boats, sometimes hunting in packs. In addition there was the threat of a break-out by German capital ships. The *Graf Spee* had gone, but others remained.

After the fall of France, the Navy had little carrier strength to spare for this task. In most cases the Walruses aboard the escorting ships were the only aircraft available. Of necessity, the German surface raiders were primarily the responsibility of the British capital ships of the Home Fleet. The sinking of the *Bismarck* in May 1941, and the abortive attempts to stop the *Scharnhorst* and *Gneisenau* in their break-out from Brest in February 1942 have been well recorded, but the Atlantic was the scene of numerous other incidents, the majority never publicised, but all forming a vital part of the Fleet Air Arm's contribution to the war.

In June 1941 the cruiser *Shropshire*, together with two corvettes and two rescue tugs, formed the escort of a valuable convoy of over 20 ships whose main cargo was iron ore from Pepel. The convoy sailed for the

United Kingdom from Freetown after assembling there on 20 June. Anti-submarine patrols were carried out by *Shropshire's* Walrus, K8548 piloted by Lt P. Francklin RN but the ship's main role was that of protecting the convoy from attack by armed raiders, and at night she took station in the centre of the convoy.

It is worth recording that *Shropshire* had sailed from the UK in the first week of August 1940, and she and her Walrus had been operating in the Indian Ocean and South Atlantic continuously so that neither the ship nor her aircraft were fitted with radar. The standard operating procedure for flying anti-submarine patrols was that of flying on cross-courses ahead of the convoy. This procedure, in a cloudless sky, had failed to prevent a number of U-boats from shadowing and concentrating on the convoy, which they then attacked with great effect on two successive nights. *Shropshire* was consequently ordered to withdraw 50 miles to the west and continue to provide anti-submarine cover. A new tactic was then adopted of flying high and approaching the convoy out of the sun, and in the morning of 28 June this succeeded in enabling an attack to be carried out on a U-boat in position 26°03′N, 24°07′W. This attack was identified after the war in records obtained by

Below: HMS *Shropshire*'s Walrus (K8548) immediately after a 'slick' landing on the ship's starboard side. This machine was originally delivered to the Ship's Flight from China Bay on 27 September 1940. In March 1941 it was temporarily transferred to HMS *Devonshire*, but returned two months later, being withdrawn at Hatston in July 1941. It later went to No 751 Squadron at Dundee for observer training.
Cdr M. B. P. Francklin

the Admiralty, the U-boat being *U-123* (Capt Hardegan). His log reading (freely translated) read: 'Four depth charges. They fell very well placed giving us a severe shaking, but nothing was affected except the water depth gauge. I was surprised at this depth. I presume that he saw where we dived by the bubbles from our air-vents in the oil-smooth sea.'

Shortly after this, *Shropshire*'s petrol supply became exhausted and the surviving ships of the convoy were ordered by the Admiralty to be dispersed and proceed independently to the UK.

Shropshire was then ordered to join the Home Fleet at Scapa Flow and another encounter, of a different kind, with a submarine took place some weeks later. Her Walrus (now P5178), operating from Scapa Flow, landed in the sea some 50 miles from Scapa to rescue the crew of Albacore N4155 from Hatston, which had crashed in the sea after engine failure. This was fortunately witnessed by a Dutch submarine at periscope depth, whose captain then surfaced and taking aboard the Albacore pilot, who was the only survivor, lightheartedly offered to tow the Walrus, which was accepted. Some eight hours later, in the sheltered waters of Stromness, the Walrus took-off and returned to Scapa Flow.

There were many successful Air-Sea Rescue operations carried out by Walrus aircraft, with their unique ability to operate not only as seaplanes but also from the decks of aircraft carriers. One of the most successful in terms of numbers rescued took place on 25 November 1942 when a Sunderland flying boat (DV972) of No 119 Squadron, operating from RAF Pembroke Dock in Milford Haven, mistakenly attacked in bad weather what was thought to be a U-boat, but was, in fact, a mine. This exploded, bringing the Sunderland down into the sea in the mouth of

the Bristol Channel. The radio operator was, however, quick enough to transmit an SOS with the aircraft's call sign, but the explosion had changed the aircraft's wavelength so that the signal was picked up by the GPO, who were able to get a rough bearing.

After some delay, the information was passed to the Naval Seaplane Station at Lawrenny Ferry in the upper reaches of Milford Haven and two Walrus aircraft of

Top: Walrus K8548 of HMS *Shropshire* taxying alongside immediately prior to hooking on to the 'Thomas Grab', with the telegraphist air gunner standing above the cockpit ready to take the hook. *Cdr M. B. P. Francklin*

Above: HMS *Furious* photographed from one of its No 801 Squadron Skuas during a trip to Takoradi on the Gold Coast, to deliver RAF Hurricanes for the Middle East squadrons. These were embarked in the Clyde without their wings attached, and then assembled on board by RAF crews en route to West Africa. On arrival they were flown off and made the trip overland in stages to Cairo. *Gordon Wright*

Left: Fulmar '6Q' of No 809 Squadron being flagged off the deck of HMS *Victorious* in late 1941. Just visible on the nose of the aircraft is the squadron's unofficial 'Donald Duck' badge. IWM

Above: A formation of Walruses from No 764 Squadron, the Seaplane Training Squadron at Lawrenny Ferry in Milford Haven, then commanded by Lt M. B. P. Francklin. The machine nearest the camera is W3079 which was written off when the pilot attempted a night landing on 9 November 1942 when off course, and it crashed into trees. The squadron also had a few Kingfishers on strength at that time. *Capt W. R. MacWhirter*

Right: Swordfish V4367 on the crane of HMS *Malaya* in Scapa Flow. This machine, one of two carried by the battleship, has ASV radar aerials on the wings struts and bomb racks can be seen under the wings. V4367 was a Blackburn-built machine delivered to the Royal Navy on 16 April 1941 and flown shortly afterwards to Lee-on-Solent, where it joined the newly formed Malaya Flight in July 1941, the ship having just been refitted following service with Force H. This aircraft was later relegated to deck landing training duties with No 769 Squadron at Arbroath. *FAA Museum*

No 764 Squadron, which was responsible for advanced Naval Seaplane Training, took off and flew a parallel track search on the bearing received, the pilots being Lt P. Francklin the Commanding Officer and Lt R. MacWhirter the Senior Pilot. After flying over 70 miles they sighted in a fading light two rubber dinghies roped together. The wind was blowing at over 20kts, and it was realised that the area was mined so that no ship could effect a rescue. Lt Francklin therefore landed and was able to get a rope to the dinghies and learn that the crew of nine were unhurt. Five were then taken on board the Walrus and Lt MacWhirter returned after signalling the position. After a rather rough night, when the tide was high, an RAF Air-Sea Rescue launch located the Walrus,

but as it proved impracticable to tow it, all 11 airmen were transferred to the launch and subsequently landed at Padstow. Bob Allerton, the telegraphist air gunner in this Walrus (L2230) recalls that, after being picked up, their aircraft was sunk by Lewis gun fire from the launch, which took them to Padstow.

As the Battle of the Atlantic ebbed and flowed, various developments took place, particularly in the attempts to bridge the gap in mid-ocean where land-based aircraft could not afford protection. In 1941 several merchant ships were fitted with aircraft catapults to accommodate modified Sea Hurricanes, which could be sent off to attack raiders if the occasion arose, though the pilot would almost inevitably have to land in the sea afterwards, with the risks that this entailed.

Early in 1943 this expedient was succeeded by MAC-ships, these being grain ships or tankers fitted with small flight decks from which they could operate three or four Swordfish. These aircraft were eventually grouped as No 836 Squadron, which continued to operate until the end of the war.

In the meantime, a captured German merchantman had been fitted with a flight deck to become the first auxiliary carrier, the *Empire Audacity*, this name being later shortened to *Audacity*. The success of this experiment led to the conversion of many more such ships in America. Known as escort carriers, the Royal Navy received a total of 38, all but two of which survived the war, the majority afterwards being returned to the United States for re-conversion.

In May 1943, No 819 Squadron aboard *Archer*, the first American conversion, helped escort the eastbound convoy HX239 from the region of Iceland. Three of her aircraft were fitted for the first time with underwing rocket projectiles. This convoy was the subject of attentions from U-boats, but these were actively engaged by the Swordfish with successful results, as recorded at the time in the squadron diary:

'**Sunday 23 May 1943** AM. The weather continued favourable and the sea calm. 04.30hrs Sub-Lt Brilliant and crew and the CO and crew flew off to search an area in which H/F D/F bearings had been reported. Nothing was sighted although both were vectored to the position in which a Liberator had made an attack some time before. On one occasion a crew reported the wake of an escort vessel as a submarine. 07.15hrs both Swordfish landed on. Lt Tuke and crew then took off on an "Adder" and at 08.10hrs reported an attack on a U-boat. Sub-Lt Nicholls and crew and a Martlet were immediately scrambled. 08.45hrs the Martlet reported an attack on a second submarine.

Above: Swordfish 'C' of No 811 Squadron taking off from the escort carrier HMS *Biter*. This squadron joined the ship in February 1943, and was soon engaged in anti-submarine patrols in the North Atlantic, during which eight attacks were made on U-boats. In addition to its Swordfish, the squadron had a flight of Martlets, or Wildcats as they were known from January 1944, and these were responsible for destroying a Ju296 with a glider bomb on 16 February 1944 whilst on patrol over a North Atlantic convoy. *FAA Museum*

This was attacked also by Sub-Lt Nicholls. The submarine had submerged by this time and no results were observed. 09.00hrs Sub-Lt Horrocks, Sub-Lt Balkwill and L/Air J. W. Wick were scrambled in "B" (RP). 09.18hrs a third submarine was attacked and reported by Sub-Lt Bowles in the Martlet. This submarine was attacked by "B" which forced the submarine to surface and the crew to abandon ship. Survivors were picked up by HMS *Escapade*. This was the first RP attack on a submarine ever made and was completely successful. The attack was made in three parts with cloud cover skilfully used to facilitate the approach. The Martlet made two successful attacks on the second and third submarines. Only the last fired back. The submarine sunk by "B" caught fire aft and suffered severe damage to the steering gear during the rocket attack. The crew appeared to be dumbfounded by the new weapon. 09.50hrs Lt Tuke and crew landed on. His attack which was from the beam resulted in a perfect straddle. The U-boat was at periscope depth at the time. No results were observed but it is certain that some damage was done. The attack by Sub-Lt Nicholls was a little short, but one DC fell very close to the submerged U-boat. 10.50hrs Sub-Lt Horrocks and Sub-Lt Nicholls landed on.'

The sunk U-boat was later identified as the *U-752*. Further patrols that day failed to sight any attackers. However, the *Archer* continued to play an active role, as recorded by Dick Yeo, then Sub-Lt (A) R. K. L. Yeo,

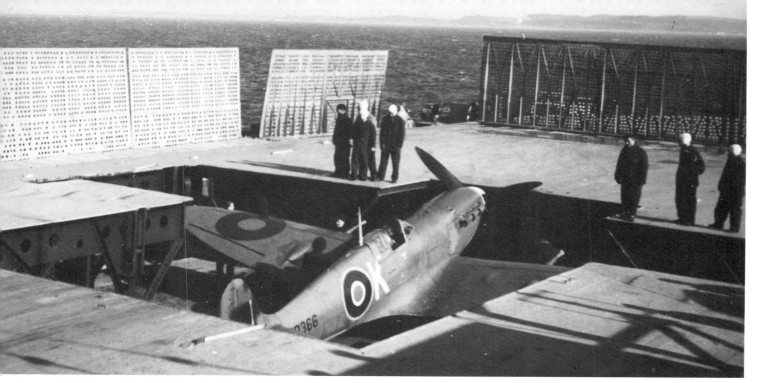

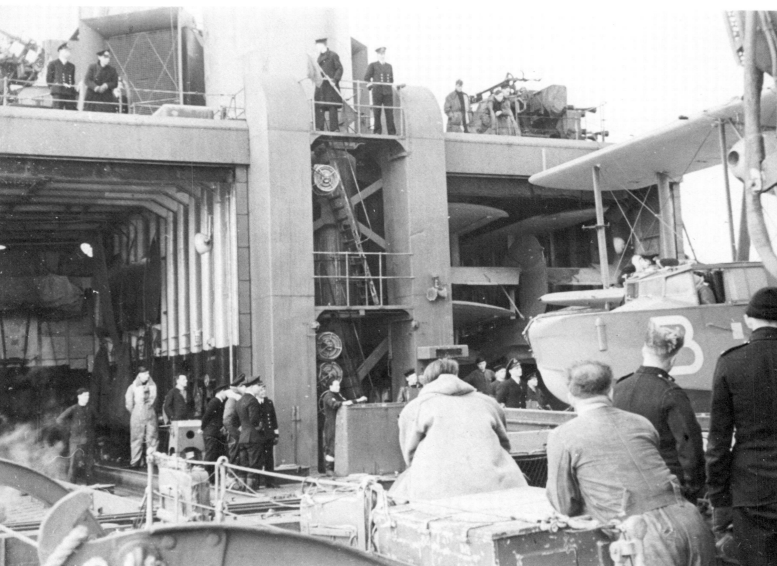

Left: Seafire IB MB366 'K' of No 801 Squadron appearing on deck from the forward lift of HMS *Furious*, whose draught screens have been raised to reduce windage on deck during ranging. This machine was very long lived, being one of the initial issue of this type to the squadron in September 1942, and remaining with them throughout Operation 'Torch' and subsequent service in home waters and the North Atlantic, including a trip to Iceland in June 1943. It was finally withdrawn when the squadron re-equipped with later variants of the Seafire in May 1944. *A. H. Thomson*

Below left: A flight deck scene aboard the cruiser HMS *Kenya* just previous to the launch of Walrus W3049 'B' to port. The ship's other Walrus can be seen ready in the starboard hangar. The type of stowage is visible in the port hangar, just vacated by W3049. The usual 'goofers' are assembled to be in at the kill. *Capt W. R. MacWhirter*

Right: Walrus W3049 is successfully launched from HMS *Kenya*. This machine had a lengthy history after its initial delivery to Donibristle on 10 January 1942. It was used by *Anson* Flight prior to joining *Kenya* Flight, being later relegated to No 772 Squadron, the Fleet Requirements Unit at Machrihanish. In May 1944 it was transferred to the RAF for ASR duties, being successively used by No 275 Squadron at Warmwell, No 277 Squadron at Hawkinge and No 278 Squadron at Thorney Island. It was sold after the war to the Essex Aero Club to become G-AJJC, being later resold to Norway to become LN-SUK, possibly for whaling purposes. *Capt W. R. MacWhirter*

Below right: Swordfish NF190 'F' of No 811 Squadron after an accident aboard HMS *Biter* some time during 1943-44, when the ship was engaged in the North Atlantic. The port oleo has evidently collapsed on landing. Rocket projectiles can be seen under the wings, and ASV radar aerials on the outer wing struts. *J. W. G. Wellham via M. Garbett*

a Martlet pilot with No 892 Squadron from June 1943:

'In early July we sailed from Lough Foyle with an escort of four destroyers and three corvettes, and went into the Bay of Biscay hunting U-boats. The Swordfish did many fruitless searches while we chased FW200s and Ju88s also without result. The snoopers appeared regularly about 09.00hrs and 15.00hrs but due to very poor visibility — never more than a hazy two miles the whole time — no interception was good enough to be turned to good account.

'We spent a week in Devonport at the end of these operations. At the end of July some very serious defects were discovered in the ship's main turbines, so the two squadrons disembarked. After a month the whole squadron (we were now the fighter flight of No 819 Squadron) was reunited on board our new ship HMS *Activity*, which up to now had only been doing deck landing training in the Clyde.'

Exercises and working-up continued for the next few months, then in mid-January 1944 the squadron rejoined *Activity:*

'After a further short work-up, our first job was U-boat hunting in the Atlantic with HMS *Nairana* and Captain Walker's 2nd Escort Group — HM Sloops *Starling*, *Kite*, *Woodpecker*, *Wren*, *Magpie* and *Wild Goose*. After days of fruitless searching — for the loss of one of *Nairana*'s Swordfish with its crew — both carriers joined a large (86 ship) homeward-bound slow convoy that was being shadowed by Ju90s, believed to be carrying radio-controlled glider bombs. We chased several of these snoopers but without result. Meanwhile Capt Walker and his group had gone off and found a pack of U-boats. For the loss (without casualties) of HMS *Woodpecker* he sank six of them — a feat for which he is now famous. We returned to the Clyde and then did a couple more convoys with HMS *Nairana* and had a week in Gibraltar also.'

Above: HMS *Pursuer* rolling to starboard in the Bay of Biscay during convoy escort duties in February 1944. Wildcats of either No 881 or No 896 Squadrons are preparing for take off on convoy patrol. *via Gordon Wright.*

Right: Wildcat '8K' of No 896 Squadron ready for boosting off for convoy patrol in the vicinity of Cap Finisterre, one day during February 1944 at dusk. Both aircraft are tethered to the deck, although the pilots are in their cockpits. A few minutes after this picture was taken the convoy was attacked by a formation of three Focke-Wulfs and these aircraft were catapulted off, two of the enemy being shot down. *via Gordon Wright.*

Gordon Wright was by now a PO writer attached to No 881 Squadron aboard *Pursuer*. He recalls an evening in February 1944 when the ship was acting as sole escort to a Malta-bound convoy:

'Round about Cape Finisterre the convoy was attacked just as dusk was falling (about 19.00hrs) by a formation of Focke-Wulfs. Two of our aircraft were immediately catapulted off to give battle, and one of these

was successful in shooting down an enemy aircraft within 2min of leaving the flight deck. Another FW was shortly shot down and the remainder chased off, but by this time darkness had covered the sky like a cloak, and we all felt extremely concerned about the safety of our own aircraft. The guiding lights were switched on along the runway (from aloft these would appear merely as a row of pinpricks, of course), and to our infinite relief the Wildcats landed on one after the other. The ship was pitching in the heavy swell, to add to the difficulty, and the DLCO (the batsman) was obliged to send the last machine round on several circuits in con-

sequence for fear of a crash landing. The pilot finally came in on his own initiative, and more by luck than judgement narrowly avoided piling his machine against the island. He weathered the batsman's subsequent indignant protests by airily mentioning that his tank was now absolutely dry, and he had no intention of choosing a "ditching" rather than a three-point landing in accordance with the best traditions!

'As a result of this particular "protection racket" the two pilots concerned, Mike Turner and Laurie Brander, both Subbies (A) RNVR were each awarded a well-deserved DSC.'

Below: A flight deck party pushing one of *Pursuer's* Wildcats towards the lift. *via Gordon Wright*

Bottom: A Corsair of No 1842 Squadron taking off from HMS *Rajah* whilst en route from America to Belfast in July 1944, after the squadron had formed and worked up at Brunswick. It later saw service with the British Pacific Fleet aboard HMS *Formidable*. Air disturbance rings from the propeller are visible in this 1/1,000 second shot. *IWM*

Operation 'Torch'

By the autumn of 1942 the tide was turning in the desert, with Rommel's forces being driven steadily westward. American forces in Europe were building up rapidly, and it was decided to mount a joint Anglo-American invasion of Vichy territories in North Africa. The date fixed for the landings was 8 November, and the operation was to be carried out under the code-name 'Torch', with the Fleet Air Arm destined to play a vital part in its success.

Available to support the amphibious operation were the fleet carriers *Argus*, *Furious*, *Formidable* and *Victorious*, and in addition the escort carriers *Avenger*, *Biter* and *Dasher*. These latter were recently-introduced conversions of a merchant vessel supplied by the Americans, and known by them as CVEs, which were basically intended for escorting convoys.

The first landings took place at 01.00hrs, with the smaller carriers lying nearby waiting to fly off dawn fighter patrols to provide cover for the troop transports. Aboard *Victorious* were the Martlets of No 882 Squadron, the pilot of machine 'C' being Lt

(A) B. H. C. Nation, RN (now Cdr B. H. C. Nation RN Rtd), who was to have a unique experience:

'Soon after dawn, *Victorious* flew off her Martlet fighters to carry out a patrol over the Vichy French airfield at Blida about 40 miles south-west of Algiers. I was the leader of this patrol and, as we climbed away heading for the North African coast we saw, spread out below us, the massive Allied invasion fleet approaching the beaches — it was a fantastic sight and one which I shall never forget.

'We crossed the coast and headed inland. Our orders were to prevent any aircraft from taking-off and to report by R/T to the ship any information on troop movements.

'We encountered a small amount of anti-aircraft fire as we approached our target, but the firing petered out after a few minutes. As we flew round the airfield we could see a large number of dispersed aircraft, anti-aircraft gunners manning, but not firing, their guns and farm workers in the surrounding fields waving their handkerchiefs. There seemed very little activity going on below us, and even the aircraft ground crews were con-

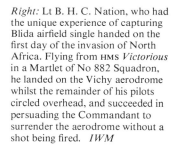

Right: Lt B. H. C. Nation, who had the unique experience of capturing Blida airfield single handed on the first day of the invasion of North Africa. Flying from HMS *Victorious* in a Martlet of No 882 Squadron, he landed on the Vichy aerodrome whilst the remainder of his pilots circled overhead, and succeeded in persuading the Commandant to surrender the aerodrome without a shot being fired. *IWM*

Far right: Seafires of No 885 Squadron and an Albacore of No 820 Squadron with wings folded, being ranged on the deck of HMS *Formidable* during Operation 'Torch'. The carrier was then part of Force H, which acted as Covering Group during the invasion. At the head of the other ships can be seen HMS *Victorious*. *IWM*

spicuous by their absence. I therefore reported to the ship that I thought the French had given in and were ready to surrender. The ship's Air Staff found this difficult to believe, and asked whether we were over the right airfield. Luckily I was able to report that the name "Blida" was written in large white letters in the middle of the airfield. I then asked the ship if I could land and accept the surrender, and a few minutes later I received a message from my Admiral that I could land "If I thought it was safe to do so". An enemy airfield may not, perhaps, be the most salubrious place to land on — nevertheless I felt it was the right thing to do, and the element of surprise would certainly be in my favour.

'I told my pilots what I was going to do and asked them to cover my approach and landing and, if the French opened fire on us, they were to "blitz" the airfield and leave me to my own devices to get away as best I could. In the event I landed without incident and taxied towards a group of officers, switched off my engine, climbed out of my aeroplane and drew my revolver. I ordered

Left: A scene on board HMS *Victorious* on 8 November 1942, the day of the invasion. All aircraft carry the 'Torch Star' insignia, and their fin flashes have been painted out. Ranged immediately behind the lowered crash barrier is a Fulmar II of No 809 Squadron, with Martlet IVs of No 882 Squadron lined up immediately following it. Also on deck are Albacores of A Flight No 832 Squadron and Seafire IICs of No 884 Squadron. The ship had sailed from Greenock on 30 October, to where she returned in due course on 23 November. *IWM*

Below left: Bombing up an Albacore of No 820 Squadron on the flight deck of HMS *Formidable* during Operation 'Torch'. The aircraft were armed with six 250lb bombs each for a squadron strike on targets in the region of Algiers. Part of the 'Torch Star' marking, painted especially for the invasion, can be seen on the fuselage beneath the centre bomb. In the background is a Seafire IB of No 885 Squadron with similar insignia underneath the wings. *IWM*

Above: Albacore 'G' of No 820 Squadron being ranged, with wings folded, on the flight deck of HMS *Formidable* during Operation 'Torch'. Its six 250lb bombs are already in position underneath the wings. *IWM*

Right: Martlet IV FN121 'Ø9Z' of No 893 Squadron crossing the lowered arrester wires as it takes off from HMS *Formidable* during the North African landings. It carries the 'Torch Star' insignia used for the operation and the inscription 'US NAVY' on the rear fuselage. The squadron had rearmed with Martlet IVs a month before the attack, their squadron numbering and lettering being painted on at Hatston on 16 October, just before embarkation. *IWM*

one of the officers to take me to his Commanding Officer — in the most appalling French — and with my revolver pointing at his back we marched to the administrative buildings. We passed a number of French soldiers with rifles, but they made no attempt to stop me. Outside the main building two sentries with fixed bayonets came to atten- tion as we walked in, which I thought at the time was a courteous gesture on their part until I realised that the salute was, of course, for their own officer.

'While all this was going on, the Martlets were flying low round the airfield in a very purposeful manner, and I had no doubts at all that they would open up with their machine guns if the French tried to interfere with my aircraft in any way. This was a comforting thought as we entered the Commandant's office. An elderly General rose from his desk and was somewhat surprised to find himself looking down the barrel of a revolver. I told him that he had no alternative but to surrender his base immediately, otherwise a striking force from the carriers would be launched with instructions to bomb Blida until they gave in. He said he needed time to discuss this with his officers, so I told him he could make one internal telephone call but that, if I was not in the air within 15min, the ship would be informed by the patrolling Martlets and his airfield would be bombed. He spoke for 2-3min on the telephone and, as he was doing this, I heard the sound of distant gunfire which meant that the American Rangers were closing in. I think this decided him for he picked up a piece of paper from his desk, and wrote that the base at Blida was at the disposal of the Allied Forces. Thus the airfield with some 60 aircraft and a garrison of 500 troops surrendered without a shot being fired.

'I had now been on the ground for nearly half an hour and was anxious to rejoin my pilots in the air and return to the carrier so, using the same French officer as a hostage in case of any last minute tricks, I walked back to my aeroplane, still keeping the unfortunate Frenchman covered. As I taxied away from him, I gave him a smile, but I don't think he had much of a sense of humour as he gave me a very cold and hostile look — perhaps one can hardly blame him for this!'

Another participant in this operation was Dennis Mudd, then Sub-Lt (A) D. R. Mudd RNVR serving with No 813 Squadron at North Front aerodrome, Gibraltar, who first saw the invasion convoy when piloting Swordfish '4M' on 6 November. He recalls: 'When the convoy came through the Straits my observer, Sub-Lt (A) D. Baring-Gould RNVR, and telegraphist air gunner, L/Air G. Machan, and I had the honour of doing the first patrol ahead of that whole convoy. We had not been told in the briefing what to expect, only that we would get a surprise. It was a fantastic sight — it went on and on for about 100 miles in length, liners, battleships, carriers, we just couldn't believe it. When we got to the end there was a signalling by Aldis lamp from a trawler, which turned out to be the Admiral in charge of the convoy asking us where certain of the ships were. One of our duties was to get ahead of the convoy and carry out the usual anti-submarine sweep, and then when we got back we were told to keep our mouths shut.

Below: A Seafire IIC of No 880 Squadron lands aboard HMS *Argus* during the North African landings. The special 'Torch Star' marking is visible on the fuselage of another machine parked at the forward end of the flight deck. The censor has been at work on the aerials in the centre of the picture. No 880 Squadron had joined the ship from Machrihanish on 16 October, and she sailed from the Clyde on 27 October. After the operation she returned to Greenock on 21 November, the Seafires having disembarked the previous day to Hatston. *IWM*

Bottom: One of the troop convoys en route for Gibraltar escorted by HMS *Biter*. The three Swordfish IIs of No 833 Squadron's A Flight are visible on deck, these aircraft being eventually disembarked to Gibraltar from where they carried out anti-submarine patrols. The escort carrier also carried the Sea Hurricane IIBs and IICs of No 800 Squadron, which had only recently re-equipped from IBs. *IWM*

Right: Seafire IIC MB156 'Ø6G' of No 885 Squadron warming up on the deck of HMS *Formidable* early in 1943. This aircraft had taken part in Operation 'Torch', but by this time had reverted to normal fuselage roundels in place of the 'Torch Star'. It had been issued to the squadron on re-equipment at Machrihanish in October 1942, and served with them until 7 April 1943 when it bounced during a landing whilst the ship was at Mers-el-Kebir. Its subsequent crash into the ship's barrier inflicted sufficiently heavy damage for it to be written off. *FAA Museum*

'On the 10th, six of our aircraft flew across to Tafaroui and landed after a flight of four hours, and the following day at dawn we again flew in "4M" to carry out the first Fleet Air Arm anti-submarine patrol from north-west Africa. On the 12th we moved to Blida.

'Although we missed out on a lot of the major attacks, we had a lot of experience and fun. We were all kitted out at some Army establishment at Gibraltar with Army battle dress a day or two before the landings, and given a .38 revolver. Once we got to Tafaroui they were all Americans, so we joined in with the messing, using army rations which were very good right down to cigarettes, sweets and toilet paper.

'It was a marvellous life for a youngster. I remember on one occasion at Tafaroui having a cook-up with an open fire, because we just slept in the hangar leaving the aircraft outside, and on this occasion a high-ranking American officer came over and asked if he could share the grub. He said, "Hey bud, I'm Dolittle" — it was General Dolittle, who had landed in his B-25 Mitchell and stayed the night, going on again the next morning.

'It was free-lance at Blida too, for the first month or two, fending for ourselves from a large box of rations which we drew. After that it became an RAF station with a proper administration — the colours went up and the whole atmosphere changed. It became a properly run establishment with all the food pooled, so we were awfully glad when we got away from it and moved on up to Bone.'

Sub-Lt (A) A. M. Sweeting RNVR was an observer with No 817 Squadron, an Albacore squadron aboard *Victorious* at the time of the landings. Now Dr Tony Sweeting, living in Canada, he recalls that he was despatched to Maison Blanche early on the morning of the invasion:

'Johnny Mills and I took off early that morning as there was apparently a "hang-up" in communications from ship-to-shore and vice-versa. The Army needed some naval W/T types to service their sets, and so a pair of No 817 Albacores were despatched with these types and some wireless parts. We landed at Maison Blanche, the main airport at Algiers, to be greeted by a dapper RAF Group Captain in immaculate light-blue battle dress and a formal salute. We were ushered over to the Flight Control tower and we sat around.

'There were some intriguing sights at Maison Blanche, this being only about five hours after the initial landings. There was a Ju52/3m parked to the side of the main runway full of loot that the German representatives in North Africa had hoped to get out, but had been forestalled. On the north side of the airfield were many parked French fighters. They were nippy little aircraft that could have made mincemeat of us had they decided to take-off, but I learnt later that they decided conditions were too "misty" — though I had not observed any mist on our flights into Maison Blanche!

'We were informed that they were having problems on the beaches getting petrol ashore, so refuelling would have to wait until the morning. It looked like a long wait at that point, so we broke into the emergency rations of our dinghies in the aircraft, as there was no food available elsewhere. The main item was a slab of almost black chocolate, but the wide-eyed Algerian youngsters who gathered in the doorway had not seen chocolate for years, some of them never, so we gave it to them.

'Our immediate problem was to find somewhere to sleep. Eventually it was a deserted barrack room, the French personnel being nowhere to be seen. The place was a scruffy mess, and the only facility was a cast-iron bed with a wired and springed frame plus a

Above: Members of No 813 Squadron and their aircraft at Blida after the invasion. From left to right they are Sub-Lt P. C. Heath, Sub-Lt F. D. Baring-Gould, Sub-Lt G. A. Donaghue, Sub-Lt D. R. Mudd, Sub-Lt R. S. Hankey (Senior Pilot), Sub-Lt H. O'Donnell, Lt-Cdr C. Hutchinson (Commanding Officer), Sub-Lt R. D. Pears, Sub-Lt D. Walker and unidentified. Also on the airfield can be seen several C-47s of the USAAF. *D. R. Mudd*

Left: Quarters for some of the crews of No 813 Squadron at Bone in December 1942. The bungalow had been occupied by a family just before the invasion, and they had only just left when the Navy took it over. Improvised beds included a wardrobe laid flat, with the door removed. On one occasion a bomb was dropped within 50yd of the bungalow, but fortunately it failed to explode and was dug up by Cornish miners from a nearby Army unit. At night frogs could be heard croaking in the nearby marshland. *D. R. Mudd*

palliasse. Johnny and I tossed up for who should get the wire frame and who should get the palliasse. I "lost" and slept on the wire, but it was Johnny who woke up covered in bites from other occupants of the mattress.

'In the meantime, our Senior Officer had been trying to find means of contacting the ship. Our own radios were useless and the Air Control tower radios unable to cope, so he conceived the magnificent idea of asking Radio Algiers, located in the city, to get on to the Fleet frequency with their more powerful transmitters. To do this, he commandeered a large old-fashioned bicycle and pumped down the road right between the desultory fire of the landed Allied troops on the one side and a pocket of reluctantly defiant Vichy outfits on the other. The spectacle of this very proper RN Lieutenant steaming down the road (in No 1s, no less) on this ponderous bicycle, serenely ignoring the sporadic shots was, to me, hilarious — despite the danger involved. Anyway, his efforts were successful, and we took-off in the morning at first light.

'It was lovely flying weather, and on the way back to the carrier I sighted a "sub" on the surface, which smartly dived into the clear waters of the Med. I could still see it under the surface, but whether it was one of ours or one of theirs I do not know. Anyway, we did not have any kind of armament, so it was useless to attempt an attack. Whilst we had been ashore the rest of the squadron had carried out attacks on two recalcitrant Vichy-held forts at the entrance to Algiers harbour. One of them was very tricky because it appeared there was a convent very close by, and to be avoided, but as far as I know this was accomplished. In any event, the Vichy French forces gave up fairly quickly. I surmise that their hearts weren't really in it.'

Arctic Convoys

The majority of the earlier Arctic convoys formed up at Hvalfiord in Iceland, switching in March 1942 to Reykjavik, then to Loch Ewe in September of that year, and finally to the Clyde in early 1945. Their destination in 1941 and 1942 was either Archangel or Murmansk, and thereafter Kola Inlet, the first convoy sailing from Hvalfiord in August 1941 and arriving at Archangel after a 10-day voyage.

Little air support was available for the earlier convoys, this consisting only of a Walrus or two aboard an escorting warship. There was at first little apparent need for such support, with only one merchant ship being lost out of over 100 which sailed up to the beginning of March 1942. Thereafter losses from both aircraft and U-boats mounted steadily, culminating in the loss of 23 ships out of 34 which sailed in June 1942 with convoy PQ17.

Air support for PQ17 included Walrus

Right: Albacore N4221 '5L' of No 817 Squadron on patrol from HMS *Victorious* off the coast of Iceland during 1941. Albacores of this squadron took part in numerous operations in northern waters, and were also involved in the North African landings. N4221 was later relegated to second line use with various units before crashing in the sea on 27 June 1943 whilst with No 785 Squadron at Crail. *via A. G. Clayton*

Below: HMS *Victorious* off the coast of Iceland, possibly around September 1941. The small number of Martlets visible on deck are most likely of No 802B Squadron. No 802 Squadron also had aircraft in HMS *Argus* and HMS *Activity* around this time, but the squadron ceased to exist when the latter ship was sunk by *U-751* off the coast of Portugal on 21 December 1941. *via A. G. Clayton*

P5706 aboard the cruiser *Norfolk*, her crew comprising the pilot, Sub-Lt (A) R. Wignall RNVR; the observer, Sub-Lt (A) G. R. N. Riley RNVR and telegraphist air gunner L/ Air G. Gibbons. On 4 July this machine was catapulted at 19.45hrs (zonal time) on a two hour reconnaissance to find the southern limits of the ice edge, but she was destined never to return to her parent ship. Geoff Riley still has the draft of his original report, of which these extracts starkly illustrate the fate of this particular Walrus. He points out that the times given are zonal times, to which one hour should be added for the corresponding Admiralty signal times:

'The position of *Norfolk* for returning was to be close ahead of PQ17; consequently the convoy was used as a basis of navigation. The outward leg was completed at 20.49hrs, half of it being flown at 1,500ft above a thick sea level mist with few clear patches. ASV was used to find ice only two small floes being found and homed on to. The return course was 210°. At 21.39hrs the aircraft flew over a unit of the convoy at 100ft in thick fog coming out at ETA on the starboard side of the convoy in comparatively clear weather. Not finding the cruiser force ahead of the convoy and seeing that it (the convoy) was splitting up for some reason, a signal by V/S to a Halycon class MS (HMS *Britomart?*) regarding the position of the cruiser force. We were told that they were last seen bearing 150°. The aircraft then flew in this direction for about 15 miles, nothing being seen. The ASV had already become u/s while searching ahead of the convoy for *Norfolk*. The only thing left to do was to carry out a suggestion made by the Commanding Officer, HMS *Norfolk* on the previous evening when an AS sweep was made in thick fog 35 miles N of Bear Island, to land alongside a member of the convoy and be taken aboard. At this time (22.25hrs) HMS *Palomares* signalled the aircraft to close her and informed the crew that the cruiser force was seen some time previously heading west at high speed. It was then decided to attempt

Left: An Albacore taking off from the flight deck of HMS *Victorious* during an Icelandic convoy around November 1941. Ahead of the carrier can be seen the battleship HMS *King George V*. At that time the ship carried Nos 817 and 820 Albacore squadrons. *IWM*

Below: The engine of Fulmar N4074 '6K' of No 809 Squadron being warmed up aboard HMS *Victorious* in Seidisfjord around November 1941. The cowling side panel has been removed. This aircraft survived until 12 January 1944, when it crashed into the sea after striking the mast of a landing craft during a co-operation exercise, whilst with No 772 FRU Squadron at Machrihanish. *IWM*

to tow the aircraft astern of *Palomares*, accordingly a signal was made requesting a grass line to be floated astern. While preparations were being made HMS *Palomares* opened fire with her 4in AA armament on a Blohm & Voss Bv 138 which was attempting to attack the Walrus from astern. On landing (at 22.40hrs) the grass was picked up from the buoy floated from *Palomares'* stern. All heavy gear was removed from the aircraft to lighten her for towing purposes. These were stowed on HMS *Palomares*.

'At this time the situation was that some German destroyers were crossing the Barents Sea to catch the remainder of PQ17 at the entrance to the White Sea. As a result of this information HMS *Palomares* made for the Matochkin Strait at full speed (12kts). She was in company with two merchant ships, *Halcyon*, *Britomart* and *Salamander*. The Strait was reached at 11.30hrs on 6th and the ships anchored at 11.50hrs. The aircraft was then hauled in and was found to contain 9-12in of water. This is thought to be a small amount when it is taken into consideration that the aircraft had to be towed at 11-12kts for 37hrs (over 400 miles), during about 12hrs of which the sea was very choppy. The

remainder of the removable gear was removed and stowed on HMS *Palomares*. At this time it was decided, if possible, to stow the a/c on a merchant ship for passage to Archangel. This was arranged by CO HMS *Palomares* with the Captain of *Ocean Freedom*. A flight was undertaken at 19.45hrs of about 20min duration in order to drop the Depth Charge which was still in the rack. It would not however leave the rack due, it is thought, to the fusing devices being corroded by sea water. On returning it was tied up astern of *Palomares*. The pilot and observer were then transferred to HMS *Britomart* for passage to Archangel. At 11.00hrs on 7th the aircraft was taxied to *Ocean Freedom*, where it was hoisted on board for passage to Archangel.'

Ocean Freedom was one of 11 merchantmen which eventually arrived at Archangel on 11 July, as part of a small convoy, having survived 10 near misses in a dive bombing attack by Ju88s the previous day. The Walrus had suffered only relatively minor damage, and various attempts were made to try to return her aboard *Ocean Freedom*. The intention was to re-stow her on the ship's

Left: An Albacore of one of the *Victorious* squadrons awaiting an engine test off the coast of Iceland. In the background can be seen the accompanying battleship, HMS *Nelson. IWM*

after-hatch cover, as she had been carried from Matochkin to Archangel, but she was still ashore when the ship eventually sailed on 11 September. On his return to the UK, Geoff Riley received a letter from the captain of *Norfolk*, in which he wrote that he would very much like to know what had happened to them.

As a result of the experience of this convoy, no more were despatched until September, when PQ18 left Loch Ewe with 40 merchant vessels on 2nd, the departure venue now having been changed to Reykjavik. Improved air cover was now available in the shape of the new escort carrier *Avenger*, which joined the convoy seven days after she had sailed, off Iceland. Aboard her were 18 Sea Hurricanes of Nos 802 and 883 Squadrons, and three Swordfish of No 825 Squadron. The enemy were keen to repeat their success with PQ17, and had strengthened Luftflotte V in northern Norway. They began their attacks on 12th and the Sea Hurricanes went up, but they made the mistake of chasing the Bv138 shadowers, leaving the convoy exposed to the attack of torpedo-carrying He111s, which succeeded in sinking eight of the merchant vessels. The fighter pilots learnt quickly from this salutory lesson, and no more successful air attacks were made whilst their carrier was with the convoy. Further attacks came on 13th and 14th, and the Sea Hurricanes were continuously in action, pausing only to land, refuel and re-arm before taking off again to repel more of the attackers. In all they had shot down five He111s and Ju88s during the three days of the operation and damaged another 21, only one of their number being lost to enemy action, although three fell foul of fire from the merchant ships, the pilots fortunately being picked up.

The Swordfish had been equally active, dropping depth charges on 16 U-boats, including the destruction of *U-589* which was

shared with the destroyer *Onslow*. Many German aircraft were shot down by anti-aircraft fire and the total losses which they suffered, 41 aircraft in all, were such that they resorted mainly to U-boat attacks on later convoys, though they never again approached the success they had achieved with PQ17 and PQ18.

This change of tactic was fortunate for the Royal Navy as the escort carriers were no longer available, being now required for Operation 'Torch'. *Dasher* sailed with JW53, which left Loch Ewe on 15 February 1943, but she had to turn back after two days due to being damaged in bad weather. It was not until JW57 sailed a year later that another escort carrier could be spared for this purpose. For this convoy, *Chaser* embarked the Swordfish and Wildcats of No 816 Squadron, joining the convoy of 43 ships and their escort on 21 February 1944, to run the gauntlet of the 14 U-boats which lay ahead. The weather was terrible for the Swordfish crews in their exposed cockpits, but on the return journey, as RA57, the *U-472* was damaged by rocket fire on 4 March, and then sunk by the guns of *Onslaught*. This was followed by two more RP successes, with

Above: An Albacore of No 820 Squadron being held down after landing on HMS *Victorious*, as a precaution against the gale that was blowing. The aircraft had just returned from an anti-submarine patrol, the ship being in the vicinity of Iceland at the time. *IWM*

Above: A Fulmar of No 809 Squadron being flagged in by the Parking Officer of HMS *Victorious* around January 1942. The squadron's 'Donald Duck' emblem can be seen painted on the nose of the aircraft, immediately underneath the engine exhausts. *IWM*

Right: Albacore X9086 '4Q' of No 832 Squadron, with wings folded, standing in front of two Fulmars of No 809 Squadron on the flight deck of HMS *Victorious* early in 1942. In the background is the battleship HMS *Duke of York*. *IWM*

U-366 being sunk the next day and *U-973* on 6th. The carrier arrived back at Scapa on 9th with only one merchant vessel being lost, on the homeward journey.

Also successful was JW/RA 58, which occurred at the same time as Operation 'Tungsten', the *Tirpitz* strike. She left Loch Ewe on 27 March 1944 with both *Activity* and *Tracker* in attendance, the former carrying three Swordfish and seven Wildcats of No 819 Squadron, and the latter 12 Avengers and seven Wildcats of No 846 Squadron. The first successes came on 1 April when *U-355* was sunk by the joint efforts of a No 846 Squadron Avenger and HMS *Beagle*, and two days later *U-288* suf-fered a similar fate at the hands of No 819 Squadron Swordfish and No 846 Squadron Avengers. Three other U-boats were damaged, and six shadowing aircraft were destroyed. When the convoy returned to Loch Ewe on 14th, the ships had emerged without loss. This was to be the only occasion on which Avengers had any success in the five such trips in which they were involved.

RA59 was purely a westbound convoy, and for this *Activity* sailed on 19 April with the three Swordfish and seven Wildcats of No 833 Squadron, these comprising part of No 819 Squadron detached to form a new unit. She was accompanied by *Fencer* carry-

Top left: Tethered aircraft aboard the escort carrier HMS *Activity* around May-June 1944, during an Arctic convoy. The photograph was taken shortly after a heavy snow squall. In the foreground are two Wildcats of No 833 Squadron, and behind them one of the No 819 Squadron's Swordfish, equipped with rockets underneath the wings. No 833 Squadron had formed on 16 April 1944 from the Fighter Flight of No 819 Squadron. On this trip the carrier embarked five Wildcats and three Swordfish. *R. K. L. Yeo*

Bottom left: A German U-boat is sighted by an Avenger during an Arctic convoy, being later sunk by a destroyer. This is almost certainly *U-355*, which was sunk on 1 April 1944 by HMS *Beagle* after being attacked by Avengers of No 846 Squadron from the escort carrier HMS *Tracker*. The squadron made several attacks on U-boats that day. After one of these, Sub-Lt Ballantyne in Avenger FN877 hit the ship's round down on returning and was killed, though his crew were saved. In another attack, by two squadron Wildcats, Sub-Lt T. D. Lucey struck the submarine with his aircraft and later had to ditch, but fortunately was rescued by HMS *Beagle* after spending 2hr in his dinghy. *FAA Museum*

ing 11 Swordfish and nine Wildcats of No 842 Squadron. They reached Vaenga Bay on 24th, and started for home with the convoy on 28th. On 1 May the Wildcats shot down a Bv138C, and on the same day a No 842 Squadron Swordfish successfully attacked *U-277*. The following day *U-674* and *U-959* were added to the toll by No 842 Squadron, who also attacked eight other U-boats before the ship docked at Greenock on 5 May.

One of the Wildcat pilots with No 819 Squadron and later No 833 Squadron was Dick Yeo, who later recorded his recollections of these two trips:

'On reaching Tail o' the Bank from a convoy, early in April, we found that another carrier there, HMS *Biter*, had had engine trouble entailing us taking her place at short notice. Buzzes were many and varied, but the embarkation of cold weather stores indicated a Russian convoy. Disembarking all but three Swordfish and embarking five Wildcat Vs with pilots, we sailed for Loch Ewe in north-west Scotland, where the convoy and escort, including another carrier, HMS *Tracker*, were all assembling.

'After battling with many snow squalls, submarines and shadowers, we reached Vaenga, in Kola Inlet, near Murmansk without losing a ship. On the way up we got two Ju88s and two Fw200s whilst *Tracker* got a Fw200 and shared a Bv138 with us. The escorts got two U-boats and the two carriers shared a third. On one day Jimmy Bowles ditched on take-off and got picked up by our own whaler. Dangerous perhaps, but a nice bit of work by the Skipper. On the homeward voyage, which was uneventful, we heard that while outward-bound we had been a decoy for the Home Fleet which followed us about 200 miles astern. Its aircraft pranged the *Tirpitz* in Kaa Fjord. The fighter types in the fleet carrier were very envious of our successes — the Fleet was undetected and unshadowed.

'No sooner had we got back to Scapa than we received orders to go back to Russia once again with a large escort and the carrier HMS *Fencer*. There was no convoy up, but we had to bring back all the ships we had taken previously. HMS *Tracker* did not come because an Avenger had flown into her round-down and caused some damage. Coming home against further hazards we damaged several snoopers, and Jack Large and I got a Bv138, a flamer in full view of the convoy. It had been trying to molest one of the *Fencer's* Swordfish. Continuous attacks were made by U-boat packs, but were driven off. Many were damaged by aircraft and escorts, and one was probably sunk. Only one merchant ship was lost — hit by two torpedoes while close on our port beam. They were probably meant for us! We did not remain long at Scapa Flow but headed southward for the Clyde. On these convoys we all qualified for the famous Blue-Nose Certificate. While up in Russia the bits and pieces of the different squadrons on board were combined in No 833 Squadron with Jack Large as CO.

'From the end of May until early September 1944 there followed a long succession of convoys, one or two monthly but mostly slow, down to Gibraltar and back. For the most part they were boring in the extreme, and rarely did we get any excitement — we chased a number of unidentified aircraft only to find them friendly.'

Above: Crews in the air operations room of the escort carrier HMS *Fencer* being briefed by Lt-Cdr (A) J. M. Glaser RN, the Air Staff Officer. The ship carried the Swordfish of No 842 Squadron, which succeeded in sinking three U-boats at the beginning of May 1942 during an Arctic convoy, and also attacked eight others. This squadron also had a fighter flight equipped with Seafires, these being later replaced by Wildcats. *IWM*

Left: The escort carrier *Nairana* with her bows hidden by heavy seas. Aboard her were the Swordfish of No 835 Squadron, which also included a flight of Sea Hurricanes, later replaced by Wildcats. Squadron aircraft shot down one enemy aircraft during a North Russian convoy in December 1944, and a further two in a similar convoy two months later. *IWM*

There were several more Arctic convoys before the end of the war. JW64 sailed from the Clyde on 3 February 1945 under the code-name Operation 'Hotbed', its escort including the carriers *Campania* and *Nairana*. The former had a new type of air warning radar, and carried No 813 Squadron equipped with 12 Swordfish III, four Wildcat VI and a Fulmar night fighter attached from No 784 Squadron. *Nairana* carried 14 Swordfish III and six Wildcat VI No 835 Squadron. On the afternoon of 6th a Ju88 shadower appeared, but was quickly shot down by No 813 Squadron Wildcats. The following morning 12 Ju88 torpedo bombers appeared, but one was shot down by a corvette and the remainder eventually withdrew after evading No 835 Squadron's Wildcats. Many further aircraft were seen on the following two days, and it was assumed that these were guiding U-boats to the convoy, but the searching Swordfish could find no trace of these. At 17.30hrs on 8 February the obsolescent Fulmar was flown off in an attempt to track down the shadowing aircraft with its AI radar, but this was giving trouble and the chase had to be called off after getting within 1½ miles of the shadower. The aircraft crashed heavily on landing and was of no further assistance during the voyage.

On 10 February further attacks were made by Ju88 torpedo bombers coming in from all directions in continuous attacks. The new aircraft radar aboard *Campania* gave ample warning of these, enabling the Wildcats to rise to meet them and the convoy to take evasive action, but several of the aircraft were damaged by the ship's own guns and only one remained serviceable as a result of their unwelcome efforts. On the return voyage U-boats had some early success, but the convoy was scattered by a hurricane force gale the second night out and it was still attempting to form up on the morning of 20 February when Ju88s were detected coming in at around 10.00hrs. No 358 Squadron sent up a pair of Wildcats and one of the enemy aircraft was sent off with a smoking engine. Many torpedoes were dropped but none hit any of the ships, and No 835 Squadron claimed another kill, with other successes and probables being claimed by the escorts and the fighters. Out of 25 attackers there was an estimated total of three kills, two probables and two possibles. The convoy eventually reached Loch Ewe on 28 February after encountering further gales.

The final convoy JW/RA67 sailed after VE-day, accompanied by the escort carrier *Queen* as a precaution should any U-boat commander decide to violate the German surrender, but the patrols of No 853 Squadron Avengers and Wildcats fortunately proved unnecessary.

Above: A frost covered Walrus aboard the cruiser HMS *Glasgow* during an Arctic convoy in the winter of 1942/43. The protective cover of the engine has been partially blown off. On the outer wing struts and on the upper mainplane can be seen ASV aerials, whilst under the lower mainplanes is a depth charge. This aircraft may be W2726, which was issued to *Glasgow* Flight late in 1941.
via E. Abrams

Mediterranean Landings 1943-1944

By the beginning of 1943 it was apparent that it would only be a matter of time before the Axis Powers were totally ejected from the African continent and that the battle must be joined elsewhere, but there were still insufficient resources to mount an invasion in northern France. At the Summit Conference in January, therefore, it was decided that the next logical step was an invasion of Sicily as an interim measure, utilising the large concentration of manpower and shipping still in the Mediterranean theatre.

After the North African landings, the two surviving escort carriers had resumed their normal duties, and *Argus* was relegated to deck landing training work in the Clyde. *Victorious* had sailed home for a month's refit, and then headed west to join the US Navy in the South-West Pacific. *Furious* remained in the Mediterranean until the end of January, then she too departed to join the Home Fleet, leaving *Formidable* as the only carrier in this arena for the next few months.

By the beginning of May 1943, the Tunisian campaign was over, and preparations could begin in earnest. There would be less need for carrier support in this next invasion, as there were now ample airfield

facilities available within striking range, both in Malta and Tunisia. However, there was still a danger from the Italian Fleet, and consequently the repaired *Indomitable* was brought in from Home waters to join *Formidable* in Force H, arriving at Gibraltar on 23 June.

The invasion took place on 10 July, as Operation 'Husky', but the Fleet Air Arm was little involved. However, during the night of 16/17 July a Ju88 came in to attack the carriers, and was mistaken for one of the returning Albacores, enabling it to get in close enough to put a torpedo into the *Indomitable*. The missile hit the carrier on her port side, and the damage to the boiler-room was sufficiently serious to put her out of action once more. Tony Sweeting, still with No 817 Squadron, now in *Indomitable*, was carrying out an anti-submarine patrol during that night and recalls:

'We were able to listen to the radios of the tank forces ashore as they forced their way into Sicily — most intriguing. Adm Lyster, commanding the carrier force, decided that we should be kept busy and ordered a night sweep to surprise U-boats charging batteries on the surface. He also intended to make his

Below: Wildcat FN114 '∅9F' of No 893 Squadron taking off from the deck of HMS *Formidable* in the Western Mediterranean during the spring of 1943 for a patrol over the Fleet. This machine ended its days with No 768 Squadron at Abbotsinch, giving deck landing training on carriers in the Firth of Clyde. *FAA Museum*

Above: Seafire LIIC LR642 '8M' of No 807 Squadron suffered a broken nose after the arrester wire parted whilst it was landing on HMS *Battler*, probably during the Salerno landings when low wind speed led to many accidents of this nature. *FAA Museum*

Left: Fighter aircraft ranged for take-off from the deck of HMS *Formidable* around the time of Operation 'Avalanche'. In the foreground are two Seafires of No 885 Squadron, and behind them are Martlets of No 888 Squadron. Both of these squadrons had joined the carrier in October 1942, and remained with her until October 1943 when they disembarked, both disbanding within a month. *IWM*

presence known, hoping to entice the Italians out to challenge us. If I recall correctly, the signal said "I intend to trail my coat along the Italian coast".

'There were six of No 817's aircraft on parallel courses on this night search, my pilot being Sub-Lt Munro, a New Zealander. The search was uneventful — no U-boats; but as we closed the carrier on the return leg, all hell broke loose. There was "flak" all over the sky. We veered away and I kept our position relative to the Fleet on the ASV. Soon the "flak" died down and, on approaching closer, it was apparent that the carrier was in trouble. We could see, in the path of the moon, that she was listing heavily, and that it was most unlikely that we were going to be able to land on. Later, we learnt that she had been hit in the port boiler room by a torpedo aircraft from the Italian mainland which had been mistaken for one of us returning early — so no avoiding action had been taken.

'A small light from the bridge blinked the signal "Go to Malta". That was all very well, but we were now unsure of our point of departure. However, I gave Neil Munro a course to steer and happily we made a landfall right over Valetta. The dicey bit was that the defences of Malta had been beefed up with night fighting Beaufighters equipped with radar, who shot first at whatever target came upon their screens. We were coming in unannounced as radio silence was still being observed, since we did not want the enemy to know that a whole carrier had been knocked out, therefore we arrived with all lights flashing. With the odd Very light recognition off, and the Aldis lamp flashing the letter of the day, we must have looked like a Christmas tree. Nevertheless we found Hal Far, a dusty strip of beaten down earth,

marked down one side by flares made of burning rags in oil cans. We counted noses and found that Freddie Bradley, our American born member, was missing, but it was not long before he and "Mac" MacLean came into dispersal — a very disgruntled crew, having tangled with one of our destroyers who shot first and asked afterwards. They had a hole through the fuselage, just aft of the air gunner's position, to prove it.'

Within two months Sicily had been occupied and inevitably the Italian mainland was the next target, with the Eighth Army crossing over the Straits of Messina in the early hours of 3 September. However, secret negotiations with the Italian Government were successfully completed that day, and consequently plans went ahead for a leap-frogging operation in the shape of a landing at Salerno, south of Naples, to be code-named Operation 'Avalanche'.

Considerable naval air support was required for this operation. Force H would provide *Formidable* again, this time accompanied by *Illustrious* which had recently been withdrawn from the Home Fleet, and these would tackle the Italian Navy if it should put in an appearance, though in the event this surrendered the following day. A specially created Force V provided more than 100 fighters, mostly Seafire IICs aboard the assault carriers *Attacker*, *Battler*, *Hunter*, *Stalker* and *Unicorn*, and this had the task of providing cover for the landing troops.

Patrols commenced at dawn on 9 September, but plans to hand over this task to British and American land-based fighters from the second day were unfulfilled owing

Right: A Martlet of No 881 Squadron just lifting off into wind after taking off from the deck of the escort carrier HMS *Pursuer*. During Operation 'Dragoon' this squadron's aircraft flew a total of 180 sorties. *via Gordon Wright*

to the unexpected presence of a resting Panzer division in the area, which prevented the land forces from taking over Montecorvino airfield. A hastily improvised airstrip was set up at Paestum, but the Seafires were unable to use this until 12 September.

This turn of events put a heavy strain on the aircraft of Force V, which had not been intended for continuous operations. There was little wind, the carriers were operating 1,000yd apart and with only a 15kt speed they were unable to make any wind. With relatively inexperienced pilots in many of the squadrons, and fragile undercarriages on the Seafires, the accident rate was excessively high, with No 899 Squadron for example losing 13 machines in three days. Typical of the experiences of these squadrons was that of No 879 Squadron aboard *Attacker*, whose diary for the first day records:

'Our first patrol took off at 06.15hrs. The wings consist of 16 LIICs and six IICs high

cover, each wing remaining airborne for one and one third hours. We all awaited the return of the first patrol. We then realised that we were going to have trouble in landing. There was little or no wind at all and speed over the deck ranged between 18 and 21kts, mostly 19. This made landing on hazardous as the normal safe minimum was 24. Our fears were justified when Sub-Lt Prentice from No 886 Squadron spun in on his approach and was drowned. All our patrol landed on safely but throughout the day tyres were being burst and wing tips and pitot heads pranged as a result of heavy landings due to low wind speed. The patrol had had no excitement with little or no flak and no e/a about. Most disappointing but it was clear that all hopes of an easy victory and landing on Italy were to be put aside.

'The Germans had obviously been prepared for our landings and had some 40-60 Tiger Tanks and the Hermann Göering Panzer Division — a truly tough prop-

Top: Looking aft from the Captain's bridge of HMS *Formidable* in the Western Mediterranean around May 1943 as a Seafire lands on. Parked on deck are three Seafire IBs of No 885 Squadron, two of which still carry only their individual letters, whilst the third has adopted the squadron prefix code '∅6'. MB345, the machine nearest the camera, crashed on deck on 27 June 1943, after bouncing during a fast approach. *IWM*

Above: Hellcat JV105 'EW' of No 800 Squadron aboard the escort carrier HMS *Emperor* around August 1944. This aircraft served with the squadron during the landings in southern France, and later took part in operations in the Aegian to clear the Germans from the Greek Islands. *FAA Museum*

Top: Martlets of No 881 Squadron are parked in the forward deck park of HMS *Pursuer* as she lies at anchor. Clearly visible is the paintwork on the side of the escort carrier, designed to break up its outline when seen from a distance. *via Gordon Wright*

Above: Escort carriers pictured soon after leaving Maddalena, Corsica in August 1944. In the van is *Pursuer*, with *Attacker, Hunter,* the cruiser *Royalist, Striker* and *Patroller* changing course to starboard to follow her. JV666 'UE', the nearest of the Wildcats aboard *Pursuer*, was damaged during a deck landing on 8 November 1944, but was repaired and later joined the fighter flight of No 846 Squadron for Arctic Convoy duties aboard HMS *Trumpeter. via Gordon Wright*

osition. Fighting on shore was most bloody and obviously towards evening things were certainly not going according to plan. The most amazing thing was the lack of air opposition. That there were e/as about we knew as the two monitors on board could keep on picking up such phrases as "Achtung Schpitfeur!", "Do not attack!", "Keep high!", and "Go home!". Jerry most certainly wouldn't play except for a very infrequent FW190 bomber who carefully chose his moment to run in. Pat Pardoe had our first serious prang and had to ram his nose into the barrier. The aircraft was a complete write-off, the engine was torn off its bearers and placed on one side of the deck whilst the fuselage was stripped and then thrown overboard.

'The other carriers seemed to be having just as much difficulty in landing on if not more and all our decks were beginning to look like graveyards. We were just congratulating ourselves on a reasonably prangless day comparatively speaking, when

George Calder, last man to land on from dusk patrol, came in far too fast, floated over wires and barriers, leaving hook and wheels on the deck, knocking one aircraft overboard, damaging two others and finishing up facing the stern dangerously perched on the focs'le. He was extremely lucky to be alive but seemed unaffected by his adventure. With this and some prangs by No 886 our deck had now become a real scrap heap. This then was the end of day one, with the aerodrome as far as we know uncaptured, with most certainly another day's flying before us tomorrow and only five serviceable aircraft. We were working from a carrier that had proved itself hopelessly slow. Most of us think the big wing formation, in view of lack of opposition, useless. We were the only carrier to do our max quota of 52 sorties today. Our troops worked till past midnight getting a/c serviceable for the morrow. Another amazing thing is the lack of enemy attempts to attack Force V. We seem to be successfully keeping e/a away from the

beach. Why can't we start strafing enemy positions etc?'

On 12 September, 26 surviving Seafires went ashore to operate from Paestum in conditions which were both difficult and hazardous, but next day they rejoined their ships, and a week later Force V disbanded. Now that the Italian Fleet was no longer a danger, Force H also disbanded, both *Formidable* and *Illustrious* rejoining the Home Fleet.

Only one more major task was to be required of the FAA in this theatre. After the Normandy landings, which took place on 6 June 1944, the battle in southern Europe began to run into difficulties, therefore plans were laid for a landing in southern France. After a postponement to enable the British and American forces to become well established in Normandy, a date was set for mid-August under the code-name Operation 'Dragoon'. The FAA was once more to play its part, the assault force consisting of

Attacker, *Emperor*, *Hunter*, *Khedive*, *Pursuer*, *Searcher* and *Stalker*, plus two American CVEs, operating as Task Force 88. Landings commenced at dawn on 15 August, and as the Luftwaffe was largely conspicuous by its absence, the naval fighters were able to roam freely and widely, with less carrier accidents than in 'Avalanche', despite similar conditions prevailing, though several aircraft were lost in operations. No 879 Squadron were once more involved, still in *Attacker*, as their diary for the second day of the operation records:
'The weather today is slightly better although there is still only 18-20kt over the deck and it is quite hazy. Most pilots have, however, got used to deck landings under these conditions and during the day there was only one prang.
'The first eight sorties went off at 09.30hrs on a bombing and strafing trip between Brignoles and Aix. Red section was sent to bomb a railway bridge along this road and, although the bridge was not claimed, the road was cratered and one armoured car, one

bowser, a lorry and two trailers and a search-light coach were all fired by strafing attacks. Light flak was reported on this mission and Leckie was hit in the tailplane by a 20mm shell. Fortunately his a/c was controllable at slow speeds and he returned safely.

'No more bombing missions were flown during the day, but TacRs by Yellow, Blue and Black sections brought back some useful information and photographs from a wide area. Yellow 1 and 2 reported a column of 16 M/T, and 30 camouflaged huts near Le Luc, and 120 stationary goods trucks at Brignoles. Flights 3 and 4 made two recces of the island of Port-Cros, which is still holding out, during the day, and reported bombing results

Right: A wind observation being taken by Lt L. S. Cullen RNVR, the Meteorological Officer of HMS *Pursuer* during the landings in southern France.
via J. D. R. Rawlings

Left: A Walrus amphibian making a deck landing on HMS *Pursuer* during Operation 'Avalanche', to bring the ship's crew some rather overdue mail. *via Gordon Wright*

and gunning up positions. TacRs to the east and south-east of Cannes only just discovered small concentrations of transport.

'One spotting mission was flown to the Racle D'Hyères during the evening, but the targets (bridges, guns) were not engaged as our own troops were in the area. Force cover was provided by the squadron at dusk and six sorties were flown.

'Sorties flown during the day — 26 (Dive bombing — 8; TacR — 10; Spotting — 2; Cover — 6).

'Aircraft serviceable 24, plus one in the morning.'

By the end of August the carriers had withdrawn, their task completed. All that now remained for the Navy was to help clear the last pockets of resistance in the Aegean, for which the 'Dragoon' carriers remained in the area initially. Strikes were made against German motor transport and ships. A force of 42 fighters from *Attacker*, *Emperor*, *Khedive* and *Pursuer* carried out an attack on Rhodes on 19 September, dropping 26,000lb bombs in a successful strike in which they suffered no losses. Three of the ships then withdrew from these operations, but the remainder continued for several weeks, the last sorties being flown by Hellcats of No 800 Squadron over Milos on 5 November. The war in the Mediterranean was now ended as far as the FAA was concerned, and they could turn their attentions elsewhere.

Left: Seafire LIII NN344 'KO' of No 899 Squadron, with starboard wing folded, aboard HMS *Khedive* in the Mediterranean during September 1944. The pilot has had the name *Jean* painted on the cowling.
L. J. Kelly via M. Garbett

Below: A Seafire of No 807 Squadron flying over a cruiser whilst on a training flight from RNAS Dekheila late in 1944. The squadron was then temporarily ashore from HMS *Hunter*, which was undergoing a refit at Alexandria after taking part in the south of France landings and the Aegean operations. *IWM*

Norway—Return to the Offensive

The entry into the war of Soviet Russia as a result of the German invasion in June 1941 added to the burdens on an already over-stretched Royal Navy. An obvious way to assist our new allies was to attack German forces in northern Norway. These had already been the target of occasional raids, but resources were limited. Now a large strike was to be mounted on the ports of Petsamo and Kirkenes.

The strike took place on 30 July, with Petsamo as the target of a mixed force of No 817 Squadron Albacores and No 812 Squadron Swordfish from *Furious*, whilst *Victorious* sent off 20 Albacores of No 827 and 828 Squadrons to attack Kirkenes. This account of the latter raid appeared anonymously some years after the war in the journal of the Telegraphist Air Gunners Association:

'A brilliant Arctic sun shines on two aircraft carriers steaming east about 80 miles north of the northern tip of Norway in July 1941. They are accompanied by a cruiser and destroyer escort. Every member of the flying crews aboard has been keyed up for 24hr wondering what comes next.

'At dawn that morning the lookouts have reported that the force is being shadowed by a German aircraft, and it looks dodgy for any operation as we know that every move is being reported. Why didn't we fly off a couple of Fulmars to shoot the shadower down? My guess is that a Fulmar would never have caught up with it.

'Anyway, at around 13.00hrs we are sent for briefing and told that we will fly off at 14.00hrs (in the brilliant Arctic sunshine) for a torpedo attack on massed shipping in Kirkenes harbour whilst the other carrier does the same thing at Petsamo. The briefing boys tell us that we should meet practically

Right: Pilots in the ready room of the escort carrier HMS *Pursuer*. Wildcats of No 881 Squadron took part in shipping strikes and minelaying operations in the Norwegian fjords during November 1944. *FAA Museum*

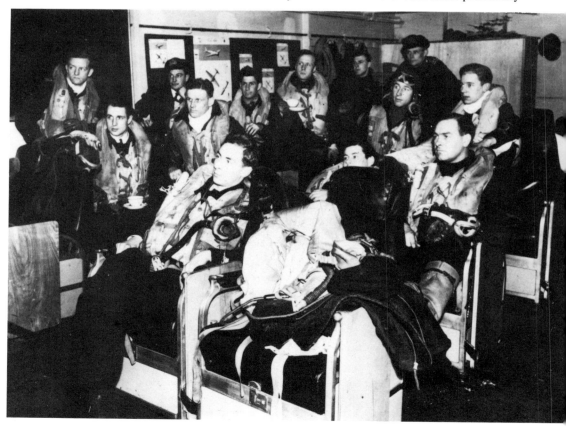

Left: An enemy flak ship blown up by cannon fire from strafing Seafires of No 801 Squadron from HMS *Furious* in August 1944, during Operation 'Begonia'. Seafires can be seen circling the target as an Avenger from No 846 Squadron, also from *Furious*, comes in from the right of the picture. The photograph was taken by another No 846 Squadron Avenger, the attack taking place at Aarumsund, near Sandoy. *FAA Museum*

Above: A Firefly of No 1770 Squadron and Seafires of Nos 887 and 894 Squadrons on the flight deck of HMS *Indefatigable* surrounded by their crews after a successful attack on enemy shipping off the coast of Norway early in August 1944. *IWM*

no opposition from aircraft as 'Jerry' had only a couple of worn out Me109s in the vicinity and the area is only lightly defended by guns. They tell us that we will go in low with the Fulmar squadron as top cover, and also that there is a German hospital ship between us and the coast and that we must not attack it.

'Anyway, we get airborne with quite a lot of misgivings on my part as I do not consider that 14.00hrs on a brilliant summer's day is the ideal time for an attack (after all, why not dawn, even though it is still daylight the Germans must sleep sometime). We climb to about 2,000ft and force on south, and after about half-an-hour sight the hospital ship about two miles to starboard; now I feel even more unhappy thinking that she is probably telling the shore base all about us. You see, there was absolutely no reason for a hospital ship to be in that position.

'We approached the narrow entrance to a fjord at cliff-top height at which time what seemed to me to be thousands of Bofors and machine guns opened up on us, with the gunners having their guns trained horizontally as we went by. I felt like throwing my little Vickers K gun at them. We climbed to get over the hill at the end of the

fjord, and down the other side was the harbour with about four small ships in it (massed shipping?). The ground gunners are still firing, and as we turn to starboard to line up for a torpedo run on the largest ship I see a nice formation of Me110s about half a mile away at about 500ft. (Of course, they didn't know we were coming; they just happened to be there?)

'Everything becomes disorganised and it's every man for himself. Torpedoes careering through the water and Albacores going all ways hotly pursued by the 110s. My aircraft did a very smart about turn and retired at full speed (100mph) the way we had come, followed by the rest of the sub-flight. We hopped over the hill and down the fjord. What with watching the ground gunners and the pursuing 110s, I nearly missed seeing my No 3 hit the sea in flames; we cleared the mouth of the fjord with my No 2 about 500yd astern. No 2 turned away towards the Russian coast hotly pursued by two 110s which eventually shot him down.

'By this time we had turned out to sea and made about eight miles; one of the two Me110s did three ranging attacks on us and then returned to base. These fighters had quite a good attack system; take station astern at about a 1,000yd and then let the cannon shells creep up on your tail; one had to wait until the last minute and then do a sharp turn away on the water.

'Arriving back over the ship I saw one aircraft in a big heap on the deck; we landed after it had been cleared and then waited for the rest of the 17 aircraft that had taken off. But in vain; the score turned out to be 11 aircraft lost and one TAG dead on arrival back on the ship. We never saw our fighter escort from start to finish, but I was told afterwards that it consisted of three Fulmars which got tangled up with a dozen 109s. "No fighter opposition." So much for daylight torpedo attacks in Albacores on a defended coast.'

A few further attacks were made from *Victorious* during the next 12 months, but carrier strength was to remain scarce, and the range was too great for attacks by land based FAA aircraft. It was therefore not until early 1944 that further operations of this nature could be carried out. By then, escort carriers were available, carrying Avenger strike aircraft and Wildcat fighters, each with a sufficient range to make extensive strikes from offshore carriers. On occasion these were augmented by fleet carriers, with *Furious, Implacable, Indefatigable* and *Victorious* all participating. Over 30 raids were made during 1944 and 1945, the last being on 4 May 1945, only four days before VE-day, when 44 aircraft from three escort carriers attacked Kilbotn, near Harstad, blowing up the depot ship *Black Watch* and sinking the *U-711* alongside her.

This account by Dick Yeo, now promoted to lieutenant and appointed as one of several Wildcat pilots attached to No 856 Squadron

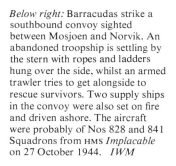

Below right: Barracudas strike a southbound convoy sighted between Mosjoen and Norvik. An abandoned troopship is settling by the stern with ropes and ladders hung over the side, whilst an armed trawler tries to get alongside to rescue survivors. Two supply ships in the convoy were also set on fire and driven ashore. The aircraft were probably of Nos 828 and 841 Squadrons from HMS *Implacable* on 27 October 1944. *IWM*

Below: Avengers of No 846 Squadron off the Norwegian coast during minelaying operations in October 1944. Flying from the escort carrier HMS *Trumpeter*, the squadron carried out a series of these operations during the month, in addition to a shipping strike, before returning to Scapa Flow towards the end of the month. *via K. R. W. Tyler*

Above: The scene immediately after an attack by Avengers of No 846 Squadron from HMS *Trumpeter* during the final wartime operation of the Home Fleet, at Kilbotn on 4 May 1945. Bombs can be seen bursting on a tanker, which later sank. The swirls on the water behind are all that remains where the U-boat depot-ship *Black Watch* had just been hit by preceding bombs. In the foreground of the Fjord is a flak ship, which was left in a damaged condition.
FAA Museum

Left: Pilots of the Fighter Flight of No 856 Squadron posed at Eglinton in front of one of their aircraft in September 1944, shortly before embarking in HMS *Premier* for minelaying operations off the Norwegian coast. Left to right they are Sub-Lt Johnny Duerdin, Lt Bill Vittle, Sub-Lt Dick Yeo and Sub-Lt Tony Hoare. *R. K. L. Yeo*

in September 1944, graphically illustrates the work of one of the squadrons involved:

'I joined No 856 Squadron at Eglinton, an Avenger squadron now having a fighter flight attached. After a week of familiarisation with Wildcat VIs, some working up and bags of ADDLs we flew aboard our new ship, HMS *Premier* off Belfast Lough. All aircraft having got safely aboard there followed an extensive working up in the Clyde and Irish Sea. There was plenty of flying, and after several visits to Machrihanish to check-swing all our compasses, we proceeded northwards through the Minches, past the Hebrides, to join the Home Fleet in Scapa Flow. One of our jobs was mine-laying in the 'Leads' — shipping lanes — that hug the Norwegian coast, thus holding up all German convoys. These 'Leads' take full advantage of the many islands and fjords that abound off Norway. We did some practice laying runs in the Orkneys and thoroughly tested our equipment, long-range tanks etc. Our first lay was at Salhusströmmen, near Haugesund, due east of Scapa Flow. Having left Scapa, the force formed up led by the light cruiser *Diadem*. Visibility was good and the snow on the rocky countryside made a grand sight, but we had little time to enjoy the scenery. On one of these runs nearly all my starboard aileron was shot away, and I got a lot of shrapnel holes in the fuselage and tailplane. We did this particular operation five or six times and so it was known as the 'Club Run'.

'In company with the fleet carrier *Implacable*, and *Trumpeter*, we intended to do a series of operations up the Norwegian coast. The weather only stayed fine long enough for Fireflies from *Implacable*, escorted by her own Wildcats (on loan from *Pursuer*) to do an anti-shipping sweep up a section of the coast. They saw nothing and after landing-on the Fleet ploughed through some dirty weather back to Scapa.

'On another occasion we went out in company with the *Implacable* and *Pursuer* for another series of operations in northern Norway including mine-laying, shipping strikes and a big beat-up of the large aerodrome at Bardufoss, near Narvik. The last operation was to have been almost on the scale of the Tirpitz 'prang'. However, no sooner had we left Scapa than an 80kt gale blew up and damaged the forward ends of

the flight decks of all three carriers. The damage to *Pursuer's* and ours was bad enough to put us out of action except in emergency so both heaved-to, put about and returned to Scapa. The *Implacable* forced on but even so she was only able to do one shipping strike which was successful. Barracudas and Fireflies attacked and smashed a troop convoy.

'In company with *Trumpeter* and the cruiser *Devonshire*, we sailed from Scapa to lay mines in Ramsöysund, north of Trondheim. Opposition was nil and even the Avengers peeled off and tried to find targets to attack. We were medium and top cover for this attack but no Hun appeared, the air was ours — and so back to Scapa.

'At Christmas 1944 the Commander-in-Chief released us for a while, so we sailed to Greenock and got 10 days leave. After re-storing we returned to Scapa. The Lepsö Rev operation was cancelled on one occasion due to very large and heavy snow squalls which would have dispersed any formation of aircraft not to mention forcing them into the 'oggin'. Apart from minelaying runs we did other types of operations.

'Several times we provided fighter cover for the withdrawal of a surface striking force from south Norwegian coastal waters, where it had perhaps smashed a convoy entering or leaving a harbour such as Egersund or the Lister in southern Norway. Attacking at night and withdrawing the next day, the forces were led by Rear Adm R. R. McGrigor in his flagship HMS *Norfolk*, and either HMS *Bellona* or HMS *Diadem* with four

fleet destroyers. We maintained a continuous fighter patrol over the fleet from just pre-dawn until the threat of air counter-attack was over. Only twice in these operations did we have any fun — once in daylight and once at night. In the daylight attack we scared off a big torpedo formation and a section from *Trumpeter* was vectored after a Ju88 that snooped too near and shot it down. The night attack was much more twitching and noisy, but our own ship's Bofors got a 'hun'. One or two of the torpedoes were seen to pass through the fleet, but they all missed.

'On another occasion we provided fighter cover for a special mine-sweeping operation, but the 1st Mine-Sweeper Flotilla carried out its task quite unmolested and we didn't see a thing. While returning from a minelaying run on one occasion, a large number of RAF Coastal Command Mosquitoes and Beaufighters passed over us after a shipping beat-up in some Norwegian fjord. Between us the 'hun' shipping got continuously harassed. I left No 856 Squadron and *Premier* in March 1945.'

The Firefly unit referred to in Yeo's account was No 1771 Squadron, then commanded by Lt-Cdr (A) H. M. Ellis DSC, DFC, RNVR, which had embarked in *Implacable* towards the end of September 1944, and was to have great success in these waters during the ensuing two months. A particularly successful day for the squadron was 27 November, which is well recorded in its diary record for that day:

'At last the weather has lifted, 5/10ths cloud,

Below: Aircraft of No 856 Squadron ranged on the deck of HMS *Premier* whilst the shipping was heading for Norway for a strike on Lepsö Rev. The carrier had just passed through a thick snow squall, and the squadron ground crews are busy sweeping snow off the Avengers and wildcats. *R. K. L. Yeo*

showers and a stiff breeze. Before dawn all our Fireflies were ranged on deck together with 12 Barracudas and Seafires for escort and CAP. As soon as it was light two Fireflies were to fly off to find targets for the striking force; this "recce" was carried out by Sub-Lts Johns and Westlake; and Lt Davies and Sub-Lt Reynolds. The striking force consisted of the following: CO and Sub-Lt Greenway; Sub-Lts Ramsden and Gullen; Sub-Lts Catterall and Manley; Sub-Lts Gill and West; Lts Turrell and Stewart; Sub-Lts Morgan and Doy; Sub-Lts Bassenthwaite and Frampton; Lt Donaghy and Sub-Lt Stevenson; Sub-Lts Lumsden and Smith; Sub-Lts Blatchley and Lander.

'The northernmost recce aircraft reported a convoy of six ships near Sandnesjöen; the other reported a large merchant ship near Rörvik which it attacked and set afire. A striking force of Fireflies and Barracudas armed with bombs was sent to deal with the convoy. After some navigational differences of opinion landfall was made just south of Sandnesjöen, and the convoy appeared to the north, proceeding south. The two larger ships were attacked successfully with bombs while Fireflies silenced the flak ship and drove another small ship ashore; the large ship of 4,000 tons proved to be a troopship, the

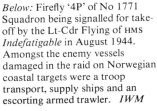

Below: Firefly '4P' of No 1771 Squadron being signalled for take-off by the Lt-Cdr Flying of HMS *Indefatigable* in August 1944. Amongst the enemy vessels damaged in the raid on Norwegian coastal targets were a troop transport, supply ships and an escorting armed trawler. *IWM*

Rigel; she was persistently strafed, but finally sunk; a motor-ship of 3,000 tons was left aground on the reef and the remaining two ships ashore. The troopship may have carried more than 2,000 men, returning from the Finnish front, and it is very satisfactory to know that few of them will find their way to the Western Front.

'Lt Donaghy narrowed his flight to Sandnesjöen itself; he met a hot reception, but shot up three ships, sinking one of 2,000 tons, harbour installations, camp positions etc; he then flew 50 miles down the railway, but unluckily finding no train returned to Sandnesjöen to finish his ammo. The sections led by the CO and Lt Turrell turned south, but found no big ships in the Leads except the 4,000ton merchant vessel set on fire by the recce aircraft; to these flames they added fuel, and set on fire two small ships nearby.

'Sub-Lts Catterall and Manley remained to take photographs, and navigate the Seafires back to base. All our crews returned safely, though Lt Donaghy's aircraft was well shot up, and Sub-Lt Gill's had a gash in the wing.

'Although weather restricted us to one sortie this time, it was an extremely fruitful one. The photographs were copious and good, and six ships were confirmed as sunk.'

Left: Avenger 'JF' of No 846 Squadron from HMS *Trumpeter* flying low over a Norwegian fjord during a minelaying operation at Haugesund on 13 January 1945. *IWM*

Below: A tangle of No 853 Squadron Avengers after a deck accident aboard HMS *Queen* on 27 April. The squadron was embarking from Hatston for a series of anti-shipping patrols and minelaying operations off the Norwegian coast. The culprit was JZ400, the uncoded machine in the centre of the picture whose arrester hook pulled out after catching No 1 wire, causing it to run into the deck park. *via R. Williams*

The Tirpitz Affair

The battleship *Tirpitz* was the largest weapon in the armoury of the German Navy after the sinking of her sister ship *Bismarck*, and she was a constant headache to the Admiralty. She was always likely to sail out to raid Atlantic and Arctic convoys, and consequently many attempts were made to put her out of action, both by the Royal Navy and the Royal Air Force.

The earliest attempt made by the Fleet Air Arm was in March 1942. The fleet carrier *Victorious* was in the escort for convoy PQ12 which sailed from Reykjavik on 1 March carrying the Albacores of Nos 817 and 832 Squadrons and the Fulmars of No 809 Squadron. On 7 March it was learned that *Tirpitz* was somewhere in the area of the

convoy, having sailed from her refuge at Trondheim, and unsuccessful attempts to sight her were made by the Albacores and also two spotting Walruses aboard the cruiser *Kenya*. Early on 9 March, however, a reconnaissance mission by six Albacores was more fortunate, the events of that morning being recorded in the diary maintained by No 832 Squadron:

'We were all woken up at 05.30hrs and we knew something was in the wind. Apparently a signal had been received early that morning giving a position of the *Tirpitz*. The search aircraft took off at 06.30hrs. At 07.35hrs the striking force, consisting of aircraft "4A", "4B", "4C", "4G", "4M", "4P" and "4R", accompanied by five aircraft of No 817 took

Right: Albacores of No 817 Squadron from HMS *Victorious* off on a strike, armed with a mixture of torpedoes and 'cucumber' mines. Aircraft of this squadron took part in the first attack by the Fleet Air Arm on *Tirpitz*, during March 1942. *via R. L. Ward*

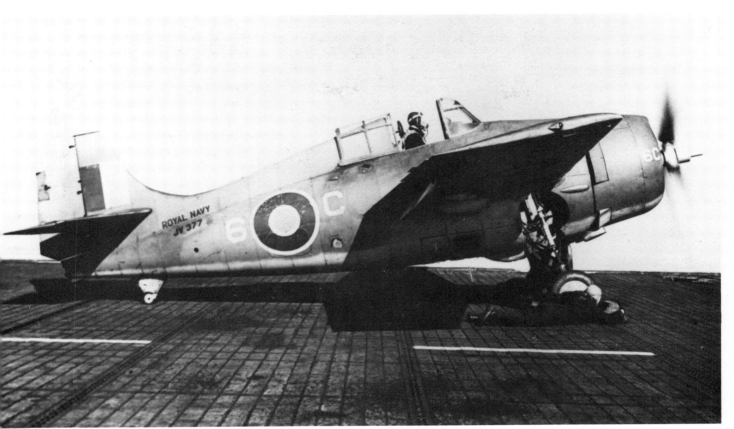

off (approx position of take off was 69°N 6′E). After forming up on the port bow the formation set course 120°, which if we saw nothing would eventually take us to Rostoy Island. However, we had not been in the air more than 40min when at 08.15hrs we received the first sighting report of the enemy from aircraft "4F". This was followed by our first amplifying report, giving the position, course and speed of the *Tirpitz*. The great accuracy of these reports soon enabled Lt George in aircraft "4A" to pick the enemy up on their ASV. At 08.40hrs the *Tirpitz* was sighted on the starboard bow.

'The weather had cleared considerably by then and visibility was anything up to 30 miles. Cloud base was at 4,000ft. The squadron started to climb and soon we were above the clouds with the *Tirpitz* about 15 miles away. The order "sub flights act independently" was given and the four sub flights widened out.

'We were guided on to the target by ASV but at 09.20hrs the first sub flights "4A", "4B" and "4C" dived to the attack with the enemy on its starboard bow below. As soon as the first sub flight came out of the clouds, the enemy opened fire and they encountered heavy flak during the dive. They dropped on the port bow at approx 1,000yd with the *Tirpitz* turning towards them.

'The second, third and fourth sub flights then dived to the attack, just after the first sub flight had successfully turned away. No 4

sub flight followed the first sub flight down and dropped on the port beam as the ship was steadying up from her vigorous turn to port. This was followed up by Nos 2 and 3 sub flights who came in out of the sun on the starboard side of the enemy who put the wheel hard over to starboard, and appeared to avoid all torpedoes. The target was thickly obscured by smoke and it is doubtful that a hit would have been seen. During the attack "4P" (Sub-Lt (A) D. J. Shepherd RNVR, Sub-Lt (A) L. Brown RNVR and L/Air S. G. Hollowood) was hit and crashed into the sea. One aircraft of No 817 was hit also, and set on fire and likewise crashed. We set course for the carrier and landed on at 10.30hrs.'

Tony Sweeting was an observer in one of the No 817 Squadron aircraft, having only been posted in to this, his first operational unit, a few days earlier. He recalls:
'For some reason, still unknown to me, I was assigned to be the Observer in Albacore "5B" piloted by Sub-Lt "Tony" Lacayo (later to become the CO of No 817 in 1945 as a Lt-Cdr), on this attack on *Tirpitz*. We had to approach the target, which was steaming eastward at 30kts into a headwind of 30kts, since we could only achieve 90kts with torpedoes on in the venerable Albacore. It is no wonder that the attack was useless, under such circumstances. Had we, with a little bit of luck, been able to deal the merest

Above: Wildcat V JV377 '6C' waiting to take off from HMS *Searcher*. This machine was lost on 27 March 1944 whilst the ship was on its way to participate in Operation 'Tungsten'. As it was landing-on the ship rolled, and it hit another machine, JV437 '6M', crashed over the side upside down and sank. The pilot, Sub-Lt M. C. Brown was unfortunately killed. *FAA Museum*

crippling blow to *Tirpitz* (a la *Bismarck*) what a difference it might have meant to subsequent events.'

All the torpedoes were dropped successfully, but the enemy ship managed to evade them. There was no opportunity to mount a second strike as *Tirpitz* sailed into Vestfjord within 2hr of the raid.

The Fleet Air Arm was never again to have the opportunity of attacking her in the open sea, as she was ordered to remain in shelter whenever Royal Navy carriers were in the area. She came out once to attack the ill-fated convoy PQ17, but quickly returned to refuge when it became known that *Victorious* was with the Home Fleet. A plan to carry out a night torpedo attack on *Tirpitz* in Altenfjord early in 1943 by six No 816 Squadron Swordfish from *Dasher* had to be called off when this escort carrier blew up off the Isle of Arran on 27 March, with heavy loss of life, due to an explosion in her aviation fuel supply. The Fleet Air Arm's foremost attack on the enemy battleship was to be that made in the spring of 1944.

The main striking force was to be the Barracudas of the 8th and 52nd Torpedo Bomber Reconnaissance Wings. The former comprised Nos 827 and 830 Squadrons and was normally embarked in *Furious*, whilst the latter consisted of Nos 829 and 830

Squadrons in *Victorious*. The latter would not be available until early March as she was undergoing a five months refit at Liverpool. Considerable preparations were made for the attack, for which the code-name Operation 'Tungsten' was selected. A dummy target was set up in Loch Eriboll, a seven mile long sea loch in Sutherland in north-west Scotland, bearing some resemblance to Kaa Fjord where the *Tirpitz* lay at anchor. These simulated attacks were not without their hazards, as recounted by Allan H. Thomson, then a TAG L/Air with No 830 Squadron, who participated in the actual raid in aircraft DP983 "5L", which now lies at the bottom of Scapa Flow after crashing into a balloon cable on 20 April 1944:

'On 23 March the whole Wing was almost shot out of the air by a broadside from a King George V class battleship. The incident happened during one of the full scale dress rehearsals for the attack. Flying from Hatston to the target area, an oblong strip marked out an island in Loch Eriboll, the Wing was at its usual height of about 50ft (ceiling 200ft) over the sea. There was a sea mist with visibility down to a couple of hundred yards, but the area west of Hoy had been reported clear of all shipping so there was no problem — until a tug was sighted. It could only mean one thing, and sure enough she was towing a target. An emergency break

Below: Wildcat V JV350 of No 842 Squadron, lands upside down on top of another machine of the same squadron on 27 March 1944, whilst embarking from Hatston in HMS *Fencer* to take part in Operation 'Tungsten'. The fighter flight of this squadron had re-equipped from Seafires only 10 days earlier. *FAA Museum*

Above: *Tirpitz* at the height of the second attack during Operation 'Tungsten' on 3 April 1944. *FAA Museum*

Left: Lt-Cdr (A) R. S. Baker-Falkner DSC, RN Wing Leader of the 8th Naval TBR Wing, who led the first striking force of Barracudas during the attack on *Tirpitz* on 3 April 1944. His machine on this occasion was Barracuda 'K' of No 827 Squadron. *IWM*

to port was immediately given, and as the aircraft scattered and climbed great spouts of water flew up around that practice target as the broadside went in. From higher up, above the mist one could see the battleship whose fire we almost ran into. If the tug had not been spotted, it is likely that the aircraft and the shells would have been in the same spot at the same time.'

The squadrons were regrouped for the operation, so that each Wing could take-off simultaneously from the two carriers. Thus Nos 827 and 829 embarked in *Victorious*, whilst Nos 830 and 831 embarked in *Furious*. Presumably due to the smaller size of *Furious*, both Nos 830 and 831 operated only nine aircraft, although No 831 normally had 12, but this was compensated by increasing No 827 from nine to 12 aircraft, so that she then had the same number as No 829 Squadron. Ample fighter cover was to be available, with the Corsairs of the 47th Naval Fighter Wing aboard *Victorious* and the Seafires of Nos 801 and 80 Squadrons aboard *Furious*. In addition there were to be a large number of Hellcats aboard the escort carriers *Emperor*, *Pursuer*, *Searcher* and *Fencer*, with the latter also carrying the Swordfish of No 842 Squadron for anti-submarine patrols.

The Home Fleet sailed from Scapa on 30 March, initially in two parts. *Victorious* joined one part, which headed for the Faroes to refuel, pretending to act as escort for outward bound convoy JW58, and was initially known as Force I. The remainder sailed as Force II later in the day on a more direct route and included *Furious* and the escort carriers. The two forces met in the afternoon of 2 April, and re-formed, the two fleet carriers now being in Force 7 and the escort carriers in Force 8.

At 04.24hrs the following morning, the first strike of 21 Barracudas of No 8 Wing took off from the two carriers, the Corsairs of No 1834 Squadron having preceded them by a few minutes. At about the same time *Searcher*, *Pursuer* and *Emperor* began to launch 10 Hellcats and 20 Wildcats, whilst *Fencer's* Wildcats and the Seafires from *Furious* also flew off. When the attacking force reached the fjord, *Tirpitz* was just about to depart her anchorage for the first time since being damaged in a midget submarine attack six months earlier. She had no opportunity to put up a smoke screen before the first aircraft came in to attack. The Hellcats and Wildcats approached from over the hills, machine gunning the battleship, whilst the Corsairs stayed at 10,000ft in case of attacks by enemy fighters. The Barracudas dived down to drop their bombs, making six direct hits, and as they attacked the second strike was taking off with a fairly similar escort. By the time they arrived, just over an hour later, a smoke screen had been laid, but this did not prevent eight further direct hits being made, in addition to a number of probables in both raids. Only two Barracudas were lost by enemy action in the attacks, these being LS569 '5M' of No 830 Squadron piloted by Sub-Lt (A) T. C. Bell RNVR which failed to return from the first raid, and LS551 '4M' of No 829 Squadron piloted by

Barracuda LS550 '4A' of
No 829 Squadron taxiing towards
the lift after Operation 'Tungsten'.
This machine was at that time the
flagship of the 52nd Naval TBR
Wing which also comprised No 831
Squadron. It is about to start the
complicated wing folding
procedure, the machine in front
having already completed folding
its starboard wing. *IWM*

Sub-Lt (A) H. H. Richardson, RNVR, which probably fell to AA fire in the second strike. A further strike planned for the next day was called off in view of the success of this raid, and the exhaustion of the participating crews.

Several other attempts were made to attack *Tirpitz* during the next few months. An attack due to take place on 26 April had to be called off owing to poor weather conditions. Aircraft took off for a raid by Barracudas from *Furious* and *Victorious* on 15 May, but were recalled owing to heavy cloud obscuring the target. Another raid due for 28 May was also cancelled owing to bad weather. The next effective raid was therefore that on 17 July, under the code-name Operation 'Mascot'.

On this occasion the carriers involved were *Formidable*, *Furious* and *Indefatigable*, and once again Barracudas were to be the main striking force. Nos 827 and 830 Squadrons were again involved, this time aboard *Formidable*, and these were accompanied by the 9th TBR Wing consisting of 820 and 826 Squadrons aboard the recently completed *Indefatigable*. The fighter support included two new types of aircraft in the shape of the Corsairs of No 1841 Squadron aboard *Formidable* and the Fireflies of No 1770 Squadron aboard *Indefatigable*. Seafires and Hellcats were also available, with three Swordfish of No 842 Squadron on board *Furious* for anti-submarine patrol work. The attack was mounted by 44 Barracudas with an escort of 48 fighters, but they were spotted from a recently built observation point on one of the nearby mountains, with the inevitable result that by the time they were ready to commence their attack a smoke screen largely obscured the

target, and none of the bombs hit the *Tirpitz*, although one fell nearby.

This attack is vividly recalled by Gordon 'Blondie' Lambert, then a TAG CPO serving with No 820 Squadron, piloted by Sub-Lt (A) Jones RNVR in '4K':

'As we approached Northern Norway we were briefed about the impending attack on *Tirpitz*. She was an ever present threat to the Russian convoys, lying in wait in a remote and almost inaccessible fjord. She was tied up alongside a jetty sheltering under almost sheer sides of the rock face which formed the fjords. Smoke generators had been built into the rock face, and at the first sign of danger they were operated which covered the fjord in a thick blanket of smoke. It was therefore necessary to try to catch them unawares and at least to start the attack before they could operate the smoke generators.

'Whilst the aircrews were being briefed (we had an excellent model of the fjord and surrounding area) the ground crews were doing their last minute checks and the armourers were busily loading up with 1,600lb AP bombs. Briefing complete we waddled out to our respective aircraft well wrapped up and carrying our survival kits. After all, if we were shot down or damaged, we could make our way to Sweden! The Flight Deck Officer gave the signal to start engines, and we knew then we were under "Starters Orders".

'The "goofers" platform was extremely well manned with all the "ghouls" waiting to see if we could get airborne. We had quite a number of aircraft lined up on the flight deck and come to think of it we had never gone off before with a 1,600 pounder slung underneath. We could feel the ship heel over as the Fleet turned into wind and the thin jet of

steam from a pipe set into the forward end of the flight deck was soon streaming back along the centre line of the deck. The Fleet was now turned into wind.

'We were the first to go off. The FDO waved his little green flag above his head and rotated it faster and faster until finally he dropped it to his side and we moved slowly forward gathering speed with every turn of the wheels until finally we ran out of deck, the aircraft dropped a few feet, the engine groaned and all I could see was the massive bow of the ship. The flight deck had disappeared from view, but the engine was equal to the occasion and we gradually gained height and circled the Fleet for the remaining aircraft to fly off and form up. Eventually all were airborne and in formation. Other carriers in company were similarly engaged, and finally the full striking force was assembled.

'It was 00.30hrs on the morning of 17 July. The sky was clear, and in that latitude at that time of year the sun never really sets, and so in spite of the time it was to all intents and purposes daylight. We set course and flew at zero feet until we reached the Norwegian coast before climbing to about 10,000ft for our dive bombing attack. We crossed the coast south of Kaa Fjord whilst a diversionary raid was being carried out to the north. One flight of fighter bombers had, in addition to their bombs, parcels of aluminium foil strips ("window") which they were to drop in the hope of confusing the German radar system, but despite their efforts the enemy were ready for us.

'As we crossed the coast, the midnight sun shining on the glaciers and the air so clear that one could see for miles, almost shut out

all thoughts of our purpose of being there. From the air the view was magnificent, and it seemed unthinkable that such beautiful scenery would soon give way to savage destruction. We eventually sighted Kaa Fjord, and caught a glimpse of *Tirpitz* as smoke began pouring from the generators. It was absolutely essential that the attack be carried out with the minimum of delay if we were to have any chance of success.

'The fighter bombers, which had come in from the north, had gone in first with a fair amount of success. Unfortunately for us, the ack ack guns were now fully manned, and the gunners had very quickly rubbed the sleep out of their eyes. They soon had our range, and in no time at all shells were bursting rather too close for comfort.

'In my opinion, it is at this stage in any

Top: Wildcat V JV406 being held down on the deck of HMS *Pursuer*, whose deck letter 'P' can be seen painted on the lift. This machine was then with No 881 Squadron, which helped to provide fighter cover for all the Tirpitz attacks during 1944. *FAA Museum*

Above: The batsman brings Barracuda '5K' of No 831 Squadron in to land on HMS *Furious* on its return from Operation 'Tungsten'. ASV aerials are visible on the aircraft wings. *IWM*

Above: A Barracuda on fire from enemy flak during Operation 'Goodwood' hits the first barrier on landing. A broken propeller blade can be seen flying into the air, but fortunately it lands in the sea, and nobody is injured. This aircraft may have been MD690 '4B' of No 826 Squadron which entered the barrier on landing on HMS *Formidable* from 'Goodwood III' on 24 August 1944. *IWM*

attack when the true value of all the training and discipline is most in evidence. It was as true in this case as it had been in the Mediterranean and was later to be in the Pacific. The cockpit drill immediately preceding the attack was carried out as though it was just another exercise. Guns were cocked, bomb switches made and fuses set. There was little point in going all that way if any single detail were forgotten, and either the bomb hung up or failed to explode because a fuse had not been set. You have no time to cock the guns if a fighter suddenly appears on your tail.

'My pilot, in whom I had the utmost confidence, called out "Stand by, we're going down". The nose dipped as he pushed the control column forward, and as our angle of dive increased so did the speed. The effect of this manoeuvre is to subject the crew to negative "g" and a feeling of weightlessness, which can be quite disconcerting if you are not strapped in and suddenly find yourself floating around the cockpit.

'Facing backwards, as was the case in the Barracuda, I could see the rest of the squadron begin their dives and follow us down. It was rather strange that in spite of all the ack ack fire, and the thought of going down into the blanket of smoke, these did not concern me so much as the thought "I wonder if they really did find a cure for those cracked locking pins?". I remember one suggestion being put forward that if a patch was put over the wing aperture it would reduce the pressure inside the wing structure, but the originator of the idea declined to fly with one of the pilots who had offered to test this theory.

'Just before we reached the smoke, which must have been about 600 or 700ft above the *Tirpitz*, I felt the aircraft lift slightly as the pilot released the bomb, and then started to pull out of the dive, but not before we had entered the smoke. It was a relief to fly out of this, so that we could at least see where we were, but then of course so could the AA gun crews. Anti aircraft fire there was in profusion, but fortunately no sign of any fighter aircraft.

'The drill on completing the attack was to make our way independently to the coast, where we would all meet together to be escorted back to the Fleet by the fighter bombers. As we arrived at the coast and circled a couple of times, I was rather concerned as to the fate of some of the others, as there were certainly not as many as started out. Eventually we set course, and arrived back at our rendezvous position to find the Fleet waiting for us. As we circled around waiting for the carrier to turn into wind for landing, several stragglers came in and joined up on us, and it was a great relief to find that all our squadron had returned. The signal was given for the fleet to turn into wind, a relief AS patrol was flown off, and finally the signal was given for us to land on. One by one we came home for an early breakfast.

'Breakfast had to wait, however, for at least another couple of hours, as there was the very detailed interrogation and de-

92

Above: The machine in the previous picture has had its fire extinguished and has been moved clear of the barrier. Damage seems relatively slight in the circumstances, and it is known that MD690 survived until at least June 1945, when it was in service at RNAS Fearn. *IWM*

Left: Barracudas of No 848 Squadron and Corsairs of No 1842 Squadron ranged on the flight deck of HMS *Formidable* ready for a strike on *Tirpitz* during Operation 'Goodwood'. The Corsairs are fitted with large long range fuel tanks under their fuselages. *IWM*

briefing procedure to go through. It never ceased to amaze me how reluctant the interrogaters were to believe what was told to them, every story and incident being checked and double-checked. Eventually, however, they were convinced that we had told all, and a very tired but relieved squadron sat down to breakfast and looked forward to some sleep.'

Further strikes were made in the latter part of August under the code-name Operation 'Goodwood', the four Barracuda squadrons involved this time being Nos 826 and 828 aboard *Formidable*, No 827 in *Furious* and No 820 in *Indefatigable*, with heavy fighter support in the shape of Corsairs, Seafires, Hellcats and Fireflies. 'Goodwood I' and 'Goodwood II' on 22 August were abortive,

Left: Corsairs of No 1842 Squadron each fitted with a bomb and a large long range tank, prepare to take off for a dive bombing attack on *Tirpitz* during Operation 'Goodwood'. The machine on the right is JT418 'N', which remained with the squadron until the end of the year, then transferred to No 1836 Squadron as 'T8F'. It failed to return from a bombing attack on 9 May 1945 during Operation 'Iceberg VIII', one of the Fleet attacks on Okinawa. *IWM*

Above: Barracuda '5M' of No 820 Squadron gets airborne during Operation 'Goodwood'. A special ramp has been raised on the deck of HMS *Furious* to give the effect of lengthening the forward end of this old carrier's flight deck to enable the aircraft to get off with the 1,600lb bomb under the fuselage. *IWM*

Right: Barracudas of No 820 Squadron making a low level run in to the Norwegian coast during 'Goodwood IV' on 29 August 1944. All 12 of the squadron's aircraft took off from HMS *Indefatigable* for this operation. *via C. H. Wood*

and the day was marred by *Nabob* becoming a casualty to an acoustic torpedo from *U-354*, putting her out of action for the remainder of the war. During 'Goodwood III' on 24 August a 500lb bomb and a 1,600lb AP bomb struck the ship, but the latter failed to explode after successfully penetrating the armoured decking. 'Goodwood IV' on 29 August was also a failure, and the battleship's career was ended by the RAF on 12 November 1944 when she was capsized by 12,000lb 'Tallboy' bombs dropped by Lancasters of Nos 9 and 617 Squadrons.

Eastern Fleet Operations 1943-1944

By late 1942 the US Navy was engaged in a bitter struggle in the islands of the Pacific, and was sorely in need of some assistance, but at this stage the Royal Navy had no carrier strength to spare. However, after completion of its task in Operation 'Torch', *Victorious* had been despatched to the Navy Yard at Norfolk, Virginia for a refit, and on completion at the beginning of February 1943 her squadrons re-embarked and she headed for Pearl Harbor. Here she suffered some damage when an Avenger crashed on deck, so it was not until 8 May that she was able to sail for New Caledonia, where she arrived on 17 May to join the USS *Saratoga* at Noumea as part of Task Force 14.

For the attack on New Georgia (Operation 'Toenail'), *Saratoga* embarked all the strike squadrons including the Avengers of No 832 Squadron, whilst *Victorious* operated purely as a fighter carrier with 60 Wildcats of both British and American squadrons. Sailing on 27 June, the carriers were stationed 250-350 miles from the inva-sion beaches, a distance which limited the time the aircraft could spend in the assault area, but they put up 600 sorties against little opposition. The aircraft were re-assigned to their parent carriers on 24 July, and the force reached Noumea the next day.

British naval strength was now building up apace in Ceylon and southern India. An Air-craft Maintenance Yard was established at Coimbatore, an Aircraft Training Establish-ment at Maharagama and an Aircraft Erec-tion Depot at Cochin. Naval air stations for operational training squadrons were com-missioned at China Bay (Trincomalee), Colombo, Katukurunda, Puttalam, Sulur and Tambaram, and squadrons were on occasion based at RAF stations in the area, of which there were many.

Tony Sweeting was still serving with No 817 Squadron, recently re-grouped as a Barracuda squadron, one of four which were despatched to the Far East in March 1944 as part of an emergency force to meet a feared attack by the Japanese Fleet. His account of

Left: A Walrus being launched from the catapult of HMS *Warspite* in the Indian Ocean towards the end of 1942. All shipborne aircraft of the Eastern Fleet had been formed into a sub unit of No 700 Squadron under the command of Lt T. W. B. Shaw, RN, and this comprised nine Walruses and two Seafoxes. All were given codes, the Walruses of HMS *Warspite* being '9A' and '9B'. The Walruses went ashore for a few days in October 1942, and one one occasion the CO led 11 aircraft in formation over Mombasa — unfortunately during the Commander-in-Chief's siesta time. *IWM*

Above: Steel-helmeted maintenance crew bringing a Swordfish of No 834 Squadron on to the flight deck of HMS *Battler* by the ship's hydraulic lift. The squadron joined the escort carrier on 17 September 1943, and then sailed with her for Eastern Waters via the Mediterranean and the Suez Canal. The carrier operated in the Indian Ocean throughout most of 1944, having also a fighter flight equipped with Seafires and later Wildcats. *IWM*

Right: In conference on board HMS *Battler* are (left to right) Maj A. R. Burch DSC, RM (Cdr Flying), Capt F. M. R. Stephenson, Lt-Cdr B. Walford RN (Air Staff Officer) and Lt-Cdr (A) E. Dixon Child RN (CO of No 834 Squadron). *IWM*

that period includes a portrayal of the primitive conditions encountered ashore:

'My flying log shows a blank for March and April, and for a good reason. We were suddenly ordered to pack up all our gear and proceed to Liverpool to board the P&O liner *Strathnaver*, now a troopship. Our aircraft were flown aboard an escort carrier and stowed on the deck. The word was that we were on our way to India as it was seen that the Japanese in Burma were massing shipping, possibly with intent to make a thrust forward towards India. It appeared we were to rejoin *Indomitable* in Ceylon, now that she had almost completed her refit in the States.

The trip out was most pleasant, almost like a peace-time cruise. It was a strange feeling to steam the length of the Med without any enemy molestation, unlike our previous sorties in that theatre. We transferred to another, smaller liner, *Aronda*, at Port Said. The accommodation was extremely comfortable and the food excellent.

'We finally arrived in Colombo after some six weeks — hardly a swift response to a threatened Japanese attack. We were not all that surprised, however, to find that the shore people in Ceylon were less than prepared for us. There were several other squadrons involved, and there was space for them but no room for No 817, so we were pushed off to Madras. This involved lowering our aircraft from the escort carrier deck on to the dock, and taxying them through the streets (with folded wings) to get to a take-off strip. It was an astonishing sight to see dhotis and saris getting whipped off the poor unsuspecting locals in the slip-stream. Our destination was a virtually abandoned RAF temporary airfield called Ulunderpet.

'Ulunderpet must have been the penance we were required to pay after our luxurious living in ex-liner troopships. It was possibly the most God forsaken location in the whole of the British war effort, barely kept alive by a dozen RAF men, who looked like something out of Robinson Crusoe. The heat was overbearing; the quarters absolutely primitive — nothing but a concrete floor with a grass roof, supported on poles. Toilet facilities were of the merest kind, a bath in a tin tub of lukewarm water was a luxury and it was disconcerting to find, when sitting over the latrine bucket, a couple of impassive, almost naked "untouchables" standing a few feet away, ready to do their job. The food was awful and the only available drink was some kind of Indian moonshine that could dissolve anything. Nasty animals like tree rats and snakes abounded and after supper, as the light went, numerous bats whizzed through the open sides of the mess.

'To top all this, we discovered that our aircraft had been affected by the salt air on the long journey out, exposed on the deck of the escort carrier, and they performed very poorly in the heat of the Madras plain. It took about an hour to reach 10,000ft with a full bomb load. The fitters and riggers toiled in the blazing sun to service the planes, and its a wonder that the whole lot didn't succumb to sun stroke. As it was, two of the aircrew came down with a mysterious disease which puzzled the doctor, and we had orders to capture what rats we could for investigation as they might have been the source. One day I found one in a tin tub of dirty bath water, scrabbling to get out! It was there I saw my first leper, who came begging. A most pathetic sight. Then on 12 June my log shows the entry "Ulunderpet to Katukurunda (Ceylon)".

'Katukurunda was as pleasant as Ulunderpet was awful. Good quarters and good food — Sunday buffet lunch was a vast array of super curries. The climate was beautiful, and

Left: The Barracudas of No 847 Squadron from HMS *Illustrious* on their way to carry out a strike. On 19 April 1944 squadron aircraft struck at oil tanks and dock installations at Sabang, and two months later made a similar attack on Port Blair in the Andamans. On its return from this latter attack to Ceylon it was absorbed into No 810 Squadron and ceased to exist. *FAA Museum*

Below left: Barracuda P9857 'G' of No 822 Squadron being rearmed with a torpedo at RAF Ulunderpet, a jungle airstrip in southern India around May 1944. 15 aircraft of the squadron were in action during Operation 'Light Baker', an attack on Sigli on 18 September 1944 whilst temporarily attached to HMS *Victorious*. *IWM*

97

Above: Seafire LIIC LR702 of No 834 Squadron comes to rest on the flight deck of HMS *Battler*, with its port wing almost over the side. The port undercarriage had collapsed during a heavy landing on 23 February 1944, whilst the carrier was on its way from Durban to Mauritius, where it arrived the following day. *FAA Museum*

we had the occasional trip into Colombo and to Mount Lavinia. We were unable to accomplish much flying, however, as the aircraft still needed extensive maintenance and the single runway, a woven metal carpet affair, gave problems. An interesting part of the scene was the horde of Italian prisoners of war, who worked on construction on the station, which was still incomplete. They must have been there almost a year, and were bronzed and healthy looking compared to us pale creatures. Then on 12 July I received my draft chit. By now I had my second stripe and had served two and a half years in No 817. I was to report to No 786 Squadron at Crail in Scotland, as an instructor in the newly established NOTU.'

In the meantime, the Eastern Fleet had been building up its carrier strength. By April 1944 it included *Illustrious* and a number of escort carriers, and was ready to mount an attack on Japanese-held territory. The target chosen was Sabang, a harbour at the northern end of the island of Sumatra, and for this operation the Fleet was loaned the services of USS *Saratoga*. The force arrived in the target area in the early morning of 19 April, and *Illustrious* flew off 18 Barracudas of Nos 810 and 847 Squadrons, escorted by 13 Corsairs. A graphic summary of this attack appears in the diary of No 810 Sqaudron:

'Flying off commenced 05.15hrs from USS *Saratoga* who launched SBDs with 1,000lb bombs each, SBFs with 2,000lb bombs and some with 4 × 500lb bombs and Hellcat escort. *Illustrious* boosted at 05.30hrs five aircraft of No 847 Squadron, then flew off 12 Corsairs for escort and four for umbrella, followed by 10 Barracudas, two of No 847 Squadron and remainder of No 810 Squadron. Three more aircraft were ranged, one of No 847 Squadron, two of No 810

Squadron and flown off to join the strike. One aircraft, DT831 (Sub-Lt Earle, Sub-Lt Bowller and PO Rogers), returned and landed on, undercarriage having failed to retract, and bombs jettisoned. Barracuda strike, armed with 2 × 500lb MC bombs and 2 × 250lb GP bombs per aircraft, and consisting of 17 aircraft, then formed up astern of *Saratoga* strike. Strike climbed to 10,500ft until it reached the target. No fighter opposition was encountered. Over target Corsair escort broke off and went down to attack and strafe. Barracudas attacked harbour installations and radar stations scoring direct hits on both. Flak was encountered but was ragged and inaccurate. Barracudas struck one minute after *Saratoga* strike. All aircraft got safely away and rendezvoused over Porto Rondo, although two Barracudas ("2H" and "2F") were compelled to make a second attack because of failure of bombs to release in first dive. One Hellcat force-landed in the sea, but pilot was picked up by one of the submarines which surfaced some six miles off the shore during the whole attack. All aircraft returned and landed safely except one of the No 847 Squadron which hit barrier causing slight damage.

'Fleet then turned west making good best speed. Hellcats shot down three "Kates" with torpedoes, and after that Fleet proceeded unmolested. During night, guns opened up on suspected enemy aircraft but no results were observed.

'Fires were started in the harbour installations and aerodrome at Sabang. The radar station was destroyed. Two 4,000-5,000ton MVs set afire by SBFs, Power House destroyed, oil tanks set ablaze (smoke rising to 7,000ft plus), many aircraft destroyed on aerodrome at Sabang and neighbouring island. Complete surprise achieved and no casualties received. Every praise must be

attached to the maintenance personnel of the squadron that such a high percentage of serviceability was available when required.'

A similar attack was made on 17 May on the oil refinery at Soerabaya on the island of Java, and for this operation *Illustrious* also embarked the Avengers of No 832 and 845 Squadrons. Ray Little, then a TAG with No 847 Squadron, later wrote this account for the TAGA Journal on the next raid:

'For two or three days before sailing, the air mechanics had been busy stripping the Barracudas of all unnecessary equipment so as to increase their speed. This led to a very strong buzz that we were to bomb Singapore, and as this meant a very long run in over Sumatra we were relieved when we learnt that Port Blair was to be the target.

'At 06.30hrs on 21 June, the 13 Barracudas flew off covered by some 35 Corsairs and once in formation we were comforted to see so many fighters stacked around us! Lt-Cdr Forde led the Barras, with "Chiefy" Pankhurst; among the TAGs were Jackie Prothero, Ted Elliott and Bob Pope.

Top: The flight deck of HMS *Illustrious* being cleared of the Corsairs of No 1833 Squadron. Flying over are several SBD-5 Dauntlesses of VB12 from USS *Saratoga*. All these aircraft had just taken part in a raid on Sourabaya, on 17 May 1944. *IWM*

Above: Avenger FN922 '5Q' of No 845 Squadron successfully picks up a wire as the batsman brings it down on HMS *Illustrious* after a strike on Sourabaya on 17 May 1944. *IWM*

'Just before we came within range of the Jap's radar a formation of Corsairs broke away and went in at sea level at top speed to catch the Jap fighters before they scrambled. This move proved very successful.

'We followed on rather more sedately, passing across the north of South Andaman Island and then turned about to attack Port Blair from the sea. The Jap gunners were unpleasantly accurate while we banked round at about 13,000ft, and we were glad when we started our dive, though my pilot, Lt Buckland, later told me that he saw plenty of light stuff coming up as we went down. Our sub-flight's target was Chatham Island, in the harbour, and the close escort fighters reported that the Island had gone up with a roar, so we must have hit something!

'In the dive my cockpit hood had been forced down over the guns by the air pressure and when we pulled out over the town the pilot was calling "Quick, gunner — the port side!" I had visions of hordes of "Zeros" coming at us and nearly ruptured myself heaving the hood open again. However, he only wanted me to shoot up a Jap tented camp! I was now trigger happy and passing low over the jungle through thick patches of morning mist I spotted a fixed undercarriage aircraft coming up in the haze. I could recognise a Barra and a Corsair — anything else was a Jap, and I was just about to let go with a burst at close range when I realised it was a Corsair with its undercarriage jammed down. I later met this fighter pilot in Cape Town and he was indeed glad I took a second look at his aircraft.

'When our sub-flight formed up again both Ginger Harris and Pete Luckett, flying in the wing aircraft, had trouble. They had both secured their hoods open with cod line and in the dive the line held, but both hoods fractured and collapsed over the gun mounting. Now both of them had jettisoned the escape panels in the hoods and were hacking at their hoods with jungle escape machetes to free the guns. Once we were safely away from the Andamans I could see the humour of the situation!

'Unhappily one aircraft, with Charlie Rogers, was lost and until after the war we thought he had bought it. It appears Charlie's aircraft was hit and went in the drink on fire. After a day in their dinghy the crew were picked up by the Japs. They had an unpleasant time and finished up in Tokyo, where Charlie had 10 months solitary confinement.

'Knocker White also had trouble. In the dive a distress signal in the back of his Mae West ignited and set fire to his clothing. The observer crawled through to him and put out the fire with an extinguisher. He came into the mess later with his back liberally covered with violet gentian. Just at that time the commander told the ship's company over the tannoy of Knocker's misfortune and it seems the flight deck party gathered around the deck speakers to listen, which upset Commander F., who ordered them back to work, commenting, "It's only some bloody fool of an air gunner who set fire to himself"!

'However, Adm Somerville seemed well pleased with the strike, especially as a group of RAF Liberators who were supposed to follow up with a night attack were unable to find the islands.'

A second strike was carried out on Sabang on 25 July, then *Illustrious* sailed for

Below: Corsairs of Nos 1830 and 1833 Squadrons on the flight deck of HMS *Illustrious*. The Eastern Fleet, in line astern, has been passed down the line by the USS *Saratoga* and her destroyer escort off the north-west coast of Australia as they part company after the Sourabaya strike. *IWM*

Above: Corsairs and Barracudas on the forward end of the flight deck of HMS *Illustrious* on 21 June 1944 after an attack on Port Blair. A Barracuda is being taken down to the hangar on the forward lift. Considerable damage was inflicted in this raid to military installations including the power house, workshops and MT yard and the seaplane base. Two aircraft were destroyed on the airfield and a radar station was completely knocked out. *IWM*

Left: An Avenger of an Eastern Fleet squadron being taken from its improvised jungle hangar late in 1944. *IWM*

Durban, where she spent two months undergoing a refit before returning to Trincomalee. During this period she was replaced by *Indomitable*, which took part in operations against Sumatran targets with *Victorious*, now returned from a refit at Liverpool. This attack was carried out in two waves on 24 August, and the Barracudas of Nos 815, 817 and 837 Squadrons inflicted heavy damage on a large cement works at Indaroeng, and the harbour at Emmahaven was also attacked, some ships being damaged. This was followed by a less successful attack on Sumatra on 18 September, and two attacks on Car Nicobar island in October.

In November, to take account of the increased British commitment in the area, the fleet carriers were transferred to a new formation, the British Pacific Fleet. The escort carriers, which formed the remaining carrier strength of the Eastern Fleet, then became part of the new East Indies Fleet.

Above: 26 Corsairs of Nos 1834 and 1836 Squadrons ranged on the flight deck of HMS *Victorious* on 18 September 1944 ready for an attack on Sigli under the leadership of Maj R. C. Hay DSC RM, the Wing Leader of the 47th Naval Fighter Wing. Damage was inflicted on a railway repair and maintenance centre. *IWM*

Right: The ship's cat walks towards the port side of the deck of an Eastern Fleet carrier as Corsairs are ranged with wings folded. Each machine has a large long range fuel tank under the fuselage. *IWM*

Left: Corsairs of Nos 1834 and 1836 Squadrons taxying out at RNAS Colombo on 11 September 1944. Shortly afterwards these aircraft, of the 47th Naval Fighter Wing, joined HMS *Victorious* for an attack on Sigli. On the right can be seen a Defiant target tug of the resident No 797 Fleet Requirements Unit Squadron. *Cdr R. C. Hay*

Below: Corsairs of the 6th Naval Fighter Wing, under the leadership of Maj R. C. Hay, flying in formation over RNAS Colombo on 27 May 1944. A month later the aircraft were part of the fighter defence of the Eastern Fleet, and also made attacks on shore targets during operations in the Andaman Islands. *Cdr R. C. Hay*

103

Channel Operations

Much vital work was performed in various theatres by Fleet Air Arm squadrons operating from shore bases. Little publicised were the invaluable efforts of squadrons based in southern England for operations in the English Channel, particularly around D-Day.

In the spring of 1944, as part of the preparations for the forthcoming invasion of Europe, several naval squadrons were moved to RAF bases on the south coast, where they came under the control of General Reconnaissance Wings of Coastal Command, these having been specifically formed for that purpose. At Manston, No 155 (GR) Wing formed in 16 Group on 1 April, and two weeks later the Swordfish of No 819 Squadron and the Avengers of No 848 Squadron moved in, these being later augmented by RAF Albacores and Beaufighters. Elsewhere in Kent, No 157 (GR) Wing formed on 14 May at Hawkinge to operate Nos 854 and 855 Avenger squadrons within 16 Group. To cover the other end of the Channel, No 156 (GR) Wing formed on 22 April as part of 19 Group to administer

the Swordfish of No 838 Squadron at Harrowbeer in Devon. Further along the coast, Nos 849 and 850 Avenger squadrons operated under 19 Group from Perranporth from 23 April, together with the rocket equipped Swordfish of 816 Squadron.

These squadrons carried out numerous shipping strikes, anti-submarine sorties and various other operations of a similar nature, operating off the coasts of Holland, Belgium and France. Attacks were carried out on German E-boats, and during the invasion period the Swordfish laid smoke to cover the movements of the convoys. No 819 Squadron Swordfish were equipped with the latest Mk X ASV in a radome under the centre fuselage, giving a panoramic presentation of the coastline and shipping.

Naval fighter squadrons were also active in the Channel. The 24th Naval Fighter Wing, under Lt-Cdr N. G. Hallett RN, was detached to Culmhead in Somerset during April, and for just over three weeks the Seafire IIIs of Nos 887 and 894 Squadrons escorted fighter-bomber Typhoons of the 2nd

Below: An Avenger of No 854 Squadron flying over southern England shortly after D-Day. The squadron operated anti-submarine patrols from Hawkinge under the control of No 157 GR Wing, in RAF Coastal Command. The invasion stripes have obliterated the prefix letters of the serial number and also the fuselage code letters, JZ456 being probably coded '4P' at that time. This machine later served with No 853 Squadron.
FAA Museum

Left: An invasion-striped Avenger of No 855 Squadron at dispersal at RAF Hawkinge during June 1944. The squadron, with No 854 Squadron, operated under No 157 GR Wing of RAF Coastal Command for a few weeks after D-Day, carrying out anti-submarine patrols in the English Channel. *J. Lees-Jones*

Below: Avengers of No 855 Squadron standing by at RAF Hawkinge in June 1944. JZ555, the nearest machine, has a Donald Duck cartoon painted on the nose, its code '5L' having been painted over by invasion stripes. The next machine is JZ550, correctly '5R', which failed to return from a patrol off the French coast on 23 July 1944. *J. Lees-Jones*

Left: Avenger '4H' of No 854 Squadron on the flight deck of HMS *Illustrious* in the British Pacific Fleet around March-April 1945, sporting credits of four bombing missions and one success against a flying bomb. This squadron shot down two of the latter whilst operating from Hawkinge after D-Day. On 9 July 1944, L/Air Shirmer, the TAG of JZ127 piloted by Lt D. P. Davies shot one down, and on 14 August another was destroyed by the front guns of Lt Voak's machine. *IWM*

105

Above: Swordfish NF119 'X' of No 819 Squadron after an accident on 3 February 1945. Nicknamed 'Black Mischief', it was taking off from the small grass airfield at Knocke-le-Zoute when it failed to clear a perimeter fence.
A. R. Wadham

Tactical Air Force in sweeps over Brittany and Normandy, sometimes operating independently.

One of the most active of these units was No 819 Squadron, then under the command of Lt-Cdr (A) P. D. Stevens RNVR who was later awarded the DFC for his work with the squadron. During the last year of the war in Europe the squadron was almost continuously engaged in operations, from the time it moved to Manston in mid-April 1944 until its disbandment 11 months later.

One of the pilots who was actively engaged throughout most of this period was Sub-Lt (A) A. Rohan Wadham RNVR who gained the DFC whilst with the squadron. He joined the squadron at Manston on 24 May 1944, only two weeks before D-Day, his observer during this time being Sub-Lt (A) A. Turberville RNVR and his telegraphist air gunner was L/Air R. Hunter. Their normal aircraft was NF119, coded 'X' and later affectionately nicknamed 'Black Mischief', which survived until being badly damaged in an accident on 3 February 1945. He recalls: 'Our task was primarily to disrupt German coastal traffic. In anticipation of the forthcoming invasion, Typhoons of the 2nd TAF had been strafing road and rail transport systems in northern France, with the Maquis also playing their part. As a consequence, the Germans began to send petrol and some armaments and troops by sea down the coast from the Scheldt estuary to Le Havre and beyond, by nightly hops. Our orders were to try and make this more difficult, and it did not matter whether we necessarily sank the targets, though if we did, then fine.

'We were armed with nose-fuse bombs, with a nose cap which came off as the bomb dropped through the air, exposing a thin tinfoil paper type of percussion cap, and it exploded

well above the surface. Our targets were mainly fast E-boats and R-boats. These were made of wood, so that if you missed by about 30 or 40yds, the chances were that with a nose-fuse bomb it would have been damaged enough to be immobilised for a time.

'We had a very sophisticated air-to-surface vessel radar, ASV Mk X, which was rather like AI, and if there were any targets around we were able to spot them on the radar at about 12 miles range. As we crossed the coast at 2,000-3,000ft after taking off from Manston, the enemy could see us coming from their own radar, so it never surprised us that they stopped when we were about 10 miles away. They were heading for such ports as Dunkirk, Calais, Boulogne, le Touquet, le Tréport and Dieppe, but they could not remain stationary all night because they knew that if they were not in harbour by first light they would be attacked by the Typhoons of No 137 Squadron from Manston, which carried rockets.

'We were operating right through each night, taking sectors of the coast, which we divided up into three or four patrol areas. The nights were fairly short at that time of year, but we started soon after it became dark and continued until first light, with different crews flying three or four consecutive patrols in each sector, usually of about 1½-2hr duration.

'Another type of operation was the dropping of flares to illuminate similar targets for the Beaufighters of Coastal Command, which were also attached to No 155 Wing. The main Beaufighter unit involved was No 143 Squadron, then commanded by Sqn-Ldr Wilmott who also acted as Wing Leader, and consequently we used the code name "Willie" for this type of operation, using this as a call sign when signalling to Manston. We undertook these operations on

Above: An invasion-striped Wildcat of No 896 Squadron standing by on the deck of HMS *Pursuer* in the Western end of the English Channel on D-Day. The carrier identification letter 'P' can be seen on the flight deck.
via Gordon Wright

Left: A Swordfish of No 816 Squadron at RAF Perranporth, shortly after D-Day, is being armed by AM/O R. J. Dick and AM/O J. Nickel, who are sliding rocket projectiles into the underwing rails. *IWM*

moonless nights, so as to create an artificial moon down which the Beaufighters could attack the targets. There were often as many as a dozen or more E or R-boats escorting two or three larger vessels, and they had generally stopped as we approached so as to avoid creating a phosphorescent wake by which we could see them. The Swordfish would drop about six flares singly in an arc behind the targets, and then the Beaufighters came out and attacked them in this artificial moon.

'With the invasion we were also given daylight duties for a time. On D-Day the squadron was given the task of laying a smoke screen to protect large convoys of troopships, supply ships and hospital ships coming down from German long range batteries in the Pas de Calais. My log book for that day records that we flew a patrol lasting 65min, to escort a convoy of 11 large ships from South Foreland, near Dover, along the south coast, but despite our smoke screen, the enemy shelling succeeded in hitting a tanker of 10,000 tons which had to be beached near Folkestone soon after we arrived. The squadron was active from mid morning to about 16.00hrs, and a message of

Above: Three Swordfish of No 816 Squadron, sporting invasion stripes, pose for the cameraman off the south coast. Their identification markings have been largely hidden by the stripes, but the centre machine is NF243 'S'. Based at RAF Perranporth under the control of 19 Group, Coastal Command, the squadron flew anti-shipping patrols over the western end of the Channel for a few weeks around D-Day, under the command of Lt-Cdr (A) P. Snow, until it disbanded on 1 August 1944. Its crews then went to No 836 Squadron at Maydown, for duty in MAC-ships. *IWM*

Right: A Swordfish of No 816 Squadron firing a demonstration salvo of eight rockets during a practice attack. Discharge can be seen behind the aircraft as it follows its missiles down. *IWM*

congratulation was later received at Manston from Gen Montgomery, who I believe had spent part of the day at Dover Castle, watching the activities in the Channel.

'The following day I had a rather alarming experience. After carrying out three daytime patrols, we took off for a night patrol, I believe in the Ostende sector. This turned out to be uneventful, but it was an extremely foggy night and on our return there was not enough visibility at Manston for me to land there, so I was redirected to Bradwell Bay. I was homed by VHF, and then Bradwell Bay guided us in on the Sandra radar beacon system. My log book shows that we were in the air for 1hr 50min, and we had been flying at 80kts all the way from Ostende. We had always been taught that if you were in cloud for a very long time you began to distrust your instruments, and although you knew it was wrong, you began to ignore your artificial horizon and start doing what felt right. On two occasions during this flight I started quietly turning the Swordfish upside down because it felt right to me. Fortunately my observer, Sub-Lt Turberville, spotted what I was doing and took me to task. We eventually landed safely at Bradwell Bay, returning to Manston the next day.

'On 16 June I had a new experience. We were in our usual aircraft, and just about to investigate a radar contact off Boulogne, when we saw three orange lights in the sky. We took them to be enemy night fighters, because the German equivalent of our AI radar showed a bright orange light when it was switched on. We took immediate evasive action, and on eventually returning to our contact we found it had reached the safety of Boulogne harbour before our poor old Swordfish managed to get there. We sub-sequently discovered that what we had seen were actually the exhausts from three "Doodle-bugs" or V1 pilotless flying bombs.

'We normally patrolled at about 3,000ft, but on a bright moonlight night we would climb to 4,000ft. We generally attacked from about 2,500-3,000ft, and were told to drop all four of our bombs by 1,000ft because there was a fear of sympathetic detonation. The early nose-fuse bombs were rather like big hand grenades in their blast effect, but it was not known whether they exploded in the order they were dropped, or if the explosion of the first set off the others in sympathy, which might have blown us up if the aircraft were too low. I later broke this order by dropping two bombs at 750ft, and then making another attack with the remaining two bombs.

'The normal method of operation was to approach the target on radar course, and then steer towards it when it came into sight, which in bright moonlight would be quite a long distance off. On a bright moonlight night we attacked up the moon path in order to protect ourselves. We had to get right above the target, and dive at about 45°, waiting until it was at least right in the angle between the engine nacelle and the wing, and then bring up the nose and do a kind of stall turn. If you were also diving into wind you ought really to have gone much further, and wait until the target was on the left of your cockpit. On 5 July, whilst carrying out an attack in bright moonlight on seven ships in the Ostende-Nieuport area, in NE995 but with my usual crew, I made the mistake of making too shallow a dive, probably due to enemy flak, and my bombs failed to reach the target.

'I had more success flying my usual

Left: An invasion-striped Swordfish of No 819 Squadron laying a smoke screen over the Allied invasion fleet on D-Day.
G. L. P. Steer

Above: Swordfish NE932 'A' of No 819 Squadron at RAF Manston shortly after D-Day. The aircraft is bombed up ready for a night attack, and on the wings can be seen the ASV aerials. This machine was flown by the squadron CO, Lt-Cdr P. D. T. Stevens and his observer, Sub-Lt Culshaw, on numerous patrols until the end of 1944.
J. Culshaw via J. D. R. Rawlings

NF119 on the night of 9 July. On this occasion I was accompanied by Lt-Cdr James Turner from the Admiral (Air)'s staff at Lee-on-Solent in place of my normal observer. Turner was very experienced in the operation of ASV X, and he was keen to fly with No 819 Squadron, which was known to be having more fun than anyone else in the Fleet Air Arm at that time, being the only squadron carrying out attacks most nights. Because of the low cloud we were flying at only about 1,500ft, which made it difficult to attack when we eventually spotted eight enemy craft near Dunkirk. During the first attack I had a very near miss with two bombs, but as I broke away at 800ft a 20mm shell went through the starboard lower mainplane, giving us a fright. Luckily it hit nothing vital, and because of the canvas wing it went straight through and simply made a hole. We were over the target for $1\frac{3}{4}$hr during which we dropped the other two bombs about 50-100yd from the ships, eventually returning to Manston after being in the air for $3\frac{1}{2}$hr.

'We had to vacate Manston on 1 August to make way for the Meteor Is of No 616 Squadron, who were sent there to chase incoming V1s. They needed our dispersal as we were near the coast in the path of the V1s heading towards London, and this early version of the Meteor only had fuel for between 20min to half an hour in the air. We were moved around for about a week, first to Inskip, then Limavady, Valley and Lee-on-Solent before coming to rest at Swingfield, an auxiliary landing strip in the Dover-Folkestone area. This already had a wire netting landing strip, probably put down for

some other purpose, but as it was only a day strip we had to make our own flare path, which consisted of a single line of lamps connected with a cable. We had to put up our own tents and live in, and we also had a mess in tents.

'On 1 October the squadron was moved north to Bircham Newton in Norfolk. By the end of the month the Allied armies had advanced well into Belgium, and so on 29 October I found myself in a detachment with six aircraft sent to St Croix airfield, near Bruges. This was an auxiliary strip constructed by Belgian labour only a few months earlier, but never used by the Germans. It had been a fine summer, but immediately we arrived the weather broke. That autumn it simply poured with rain, and the airfield quickly became totally waterlogged. It was later discovered that the Belgian labour had filled all the concrete drainage pipes with extra lumps of cement, to make the aerodrome unserviceable for the Germans. Unfortunately the first users were ourselves, and the pipes could not be unblocked, so we were waterlogged there for 11 days.

'The detachment then moved north to Maldeghem, an RAF-occupied aerodrome about eight miles away, just south of the Bruges-Ghent road, where I rejoined them on 24 November after spending a few days back in England at the squadron headquarters. The following night we carried out an anti-shipping patrol in NF132, attacking two groups of small motor vessels near the Hook of Holland. This was another instance of the wind being against us and the dive too shallow, but we sprayed out our four bombs, and although the first three dropped short,

we squirted the fourth in the right direction and scored a direct hit on an M-class minesweeper, my port lower mainplane being holed during the attack.

'By mid-December we had moved to the little prewar civil aerodrome at Knocke-le-Zoute, the casino resort on the north coast of Belgium. This had packed mud and wire, and from here we were to help protect the Scheldt estuary, now the main shipping lane supplying the armies in Holland. It was thought that E and R-boats, and possibly even bigger ships such as U-boats, would try to attack our shipping, so we patrolled the whole of the coast. I had a slightly alarming experience on 29 January in NF119 when we got icing on the wings. I could see the ice forming, and began to lose flying speed. Eventually the aircraft was in a nose up attitude flying at full throttle but still losing height. The aircraft had of course become very heavy and was slowly sinking towards the sea, but when we were at only a little over 1,000ft there was a loud crack and all the ice fell off. This was the first time I had experienced this. It can happen in a very moist atmosphere, very close to freezing point, where water droplets, such as dew or cloud, turn to ice on hitting the wing surface which is below freezing point, and gradually build up. This would not happen on, for instance, a Russian convoy, however, as the temperature would be too far below freezing point.

'My last attack with No 819 Squadron was on 21 February in NF314. We sighted six enemy ships, either TTA's or M-class minesweepers, three miles off the Hook of Holland, and attacked up the moon path after seeing them stop whilst we were five miles from them. In the first attack our two bombs dropped very close on the port quarter of one of the ships. In our second attack, our remaining two bombs landed 100yd on the starboard of another. We then dropped flares, which illuminated two vessels within 50yd of each other, one apparently awash amidships. The other four were seen on our radar to return to the Hook, followed 20min later by a fifth, but there was no sign of the sixth, which had presumably sunk. Five days later the squadron returned to Bircham Newton, where it disbanded on 10 March.'

111

East Indies Fleet 1945

After the departure of the fleet carriers with the British Pacific Fleet, only the escort carriers *Ameer* and *Shah* remained to comprise the nucleus of the carrier strength of the East Indies Fleet at the beginning of 1945. The former carried the Hellcats of No 804 Squadron, whilst the Avengers of No 851 Squadron were aboard the latter.

This Fleet was for the most part engaged in support of the activities of the British 14th Army in Burma, making many attacks on Japanese land and sea communications lines. The first major operation of the Fleet in which carriers participated was the invasion of Ramree Island, off the Burmese coast. No 804 Squadron Hellcats provided cover for the landings by the 26th Indian Infantry Division on 21 January, flying CAPs and spotting for the artillery bombardment. These activities continued until the end of the month, including providing cover for the landings on nearby Cheduba Island on

26 January by Royal Marines, then the Fleet returned to Trincomalee and No 804 Squadron disembarked on 3 February to China Bay.

The tide had now turned in this theatre of war, and Lord Louis Mountbatten urgently required strategic reconnaissance of those areas where future landings were likely to be made, particularly Sumatra, Malaya and Singapore, but RAF Liberators in Ceylon had insufficient range to remain long over the target areas. The use of PR Seafires was originally planned, but when the Fleet again left port on 22 February with *Empress* taking the place of *Shah*, she had aboard her No 888 Squadron equipped with PR Hellcats. *Ameer* again carried No 804 Squadron, except for one flight which was detached to *Empress* which also carried the Avengers of No 845 Squadron.

The original Hellcats of No 888 Squadron were equipped with one K17 camera of 9in ×

Below: Hellcats of No 888 Squadron aboard HMS *Indefatigable* being ranged prior to the attack on Pangkalan Brandan on 4 January 1945.
B. A. MacCaw

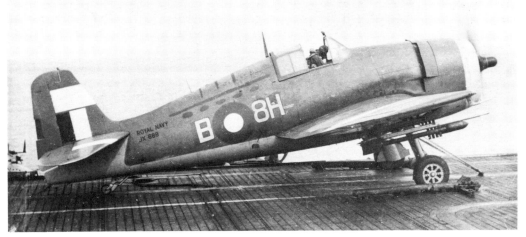

Above: A Hellcat flies low over native workmen engaged in building a road leading from the perimeter track to dispersal points at a jungle airfield in Ceylon. *FAA Museum*

Left: Hellcat JX688 'B8H' of No 896 Squadron on the catapult of HMS *Empress* awaiting take off, armed with rockets, just before the end of the war in the Pacific. This squadron continued to be active in the early part of September 1945, during the occupation of the Malayan Peninsula. *J. W. G. Wellham via M. Garbett*

9in format fitted with a 6in focal length lens for survey work, and one K18 camera of 9in × 18in format with a 24in lens for large scale intelligence cover, both of these being American service models fitted vertically. In order to provide considerably more photographs, two aircraft were specially equipped with two British F52 cameras fitted with 36in lenses and overlapping by 10%. These had 500 exposures in each magazine as opposed to the 125 exposures of the K18, but the additional weight aft made these aircraft grossly tail heavy. However, these were used successfully, despite orders that they must not be flown in this condition.

Most of the armour was removed from the No 888 Squadron aircraft, and guns were only carried when engaged on low level work. In order to minimise the risk of being spotted by enemy aircraft, the Hellcats were painted a specially concocted shade of sky blue, made by mixing dark blue paint with

Top: Hellcat 'B7B' of No 896 Squadron comes in to land on HMS *Ameer*, its starboard oleo being likely to suffer damage unless the pilot can very quickly straighten her up. On the lift is painted the current identification letter 'R', these letters being changed from time to time for security reasons. *R. A. Shilcock*

some white, with the red being omitted from the centre of the roundels. For similar reasons no squadron identification markings were carried, but the flights were distinguished by their spinners, aircraft of No 1 Flight carrying one white ring and those of No 2 Flight two white rings, the flight commander's aircraft having plain spinners. Aircraft strength varied between six and 10, but in fact pilot strength was sometimes as low as

four. The aircraft proved ideal for their task, and serviceability was maintained at a high rate.

Commencing on 26 February, the PR Hellcats flew at heights of up to 30,000ft or more over large areas of the Kra Isthmus, Penang, Phuket Island, northern Sumatra and other regions. There was some initial trouble with camera failures, but the weather remained clear and generally good results

Above: Hellcats of No 896 Squadron flying in box formation over RNAS Wingfield, Capetown early in 1945, before joining HMS *Ameer* to join the East Indies Fleet. *R. A. Shilcock*

Left: No 896 Squadron being inspected at Wingfield early in 1945 by Vice-Adm Sir R. Burnett, the Commander-in-Chief. Shortly afterwards the squadron sailed for Southern India in HMS *Ameer* and subsequently carried out operations from both this carrier and HMS *Empress*. Aircraft JX690 in the centre of the picture was coded '2AB' at that time and was one of the original equipment of the squadron, having been shipped out to Wingfield from the United States aboard HMS *Ranee*. *R. A. Shilcock*

were obtained. The preferred height over the target area was between 32,000 and 35,000ft, but they could get up to 42,000ft if necessary, or if there was cloud cover they would drop down to as little as 8,000ft. The Hellcat's fuel capacity with a large long range tank under the fuselage enabled them to stay over the target area for considerable periods, and trips averaged a total of six or seven hours and occasionally longer. These were almost certainly the highest and longest operational sorties performed by any FAA squadron, notwithstanding that the aircraft were unpressurised and pilots flew on oxygen masks.

After taking off from the carrier, the Hellcats flew low over the water on a dog leg course so as to mislead the enemy as to the point of departure, flying about 80 miles at right angles to the intended approach before turning inland. They would then climb and fly at height for about 300-400 miles over the area to be photographed, after which they would adopt the same tactics in reverse, again at sea level on the last 80 miles of the dog leg. This created navigational problems, and it was not uncommon to have difficulty in locating the Fleet on return, as this could have moved a considerable distance by that time, and consequently pilots were given freedom to land on any carrier which they could find.

Navigation had to be carried out entirely by dead-reckoning on a knee-pad. On the homeward trip the pilots could be guided by the ship's YG beacon, but unfortunately it was not uncommon for the aircraft's beacon aerial to be knocked off by the long-range tank when it was jettisoned after exhaustion to save weight and drag on the return journey.

One of the main tasks of the squadron was to fly over potential landing beaches in order to assess gradients at different states of the tide. The technique depended on the pilot flying very accurately at a specified time over the beach. The camera automatically photographed a stop watch, and the distance travelled by a wave in a given time between exposures allowed the interpreters to gauge the depth of the water. Film processing on return was a problem due to the heat, but the ward room ice helped to keep temperatures down to a suitable level.

Briefing by Maj Farmer, the Army Liaison Officer, was excellent, and a considerable amount of mapping and survey work was successfully accomplished. There was a danger from enemy fighters, although the 'Zekes' and 'Oscars' could only catch the fast Hellcats if they were prepared. Since the Japanese were unaware that the aircraft were unarmed, this tended to deter the slower enemy fighters. The CO, Lt-Cdr Brian MacCaw, had an unusual experience on the Pangkalan Brandan strike when flying over the target area at a height of over 30,000ft. He suddenly saw a Japanese fighter also circling and, as he accelerated away, he was surprised to see the enemy also departing at great speed in the opposite direction, presumably having spotted him at exactly the same moment. MacCaw later learned from the Intelligence Section responsible for monitoring enemy frequencies that the pilot was an important Japanese Army Major who had been directing his own fighters over the target area, and presumably did not want to stay and run the risk of being shot down by what he imagined to be an armed Hellcat in sight of his own airmen, and thus lose face.

On 1 March, Hellcats from the detach-

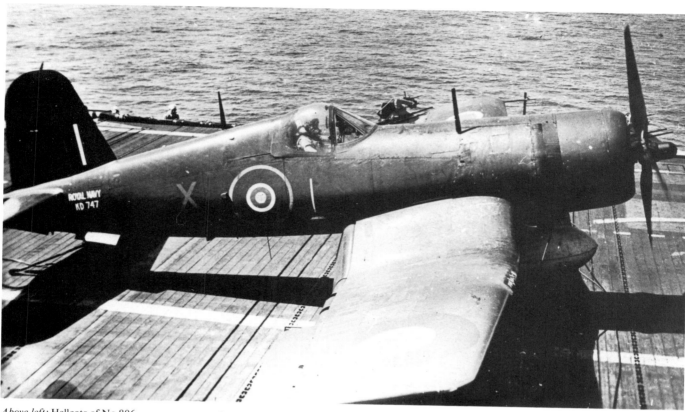

Above left: Hellcats of No 896 Squadron ranged on the flight deck of HMS *Ameer* in May 1945. Chocks are being withdrawn from the two leading machines. The squadron disembarked to RNAS Tambaram, near Madras on 12 May 1945. *R. A. Shilcock*

Left: Three PR Hellcats of No 888 Squadron, fitted with long range tanks under the fuselage, fly in formation over the jungle. They carry the special paint scheme used on aircraft of this squadron, but there is some variation in the method of applying this as can be seen from the different diameters of the blue portion of the fuselage roundels and the different widths of fine stripes. *B. A. MacCaw*

Above: Corsair IV KD747 'X' of No 1843 Squadron coming to rest after landing on HMS *Arbiter* in the Indian Ocean early in 1945. This aircraft suffered minor damage on 25 March 1945 when it made a fast approach and floated over all the arrester wires to land in the ship's barrier.
P. C. S. Chilton via J. D. R. Rawlings

ment of No 804 Squadron aboard *Ameer* shot down a 'Dinah' and two 'Oscars' whilst providing CAP for the Fleet, these being the first successes against the Japanese by fighters operating from British escort carriers. The ships then returned to Trincomalee on 7 March.

Carrier strength was now further increased by the arrival of *Khedive* and *Emperor*, both of which sailed with the Fleet on 8 April for another PR task. The main objective was photo coverage of the Kuala Lumpur, Port Dickson and Malacca areas of Malaya, with emphasis on airfields, beaches and ports. Activities over the target areas tended to be restricted by the distance travelled from the carrier, which was sometimes as much as 300 miles offshore. Poor weather also hampered operations, and Sub-Lt (A) J. W. Tomlinson RNVR an American pilot serving with No 888 Squadron, lost his life when his machine (JX683) crashed 10 miles west of Port Dickson on 14 April following an engine failure. He survived the crash and was rescued by a fishing boat, but he was taken prisoner and later beheaded.

No 808 Squadron, aboard *Khedive*, shot down three aircraft which attacked the Fleet, but they were dogged by operating difficulties including the destruction of three aircraft in an accident on 10 April when JV144 bounced on landing, hitting JW719 and JV298, the latter being knocked overboard with the loss of the pilot, Lt (A) P. A. Sherry RNVR.

Shortly after returning from this trip on 20 April, certain carriers of the East Indies Fleet, which had been known for a time as the Escort Carrier Squadron, became re-grouped as the 21st Aircraft Carrier Squadron, initially comprising *Emperor*, *Hunter*, *Khedive* and *Stalker*, these being shortly joined by *Ameer*, *Attacker*, *Pursuer*, *Searcher* and *Trouncer*. The initial four carriers were all engaged in the next operation, the long awaited invasion of Rangoon, known as Operation 'Dracula'. On this occasion no Avenger squadrons were embarked in the main attack, Nos 800 and 808 Hellcat squadrons being aboard *Emperor* and *Khedive* respectively, whilst *Hunter* and *Stalker* carried the first Seafire squadrons to join the Fleet, being Nos 807 and 809 Squadrons respectively. The amphibious landings took place on 2 May, the fighter squadrons flying 110 sorties that day, but little opposition was encountered as they strafed and dropped bombs.

The anti-climax provided by the operations may be surmised by the few brief notes devoted by the diarist of No 807 Squadron's line book:

'Operation "Dracula" D-day Wednesday 2 May to D+2 Previous to this operation we all imagined that the capture of Rangoon would present many difficulties and demand the best efforts of all the forces concerned.

'In this, however, we were proved to be mistaken as the Army met with slight resistance that was easily overcome.

Seafires of No 807 Squadron, ashore from HMS *Hunter* being equipped: (above) being fitted with a bomb under the centre fuselage, (left) armourers preparing ammunition for the wing guns, and (right) a camera gun being fitted in a reconnaissance machine.
all FAA Museum

'We found our flying time almost equally divided into Force Cover and Beach Cover. One strike only was sent off. Four Seafires and four Hellcats, led by our CO, Lt-Cdr Clarke, dive bombed some gun positions on the west bank of the Rangoon river.

'The patrol lines, which we flew when briefed for Beach Cover are marked on the $\frac{1}{4}$in map on the preceding page (of the line book). The patrol "Bitter" was the one most frequently flown as it covered the inner anchorage of the Landing Ships.

'That was "Dracula". Consequently, AC21's thirst for blood remained unquenched and the carrier force proceeded south in search of prey.'

Two days later, after a spell of poor weather, the Carrier Group attacked airfields and shipping off the Tenasserim coast, further south on 5 and 6 May.

In the meantime, the 3rd Battle Squadron was in action in the Andaman and Nicobar Islands, preventing Japanese air units in the region from flying to resist the invasion. Aboard *Empress* and *Shah* with the force were the Hellcats of No 804 Squadron and the Avengers of No 851 Squadron, and a few Seafires of No 809 Squadron. During eight days of activity, commencing on 30 April, these carried out diversionary strikes with rockets and bombs on Japanese airfields, and enemy shipping in the area was attacked by the Avengers. Altogether the six carriers put up over 400 sorties before withdrawing, and although there were a number of accidents, only one aircraft was lost to enemy action, this being Hellcat JX803 of No 804 Squadron which ditched near the Fleet after being hit by enemy anti-aircraft fire, the pilot, Sub-Lt (A) J. A. Scott RNVR regrettably losing his life.

The Fleet returned to Trincomalee on 9 May, but was soon back at sea for strikes on the Nicobar Islands. However, *Shah's* accelerator broke down, and her Avengers had to be transferred to *Emperor* on 11 May. A search was made for the enemy cruiser *Haguro*, and she was found during the morning of 15th by a No 851 Squadron Avenger, but owing to operating difficulties the only attack made was by three aircraft of that squadron, and none of these succeeded

in hitting the target, although a near miss was claimed by Lt (A) K. C. Crompton RNVR in FN939 '1M' during the dive-bombing attack. She was sunk early the following morning in a torpedo attack by the 26th Destroyer Flotilla.

Mechanical problems now bedevilled the carriers, and when the next operations occurred in mid June only three of the seven with the Fleet were serviceable. *Khedive* carried No 808 Squadron Hellcats. *Stalker* had No 809 Squadron Seafires, and *Ameer* had **the Hellcat fighters of No 804 Squadron and the PR Hellcats of No 888 Squadron. The** main task on this occasion was a photographic survey of southern Malaya and the Penang area, commencing on 18 June. No strikes were permitted until the last PR sortie was launched two days later, to avoid provoking the enemy whilst this invaluable work was carried out. Then 29 aircraft from the three fighter squadrons were launched to attack shipping, airfields and communications in Sumatra and southern Burma. Heavy damage was inflicted, but the recently appointed CO of No 808 Squadron, Lt-Cdr (A) C. F. Wheatley RNVR, was killed when his Hellcat (JW868) was shot down in flames over Medan.

Further attacks in July were to prove the last major operation of the war by this carrier force. Between 5 and 11 July, Hellcats of No 896 Squadron in *Ameer*, and No 800 Squadron in *Emperor* struck at the few replacement Japanese aircraft on Car Nicobar. Strikes were also made on shipping in the area; during one such attack on 7 July, Hellcat JX680 piloted by Lt-Cdr (A) R. M. Norris RNVR the CO of No 896 Squadron since it reformed the previous October, was hit by light anti-aircraft fire and crashed in the sea.

Similar operations were carried out from 24 July in North Malaya, and cover was provided for a minesweeping operation off Phuket Island. Considerable damage was inflicted by Nos 804 and 896 Squadrons in three days of operations, with attacks on railways, road transport and airfields. In a raid on Phuket on 26 July, JX703, a Hellcat piloted by Sub-Lt (A) I. T. Dean of No 896 Squadron, had the misfortune to fly into a locomotive during a strafing run, bursting into flames on impact.

This was to prove the last operation by the 21st Aircraft Carrier Squadron, a planned strike by five carriers on Penang being cancelled. However, the Squadron participated in Operation 'Zipper', the re-occupation of Malaya, with six carriers anchored off Singapore on 10 September.

Right: Seafire 'D5V' of No 807 Squadron from HMS *Hunter* flies low over the jungle. *FAA Museum*

Below: A Hellcat has drifted over the side of an escort carrier whilst landing, and is being pulled back on board by the maintenance crews, watched by a crowd of 'goofers'. *IWM*

Sumatra Raids

Under the command of Rear-Adm Sir Philip L. Vian, the British Pacific Fleet's first major carrier operation was another attack on Sumatra towards the end of 1944. Mounted on 20 December, bad weather caused the striking force to be diverted to the secondary target of Belawan Deli, a port serving Medan, but results were poor. A further attempt was therefore mounted early in the New Year as Operation 'Lentil'.

The carrier strength now comprised *Indefatigable*, *Indomitable* and *Victorious*, each with an Avenger squadron and two fighter squadrons, and these reached the target area on 4 January in clear weather. An innovation was an offensive sweep before the main strike by 16 Corsairs and Hellcats, this tactic being code-named a 'Ramrod'. After taking off at 06.10hrs they attacked airfields 80 miles inland to destroy seven out of 25 aircraft on the ground in a surprise attack. The main striking force of 32 Avengers and 12 Fireflies left at 07.40hrs with an escort of 32 fighters. On nearing the target the Fireflies broke away to attack the port of Pangkalan Soe Soe with rockets, scoring hits on electrical and oil installations, and these were followed by the Avengers which dropped about 30 tons of bombs. The escort shot down five of about a dozen Oscars which attacked them, and enemy flak was light, consequently losses were minimal.

After this operation the force returned to Trincomalee, but on 16 January they sailed again, this time headed for Australia, from where future operations were to be undertaken using Sydney as the main base. The carriers, now augmented by *Illustrious*, were

Below: The CO of No 857 Squadron from HMS *Indomitable*, Lt-Cdr (A) W. Stuart DSC RNVR in Avenger JZ594 'W1A', is about to turn in for the dive on the secondary target of Belawan Oil Refinery during the attack on 20 December 1944. Flying at 12,000ft, he is photographed from his No 2's machine, JZ592 piloted by Sub-Lt (A) A. G. Clayton RNVR. Smoke can be seen rising after the attack by earlier aircraft. *A. G. Clayton*

Above: Smoke rising from the oil refinery at Pangkalan Brandan during Operation 'Lentil' on 4 January 1945. The strike, which took place in good weather, was highly successful. *IWM*

Right: Corsair 'T7L' of No 1834 Squadron from HMS *Victorious* being ferried by pontoon in Colombo harbour. This squadron participated in the successful raids on the Palembang oil refinery in January 1945. *FAA Museum*

grouped together as the 1st Aircraft Carrier Squadron, and strikes were planned to take place en route on targets in Sumatra as Operation 'Meridian'.

Bad weather postponed the first attack, on the oil refinery at Pladjoe, but this eventually took place on 24 January and inflicted heavy damage despite the sudden appearance of a balloon barrage as the Avengers dived to attack. The second attack, five days later on the oil refinery and installations at Soengei Gerong benefited from the lessons of the earlier raid, and was again highly successful. In all, these three raids during January accounted for about 140 Japanese aircraft and inflicted considerable damage to the enemy's oil supplies, in addition to other damage.

One of those who took part in these operations was Glyn Clayton, who as Sub-Lt (A) A. G. Clayton RNVR was serving as an Avenger pilot of No 857 Squadron aboard *Indomitable*:

'Sailing from Trincomalee we all knew whether we were simply going out on exercises or on a raid because in the latter case the ship's Royal Marine band always played us out of harbour — we were going into action!

'We had attacked some small refineries in the north-east of Sumatra, at Pangkalan Brandan and Belawan Deli, and Palembang was obviously just over the horizon. However we knew nothing of it until we actually sailed. Then some of the aircrew, possibly by inspired guesswork, got hold of

Left: Seafire NN460 'H6Z' of No 894 Squadron entering the barrier of HMS *Indefatigable* after making a heavy landing during which the starboard oleo collapsed on returning from the raid on Pangkalan Brandan on 4 January 1945. *IWM*

Below left: Seafire NN460 'H6Z' being manhandled by the deck party after its encounter with *Indefatigable*'s barrier. This squadron was later active with the 24th Naval Fighter Wing during numerous attacks on the Sakishima Gunto and later the Japanese mainland. *FAA Museum*

Above: Firefly DT934 '4K' of No 1770 Squadron waiting to take-off from the deck of HMS *Indefatigable* for a rocket attack on the oil refinery at Pangkalan Brandan during Operation 'Lentil'. This machine was later damaged when it floated into the barrier after a fast approach on 13 March 1945, whilst the ship was at Manus.
Crown Copyright

Right: Seafire 'H6Y' with wings folded, surrounded by a deck party during the Sumatra raids.
B. A. MacCaw

the word Palembang. There was intensive briefing with scale models etc for what was for most of us the most ambitious job we were to undertake. Any who were shot down and survived were to make their way with the help of (hopefully) friendly natives to a certain point on the west coast where a submarine would appear for I think two nights in 27 days time after the raid. This seemed feasible until we saw the mountains! Aircraft were checked and rechecked, cleaned and worried over endlessly.

'I missed the first raid because I led the small raid on Mana airfield on the west coast, in a way as a diversion but mainly to put out of action the runway and the reconnaissance bombers which were known to be there. We were then to fly south down the coast at tree top height to strafe some of the many airfields there. In the event, after the bombing of Mana, which certainly put the runway out of action, Lt Westfield, who led our Hellcat escort, was wounded in one eye and had to return to the ship, and we were all recalled,

since a loss of two of, I think, our four escorting fighters was thought to be rather asking for trouble.

'The first Palembang raid was a success and that night Japanese broadcasts were decoded: they claimed that the raid had been beaten off with great losses and that we would never attempt it again!

'Five days later we were back in the flying-off position at dawn. I was late getting into my aircraft and was soaked through by a sudden torrential rain storm which swept down the flight deck. I was hanging on to one of the wheel chocks, against the driving rain and the slipstreams of other aircraft running up, soaked to the skin!

'We crossed the coast and climbed over the western mountain range, I believe some 12,000ft high and clothed in dense jungle right up to the top. What hope I wondered would we have of making it on foot in 27 days, with Japanese troops to avoid, possibly friendly villagers, animals, snakes, leeches, jungle etc, it seemed a forlorn hope.

'Back to reality when the starboard wing tank emptied, engine momentarily cut out in the fraction of a second taken in switching

Above: Forming up for Operation 'Lentil' are the Avengers of No 857 Squadron from HMS *Indomitable,* No 849 Squadron from HMS *Victorious* and No 820 Squadron from HMS *Indefatigable.* IWM

Left: Sunday morning service aboard HMS *Indefatigable* during the period of the Sumatra raids in January 1945. In the rear are Seafires of Nos 887 and 894 Squadrons, which comprised the 24th Naval Fighter Wing. B. A. MacCaw

Below: Seafire 'H5T' of No 887 Squadron catches the wire after a successful landing during the Sumatra raids. B. A. MacCaw

Above: Smoke rising from the oil refinery at Soengei Gerong after a successful strike by aircraft from four fleet carriers during Operation 'Meridian II' on 29 January 1945. The aircraft had to fly through considerable flak, which can be seen in the photograph.
Cdr R. C. Hay

Right: Avenger 'Q4V' of No 854 Squadron bombing up on the flight deck of HMS *Illustrious* during Operation 'Meridian II'. Included in this group are Sub-Lt (A) H. L. Taylor RNVR, AMO A. B. Hall, AMO S. W. Keene, AMO J. Frene, AMO J. H. Camden and N/Air D. Thomson. Sub-Lt Taylor lost his life during an attack on airfields in the Sakishima Gunto on 26 March 1945, when his machine, FN863, was hit by flak and subsequently exploded over the sea.
IWM

over to the main fuel tank. Then a gentle descent, all four squadrons in good formation, and the escorting fighters weaving about — very encouraging.

'I think I remember correctly that we had to pass over or near five enemy airfields, and they by then were expecting us. There was a confusion of aircraft flashing about, some in flames, and I remember well that the Jap fighters would dive almost vertically through our formation then climb again vertically, firing on the way up.

'When the target lay ahead we saw first of all the AA barrage, black shell bursts directly in our path — then the balloons — the box barrage being laid just above the balloons so that you had a clear choice — down through the balloons or over the top and into the flak. The CO of No 854, Lt-Cdr Mainprice, and his wingman were of course brought down by balloon on the first raid.

'Then suddenly my aircraft seemed to stop in mid air. We knew afterwards that we had been hit by flak almost in the centre of the underside engine cowling — miraculously the engine was not hit. The impression was of riding a bicycle past someone who suddenly caught hold of the saddle to pull the bicycle backwards. I suppose the hit, directly opposite to the line of flight produced that remarkable deceleration. Not knowing what had happened, we dived over the balloons and dropped our bombs on our particular target — but I realised that something was wrong when the aircraft did not lighten. I asked my air gunner (PO W. A. Taylor), who was down at the belly gun, to look into the bomb bay through the window and he reported that the bomb bay doors were closed, so I knew that we had probably been hit and that the hydraulics had gone. I tried several times but failed to open them.

'By this time we were away from the target, flying east to turn through south to our rendezvous south-west of Palembang. The defending fighters of course knew this and we were jumped by an all silver "Tojo". He approached us very fast from underneath and astern, and I am almost sure I engaged the supercharger to try to get some extra speed! He was firing but did not hit us, and purely on instinct I flew down to almost ground level. He followed, and being below us and perhaps not noticing what was happening, flew at great speed into a clump of trees and exploded into flames.

'We formed up with the rest of the squadron, some obviously the worse for wear, and having tried to get the wheels down by diving and pulling out sharply, we finally managed to operate wheels and flaps by the emergency hydraulic system. I made a very good landing and, on looking around the aircraft, was bothered to find that although these things could not, in theory, happen, one bomb had been released, and its nose was poking through the gap in the bomb doors!'

Operations in the air during these raids were supervised by Maj R. C. Hay, RM, an extremely experienced fighter pilot, who had been appointed to the new post of Air Co-ordinator, using the R/T callsign 'Father', his title being changed shortly afterwards to Air Group Leader. For his part in 'Meridian' he was later awarded the DSO. Flying Corsair JT427 'T-RH' he commenced photographing the second attack at 08.50hrs as the first bombs fell, and saw severe damage being inflicted, which his photographs subsequently confirmed. Bombing by the first wing of Avengers was very impressive, but the smoke from their efforts made it difficult for the second wing to see their targets. However, No 854 Squadron from *Illustrious* in this wing succeeded in setting fire to some oil tanks very close to

their objective. Later aircraft used their initiative and chose other targets, as their correct ones were obscured, one stick of bombs apparently bursting along the wharves. It was perhaps regrettable that the efforts of so many aircraft were concentrated on one small target when nearby Pladjoe was equally important and clearly visible.

Maj Hay finished filming about 3min after the last bomb had been dropped, and as the flak had subsided he climbed to 10,000ft for a vertical line overlap. He had to abandon this idea when a 'Tojo' approached, and in the ensuing dogfight they descended to ground level. After shooting this aircraft down, he also destroyed an 'Oscar' which had been attracted by the gunfire.

During this time the Avengers departed from the target area towards their rendezvous 30 miles away, though a number failed to find it, as was also the case with Maj Hay although he searched for some time. Several aircraft were lost during the hectic battle which took place at this period.

In his subsequent report Maj Hay concluded that Meridian I and II were the most interesting and successful operations he knew of, and especially praised the determination of the Avenger pilots for their accurate bombing in the face of maximum discouragement. He also commended the efforts of the fighter escort against stiff opposition, but criticised several aspects of the overall plan. One of these was the decision to concentrate the first attack on Pladjoe and the second on Soengei Gerong. The later Avenger pilots in each attack found their targets hidden in smoke, when there was a very clear alternative just beside them which they had to ignore.

Having carried out one of the Fleet Air Arm's most outstanding feats of the war, the carriers now continued with the Fleet to Sydney, where they arrived on 10 February.

Above: HMS *Indomitable* in Chesapeake Bay, Virginia on 11 April 1944, with No 854 Squadron Avengers embarked for passage to the UK. By the New Year they were in action in Sumatra, being homed on to their target by HM Submarine *Thule* during Operation 'Meridian II'. Regrettably the CO, piloting JZ112 'Q4A', was lost when his starboard wing struck a balloon cable whilst he was leading a flight of six aircraft in a steep glide-bombing attack. In this attack, Lt G. J. Connolly in 'Q4P' shot down with his two front guns one of two 'Tojos' which were attacking 'P1G' of No 849 Squadron, and was later awarded the DSO. *via F. S. Martin*

The Sakishima Gunto

On 27 February 1945 the British Pacific Fleet sailed from Sydney, at reduced strength due partly to mechanical problems and partly to industrial troubles in the docks. By 7 March they had reached Manus, in the Admiralty Islands, where they became part of the formidable Task Force 57 in the American 5th Fleet. Staging through Ulithi, an atoll in the Caroline Islands, they prepared to carry out a series of attacks on the Sakishima Gunto group of islands between Okinawa and Formosa, in the East China Seas. These attacks were to form part of Operation 'Iceberg', the American invasion of Okinawa.

The first raid took place on 26 March, with attacks being made on six main airfields on the islands of Ishigaki Shima and Mujako Shima. Due to refuelling difficulties, the ships sailed slowly to conserve fuel, and the low windspeed over the pitching decks resulted in a high incidence of accidents, especially to the Seafire escorts. Another attack was mounted the following day, further losses being sustained, then the British Pacific Fleet withdrew to refuel and replenish. The aircraft had flown 548 sorties of all kinds, and 64 tons of bombs had been dropped and 151 rockets fired, but 17 aircraft and nine aircrew had been lost in two days. Permanent damage was not as great as hoped, the Japanese being adept at filling the runway craters overnight, being unmolested at this time as there were then no night intruder squadrons attached to the Fleet.

This pattern of two days of strikes

Below: Avenger '385/W' of No 857 Squadron, piloted by Sub-Lt M. Dee with Sub-Lt D. Gardiner as observer, awaiting form up over HMS *Indomitable* on 25 May 1945, during fleet attacks on Sakishima Gunto. *via D. Gardiner*

followed by withdrawal was to become a regular feature at intermittent intervals over the next two months. The same targets were attacked on 31 March and 1 April, and again on 6 and 7 April. The attacks on 1 April were met by the first major counter-attack, when the Fleet was attacked by up to 20 Japanese aircraft whilst the Ramrods were on their way to attack Ishigaki. Two aircraft were shot down, but a 'Zeke' which had been attacked by Sub-Lt (A) R. H. Reynolds RNVR of No 887 Squadron made the first successful kamikaze or suicide attack on the British Pacific Fleet, when it dived on to the flight deck of *Indefatigable* and inflicted heavy damage despite the armoured deck. Sub-Lt Reynolds stayed aloft in his Seafire and helped combat further such attacks, destroying two other 'Zekes' before landing on the battered deck. These attacks led to one or two destroyers being stationed at each end of the line with a Hellcat flying overhead to identify returning friendly aircraft before allowing them to land; a practice known colloquially by the Americans as 'de-lousing', but officially by the code-name 'Tomcat'.

Gordon Lambert, serving with No 820 Squadron, was aboard *Indefatigable* at the time of the kamikaze success:

'It would be some time before 08.00hrs that I had washed and shaved and was preparing to go to breakfast in the wardroom, which was our action mess. The rest of the ship's company was at early morning action stations. There was some firing although I believed it to be that some spotter plane had come too close. Anyway our cover air patrols were in the air, and we were some distance from the nearest land, so all was well — or was it? Suddenly the anti-aircraft fire seemed to get more insistent, and as our mess was down near the water line I thought it prudent to get up to our crew room in the island superstructure.

'Whilst I was on my way up to the crew room there was an almighty explosion, and I could feel the blast wave come down the ladder I was ascending. My immediate thought was that we had been hit by a bomb and if it had penetrated the flight deck to burst in the hangar we were going to be in real trouble. I raced up the remaining ladders to the crew room, to find a few others assembled and all speculating on what had happened. A voice on the tannoy system called for all doctors and sick berth attendants to report to the flight deck, and for damage control parties. The quartermaster rang eight bells — it was 8 o'clock on the morning of April fool's day 1945.

'We went to the flight deck to see what had happened, and lodged between the side of the island and the flight deck was the remains of a Japanese suicide plane — a kamikaze!!! The medical staff moved about the dead, the dying and the injured, giving injections and

Below: Corsair JT586 '125/Q', piloted by Lt (A) P. S. Cole DSC RNVR, the Senior Pilot of No 1830 Squadron trying to make the crash barrier of HMS *Illustrious* on returning from a strafing attack on Formosan airfields. *IWM*

Bottom: Lt Cole's machine ends up against the bridge of HMS *Illustrious* after being caught by the wires. He was able to climb out unhurt as the ship's firefighters raced to prevent the machine from catching fire. *IWM*

generally making people comfortable until they could be got down below to the sick bay. The damage control party set about removing the debris from the flight deck in an attempt to get the ship fully operational again. By 08.30hrs we were almost back to normal. Seafires which had been up on early morning CAP came into land, and only one crash barrier remained inoperable. In all other respects we were back to normal. Later that day even that was repaired. So much for the feared suicide bomber.

'As soon as the initial excitement died down I decided to go to breakfast. As I was descending one of the ladders, just ahead of me was a stretcher party carrying down to the sick bay a badly injured seaman. His leg had been injured, the temporary dressing had fallen off as he was being carried down the ladder on a straitjacket type stretcher, and I could see the torn and mutilated flesh and bone. When I sat down to breakfast and was offered bacon and tomatoes (train smash) I had to refuse.

'We spent almost the whole of April carrying out raids on Japanese airfields and shipping around the islands. One of these raids was an attack on the port of Kiirun in northern Formosa. The attack itself had been successful, although one crew at least would probably not agree. As we left the target area one aircraft, not from our squadron, came down in the sea. We saw the crew manage to get out of the aircraft, but there was a motor boat on its way to collect them. Knowing of the atrocities performed by the Japs, they would probably have been better off had they been killed outright.

'The raids were in the main uneventful. There was always AA fire to contend with, and of course the enemy fighters, but at least those of us in No 820 Squadron kept coming back. One or two incidents did cause the blood to flow a little quicker, such as the occasion when we were approaching a target and saw a flash of gunfire. I reported it to the pilot, who said "It's too far away to bother us". In a matter of seconds there was a resounding crack right underneath us and the aircraft was peppered with shrapnel. It never ceased to amaze me that when flying through anti-aircraft fire one could see the shells burst but did not hear any noise above the roar of the engine, unless of course it was very close. We did a bit of bobbing and weaving, but could not shake off their extremely accurate fire. We turned away and went round the island and attacked from the opposite side with considerable success, and more important — no losses.

'On another occasion we had to approach our target from the opposite side of the island from our direction of approach. Attack out of the sun and all that!!! We had got round to the far side and were flying at about 10,000ft when suddenly the engine cut out. We dropped several hundred feet and I for one thought it was curtains for us. Just as suddenly it cut in again, and as we regained height and our position the pilot calmly informed us that he had forgotten to switch tanks.

'One evening I was strolling up and down the flight deck with my pilot having a yarn, and I expressed my concern about the way we dropped off the front of the flight deck, and how I could see the turbulence created by the slipstream. "Don't worry about that" he said, "It gives the aircraft a bit of extra speed and assists in getting some lift". As we were talking, one of the other carriers was flying off some strike aircraft and we were watching them adopt more or less the same drill. Unfortunately one pilot obviously tried to pull his aircraft up before reaching the front of the flight deck. He didn't have enough flying speed, stalled and crashed into the sea. I needed no further convincing.'

After these attacks the Fleet withdrew to Leyte in the Philippines for a full replenishment. Arriving on 23 April after a voyage of 1,000 miles, they had been at sea for over a month since leaving Ulithi, a record in British naval history since the time of Nelson. They had achieved their main objective of neutralising, at least temporarily, the

Below: A near miss by a Kamikaze on HMS *Victorious.* *A. G. Clayton*

Above left and left: Scenes on the deck of HMS *Formidable* immediately after a Kamikaze attack on 4 May 1945. *IWM*

Above: Repairing the deck of HMS *Formidable* following a Kamikaze attack. The steel decking of the British fleet carriers afforded considerable protection, unlike the wooden decking of their American counterparts. *Cdr R. C. Hay*

Right: A Barracuda of No 812 Squadron tries desperately to gain speed and go round again after missing the wire of HMS *Vengeance* during March 1945. The carrier deck letter 'A' can be seen in a circle aft of the deck lift. *C. H. Wood*

Sakishima airfields during the invasion of Okinawa, having flown 2,444 sorties, dropped 412 tons of bombs and fired 325 rockets. 47 aircraft had been lost operationally, but many of the crews were saved, only 29 being listed as killed or missing.

Respite was welcome for the weary crews, but on 1 May they put to sea again and were in action within three days against the same targets. The Japanese had taken full advantage of the lull to make good much of the damage and flak over the target was as heavy as ever. Shortly after 11.00hrs enemy aircraft began a series of attacks on the carriers, and at 11.31hrs a 'Zeke' succeeded in hitting *Formidable* in a kamikaze attack, the resulting explosion creating a 2ft hole and surrounding dent in the flight-deck, causing considerable damage and casualties. Similar attacks continued until 9 May, with five carriers being hit, but all continued in service. The Fleet finally withdrew to Manus on 25 May, where it arrived five days later.

Two Shades of Blue

Late in the war, a number of RAF pilots were offered the opportunity of transferring to the Fleet Air Arm. One of these was Plt Off J. P. D. Rafferty, who had originally been accepted into the RAF in September 1942, eventually going to St Andrews the following March for a university short course lasting six months. Soon after he was posted to 14 EFTS at Elmdon for a few weeks' initial training on Tiger Moths, but after this he found himself to be one of many such partially trained pilots awaiting transfer to Advanced Training in South Africa, the USA and Canada. In May 1944 he found himself aboard HMT *Andes* bound for Canada where, after a few days at Personnel Depot, Moncton, his course entrained for No 5 British Flying Training School, Riddle Field, Clewiston, Florida. He recalls:

'This was a very efficient unit, one of about six of its kind in the United States. The Commanding Officer, a Squadron Leader, together with a small staff of about five Officers and NCOs were responsible for administration, but all training was undertaken by a commercial company employing its own civilian staff of flying and ground instructors. We were told on arrival that those who survived the course would graduate and get their wings on 21 January, and after an integrated course of primary flying training on Stearman PT-17s, followed by basic training on North American AT-6s, that is exactly what happened. On completion of the course we returned to Personnel Depot, Moncton where, as the European war was in its closing stages, we had another period of waiting before embarking for the UK in HMT *Louis Pasteur*, in which I was given hull space in which to sling a hammock right above the ship's propellers, a foretaste of naval life had I realised it.

'We were sent initially to the Air Crew Disposal Centre at Harrogate, where there were a considerable number of newly trained pilots and other air crew, all anxious to get into the war. Then one day a notice was posted telling us all to assemble in the ante room at 14.30hrs. A large number of us crowded into the room at the appointed time, and the Adjutant introduced us to a Squadron Leader from the Air Ministry, who turned out to be the officer in charge of postings. He announced that he was there to explain to us the AMO covering a voluntary scheme for transfer to the Fleet Air Arm. This, of course, produced a chorus of loud catcalls. After these had subsided he went on to say that before we condemned the idea out of hand we should consider what might happen to us if we didn't, listing such things as becoming a glider pilot, a flight engineer on York transports or an Air Traffic Control Officer in the Outer Hebrides. Our loyalties were, naturally, firmly with the RAF but impelled by a desire to fly, and the possibility that we might see some action in the Far East, around 50 or 60 of us said we would be interested. As a consequence, on 8 May 1945 we found ourselves after a day's train journey reporting to HMS *Macaw*, a FAA reception centre at Bootle in Cumberland.

'Here we were introduced gently but firmly to the Navy, and after two weeks we had to decide whether to remain or revert to the RAF. Of those who opted to remain the officers transferred to equivalent ranks, some NCO pilots were commissioned to Sub-Lts and the remainder became PO pilots. I was one of those who decided to remain, and after two weeks leave, during which we had to shave off our moustaches and buy the right colour uniform, we returned to Bootle to get to know Nelson better. We then went on to an Advanced Flying Unit at RAF Atcham for grading, followed by our first real FAA unit, the Naval Advanced Instrument Flying School at Hinstock, where we flew Oxfords and Harvards. On completion of a brief course here, we were sent on the Greenwich course in late July.

'After this we returned to Bootle for dispersal to advanced training squadrons, which at that time were principally equipped with Seafires and Barracudas. I was in fact appointed to RNAS Crimond, near Rattray Head, where on 10 August I joined No 714 TBR Training Squadron, but the dropping of the two atomic bombs on Japan ended any possibility of my seeing active service in that theatre. However, I remained at Rattray, training on Barracudas until 3 November when I moved to Crail and joined No 786 Squadron. By now the FAA was being run down, and all flying training ceased on 1 January except for those who had opted for a four year short service commission. I was eventually demobilised in November of that year.'

The Finale

The battle-weary British Pacific Fleet reached Sydney on 5 June, to spend the next few weeks making good its losses. The ships were repaired and replenished, and their personnel partook of Australian hospitality. The carrier squadrons took full advantage of the welcome break to re-arm and work up on their new machines.

Meanwhile *Implacable* had joined the Fleet, having arrived at Colombo on 6 April. She sailed to Australia later that month, then at the end of May was despatched to Manus to gain experience in modern combat techniques before participation in a major operation. On 12 June, in company with the escort carrier *Ruler* and five cruisers, they left Manus as Task Force 111/2 (Operation 'Inmate') for an attack on Truk Atoll in the Caroline Islands. Arriving in the target zone on 14 June, the carrier aircraft spent two days in a series of attacks, although targets were few owing to previous attentions by the Americans in Task Force 58. An assortment of Ramrods and strikes was made in over

200 sorties against such targets as could be found, being mainly shipping, airfields and installations. *Ruler* provided a spare deck and saved many aircraft from being forced to ditch through fuel shortage whilst queueing to land on.

The force returned from Manus on 17 June to await the arrival of the remainder of the Fleet. The 1st Aircraft Carrier Squadron was now to become part of Task Force 37 for their next and final task, a series of strikes on the Japanese home islands. They were to be accompanied by the escort carriers of the 30th Aircraft Carrier Squadron operating as a Fleet Train under the code name Task Force 112. They joined the American Third Fleet on 16 July, operating as an independent addition to this because of their experience. Although the typhoon season was in full swing, operations commenced the next day, despite the bad weather which caused the recall of the American strikes. The first machines took off at 03.50hrs whilst the ships were 250 miles

Below: A Barracuda of No 812 Squadron from HMS *Vengeance* lands in the water on 29 May 1945. The crew can be seen clambering out, and the inflated dinghy is floating in the water, still tethered to the aircraft. *C. H. Wood*

north-east of Tokyo, and aircraft from *Victorious* and *Implacable* struck at airfields on the east coast. Amongst the aircraft taking part were the Fireflies of No 1771 Squadron, commanded by Lt-Cdr (A) W. J. R. MacWhirter DSC RN. Their diary record for that day reads:

'The big day has arrived — the day on which we join in the attack on the Jap mainland; for a good many it began too early, with a shake at 02.00hrs.

'The Ramrod of eight Fireflies was comprised as follows; CO and Lt Greenway; Sub-Lts Gill and Izatt; Sub-Lts Catterall and Manley; Sub-Lts Kynaston and Gullen; Lts Turral and Westlake; Sub-Lt Edmundson: Lt Corrin and Sub-Lt West; Sub-Lts Reekie and Straughton. A press representative who

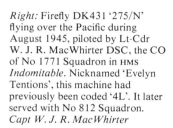

Right: Firefly DK431 '275/N' flying over the Pacific during August 1945, piloted by Lt-Cdr W. J. R. MacWhirter DSC, the CO of No 1771 Squadron in HMS *Indomitable*. Nicknamed 'Evelyn Tentions', this machine had previously been coded '4L'. It later served with No 812 Squadron. *Capt W. J. R. MacWhirter*

Below: Barracuda '377/A' of No 812 Squadron flying past the extended wireless aerial of HMS *Vengeance* in July 1945. *C. H. Wood*

was to have flown with Sub-Lt Edmundson failed to turn up in time and missed the fun.

'These two flights crossed the coast at Arahama, in Honshu; Lt Turral claims to be the first British pilot to fly over Japan; thus No 1771 Squadron again makes history! Targets attacked included Masadu, Sendai and Matsushima airfields, as well as some shipping and radar stations. The aircraft, which were all carrying a large long-range tank and four 60lb rockets, were forced to fly on the deck by the low cloud ceiling; all rocket attacks had therefore to be low level. This is, no doubt, why two aircraft sustained minor damage from the explosion of their own rockets. Both the CO's and Lt Turral's aircraft were hit by flak, the former in the pilot's cockpit and the latter in the wing tank, whose self-sealing properties proved their worth.

'As the weather deteriorated during the day, and visibility became greatly reduced, a later strike, which included Fireflies, was cancelled.'

The following day targets were attacked to the north-east of Tokyo, the pattern being similar to that of the first day, with bad weather restricting activities, but 12 aircraft

being destroyed and 18 damaged by Corsair and Seafire attacks on airfields amidst heavy anti-aircraft fire. After turning from these targets they turned their attention to shipping, attacking and sinking a number of junks. The force then withdrew for the normal two days refuelling and replenishment, but bad weather continued and prevented a resumption of activities until 24 July.

On the first day of these next operations, 416 sorties were flown, including 260 against targets in and around Japan, the remainder being AS patrols and CAPs. The airfield at

Below: Hellcat JZ935 '145/W' of No 1844 Squadron picking up a few wires on landing on HMS *Indomitable* after a raid on Japan late in the war. *via G. S. Leslie*

Bottom: Corsair IV KD780 '122/D' of No 1846 Squadron goes round again during a landing on HMS *Colossus.* The large long range belly tank is visible between the undercarriage legs.
John W. Adams collection, restored by C. F. E. Smedley

Above: A Barracuda of No 812 Squadron on the lift of HMS *Vengeance* in June 1945. On deck are another Barracuda and several Corsairs of No 1850 Squadron. *C. H. Wood*

Right: Corsair KD344 'U6K' of No 1846 Squadron from HMS *Colossus* ashore in Australia. On 8 July 1945 this machine hit the ship's barrier after its hook had bounced over three wires during landing. *FAA Museum*

Tokushima was particularly well defended with almost 200 anti-aircraft guns, and these accounted for a Seafire and an Avenger. During the day six Avengers from *Victorious*, escorted by two Corsairs and two Fireflies, carried out an attack on the Japanese carrier *Kaiyo*, scoring a direct hit and leaving her ablaze with a broken back. This turned out to be the only attack made during the war by the Fleet Air Arm on an enemy carrier, the ship being finished off later in the operations by American aircraft.

The usual two days replenishment

followed, then a further three days of attacks. On 28 July the force returned to the attack, on further targets in the Inland Sea, including a dawn strike by 20 Avengers on Harima dockyard. Fighters struck at airfields and the naval base at Maizuru, north of Kyoto on Honshu, the main island of Japan. More bad weather prevented strikes on the following day, but 336 sorties were flown on 30 July despite fog in the Tokyo area, and heavy damage was inflicted on enemy warships.

The next operations were postponed in

order to keep the Fleet out of the Hiroshima area for the dropping of the first Atomic bomb, and bad weather again intervened, but an improvement on 9 August enabled strikes to be resumed, despite the dropping of the second Atomic bomb that day, on Nagasaki. Flying commenced at 04.10hrs, and the expertise now gained was put to good effect, considerable damage being inflicted in 267 offensive sorties, a further 140 CAP sorties being flown. On this day the Fleet Air Arm achieved its peak effort of the war in terms of bombs and ammunition expended.

On this same date the Fleet Air Arm gained its second VC of the war again posthumously, this being awarded to Lt (A) R. H. Gray RCNVR of No 1841 Squadron from *Formidable* for his great valour in leading an attack on the Japanese escort ship *Amakusa* in Onagawa Wan, in Honshu island. He lost his life pressing home the attack, obtaining at least one direct hit which sank the enemy ship after his own aircraft had been hit and burst into flames.

Attacks continued the following day, but worthwhile targets were by now becoming rare as carrier aircraft flew freely over Honshu. On 11 August, all but *Indefatigable* withdrew to Sydney. In the last fighter combat of the war, Seafires of the 24th Naval Fighter Wing shot down eight of a formation of 12 enemy fighters whilst escorting an Avenger attack on the Tokyo area on 15 August. One Seafire and an Avenger were lost, but the gunner of the latter shot down another Japanese fighter before the aircraft ditched. One of the successful fighter pilots subsequently completed the following combat report:

'Type and number of aircraft — No 887 Sqn Seafire LR866.
'Fired — 150 cannon rounds and 1200 .303.
'Height — 13,000 to 8,000ft.

'Eight striking aircraft in two group flights at 3 o'clock 1,000 above my flight which was top cover. Four(?) enemy aircraft behind and above from same direction. Two single decoys below. Attacking enemy aircraft moved to 1 o'clock on Avengers almost directly above same and peeled over in three-quarter roll into 80° dive from 4,000ft at Avengers from echelon formation. Enemy aircraft little evasion when attacked (no time). They attacked with height advantage joining in dog fight circle. Accuracy of enemy fire — very poor for the amount of firing they did.

'Fighter escort in model position. Naval cover of four Seafires at 1,000ft above strike with top escort (3) a further 3,000ft above that. At time of sighting enemy aircraft broke through the escorts from directly over strike to 500ft astern and enemy aircraft accordingly moved from the beam to 1 o'clock, closing rapidly so that four aircraft got into attacking dive out of range of top escort.

'I deployed my own (top) flight using full throttle as smartly as possible. I gave up the first four enemy aircraft as being out of range. A final verbal warning was given and middle cover effectively engaged two on their pull away from attacking dive. That was the total of the "Zeke" offensive in the strike. My flight engaged the second four just before they reached the peel over position and spattered them so effectively that on finishing my "B" combat there were three flaming Zekes on the way down.

'Assessment — 2 destroyed and 1 shared.

'Arrived at Tomcat 1 by using Y/JB Course. Tomcat 1 gave a course which took three aircraft to the American Fleet and gave the call sign.

'Own tactics in brief stating the relative direction of attack — I took my flight of three aircraft at 100yd abreast spacing to attack four "Zekes". Taking the second from the right I signalled the commencement of firing by opening fire at 800yd (using GGS and cannon alone). On a 10° port attack, closing to 450yd astern, firing two (2½sec) bursts. The starboard oleo and then the port oleo legs dropped and the enemy flamed nicely going down. My No 3 was also firing at this aircraft, hitting the aircraft. I then fired at the extreme starboard enemy aircraft giving a quick stern burst at 300yd as he dived to starboard. A shallow climb to starboard ensured that I got slight deflection angle shot at 250yd with a close to stern two

Left: Avengers of No 848 Squadron on their way to bomb targets on the Japanese mainland in August 1945, after taking off from HMS *Formidable*. In the distance can be seen the island of Honshu. The two nearest machines are JZ466 '380/X' and JZ114 '376/X'. *FAA Museum*

second burst to 200yd when the under-carriage dropped. Bits flew off and the enemy aircraft burst into flames and disappeared in an aileron dive at high speed into cloud. Cannon and MG were used together throughout this attack.

'I then found one of the original attacking "Zekes" climbing at 8,000ft and about 500ft and 1,000yd from me. I closed to 100yd at 11,000ft kicking on rudder to have a look at the markings, and went back astern and fired two two second bursts of MG cannon being finished. Strikes all over the aircraft and the pilot baled out, his aircraft diving past him and smoking somewhat. Three "Zekes" then attacked me from 15,000ft and I finished my MG ammunition in two short bursts on attacks at 400yd before leaving the area hurriedly.
SIGNED Sub-Lt Victor S. Lowden (A) RNVR'

Sub-Lt Lowden was credited with two enemy aircraft destroyed and another shared in what turned out to be the last fighter combat of the war, over Tokyo Bay. After returning to the carrier, several immediate awards were made, but by an ironic twist of fate the pilot of the only Seafire to be lost in this action, Sub-Lt Freddie Hockley, was beheaded after being taken prisoner by the Japanese.

Operations ceased when all further strikes were cancelled at 07.00hrs following the Japanese agreement to an unconditional surrender. Just as *King George V* was hoisting her flags 'End hostilities', however, an enemy aircraft came out of the cloud heading straight for *Indefatigable*, whose surviving aircraft were now safely back aboard. Fortunately he was followed by a Corsair which shot him to pieces just in time.

Above: Manus, in the Admiralty Islands was used during 1945 as a fleet refuelling base. The airstrip at RNAS Ponam, a small island, was officially opened as HMS *Nabaron* on 2 April 1945 for Mobile Naval Air Base No 4 (MONAB 4). It held a reserve of Avenger, Corsair, Hellcat, Seafire and Firefly aircraft until it was paid off on 10 November 1945. *K. Chambers*

Right: A photograph taken during a strike on Matsushima airfield on Honshu island, during a raid on 9 August 1945, by Sub-Lt M. J. Brown, a reconnaissance pilot of No 887 Squadron from HMS *Indefatigable* flying Seafire '135/S'. Smoke is rising from installations behind the bombed out hangars. A number of Japanese aircraft can be seen in front of the remains of the hangars, and elsewhere on the aerodrome. *M. J. Brown*

Maps

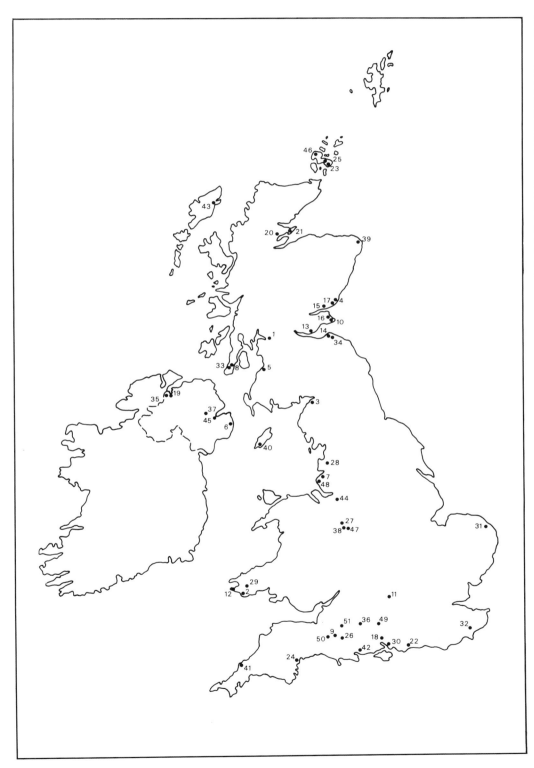

Royal Naval Air Stations in the United Kingdom 1939-45

1 Abbotsinch (HMS Sanderling),
2 Angle (HMS Goldcrest),
3 Anthorn (HMS Nuthatch),
4 Arbroath (HMS Condor), **5** Ayr
(HMS Wagtail), **6** Ballyhalbert
(HMS Corncrake), **7** Burscough
(HMS Ringtail), **8** Campbeltown
(HMS Landrail), **9** Charlton
Horethorne (HMS Heron II),
10 Crail (HMS Jackdaw),
11 Culham (HMS Hornbill), **12** Dale
(HMS Goldcrest), **13** Donibristle
(HMS Merlin), **14** Drem
(HMS Nighthawk), **15** Dundee
(HMS Condor II), **16** Dunino
(HMS Jackdaw II), **17** East Haven
(HMS Peewit), **18** Eastleigh
(HMS Raven), **19** Eglinton
(HMS Gannet), **20** Evanton
(HMS Fieldfare), **21** Fearn
(HMS Owl), **22** Ford
(HMS Peregrine), **23** Grimsetter
(HMS Robin), **24** Haldon
(HMS Heron II), **25** Hatston
(HMS Sparrowhawk), **26** Henstridge
(HMS Dipper), **27** Hinstock
(HMS Godwit), **28** Inskip
(HMS Nightjar), **29** Lawrenny Ferry
(HMS Daedalus II), **30** Lee-on-Solent
(HMS Daedalus), **31** Ludham
(HMS Flycatcher), **32** Lympne
(HMS Daedalus II),
33 Machrihanish (HMS Landrail),
34 MacMerry (HMS Nighthawk),
35 Maydown (HMS Shrike),
36 Middle Wallop
(HMS Flycatcher), **37** Nutts Corner
(HMS Pintail), **38** Peplow
(HMS Godwit II), **39** Rattray Head
(Crimond) (HMS Merganser),
40 Ronaldsway (HMS Urley),
41 St Merryn (HMS Vulture),
42 Sandbanks (HMS Daedalus II),
43 Stornoway (HMS Mentor II),
44 Stretton (HMS Blackcap),
45 Sydenham (Belfast)
(HMS Gadwall), **46** Twatt
(HMS Tern), **47** Weston Park
(HMS Godwit II), **48** Woodvale
(HMS Ringtail II), **49** Worthy Down
(HMS Kestrel), **50** Yeovilton
(HMS Heron), **51** Zeals
(HMS Humming Bird).

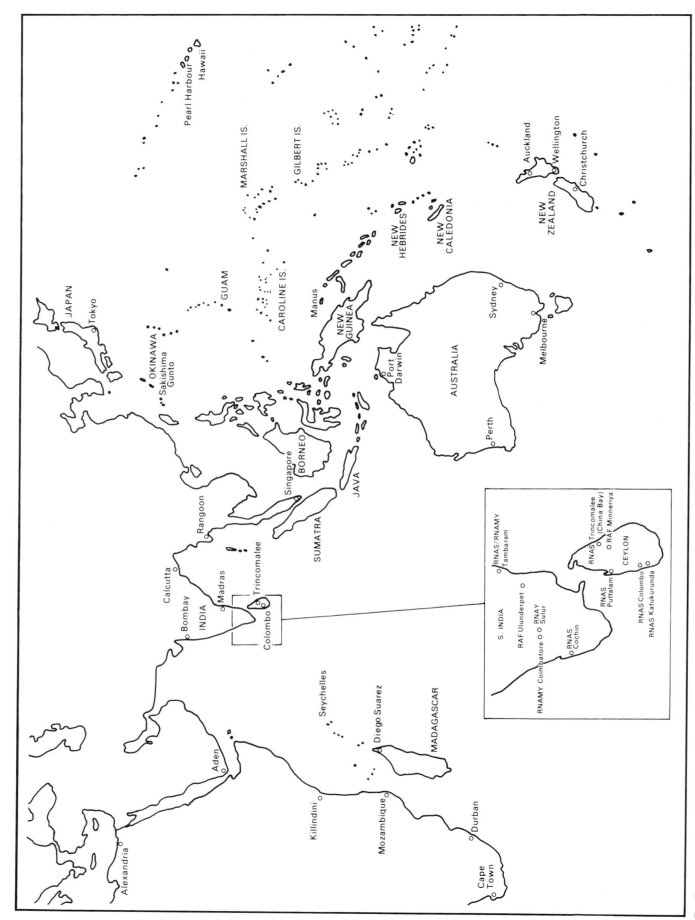

Far Eastern operations with (inset) details of Airfields used by RN units in Ceylon and Southern India.

STOPPING SCHOOL PROPERTY

John Zeisel
Architecture Research Office
Graduate School of Design
Harvard University

DAMAGE

Design and Administrative Guidelines to Reduce School Vandalism

Published by American Association of School Administrators
and Educational Facilities Laboratories in collaboration with City
of Boston Public Facilities Department

Sponsors
City of Boston Public Facilities Department
   Kevin H. White, Mayor
   Robert J. Vey, Deputy Mayor
   Victor E. Hagan, Director
   Stuart Lesser, Chief Architect
   Roger C. Roman, Senior Architect
   Ralph Clampitt, Systems Project Coordinator
Educational Facilities Laboratories, New York
Advisory Council on Education, Massachusetts

Research Team
Andrew Seidel
Mary Griffin
Deana Rhodeside

Graphics
William March, Brenda Levin, William Bricken

Design
Brooke Todd & Associates

Edited by
William E. Henry, Associate Director
American Association of School Administrators

Copies of this publication are available for $4.95 each from
AASA, 1801 North Moore Street, Arlington, VA 22209. 2-9 copies
receive a 10 percent discount, 10 or more copies, 20 percent.
Orders for $15 or less must be accompanied by payment in full and
include $1.00 for postage and handling.

Stock Number: 021-00472

Preface

In April, 1975 the Subcommittee to Investigate Juvenile Delinquency released a report on the nature and extent of violence and vandalism in American public schools. This report, "Our Nation's Schools — A Report Card: "A" In School Violence and Vandalism" was the result of a nation-wide survey of 757 school districts containing over half of the public elementary and secondary students in the country. The sobering survey findings prompted the Subcommittee to hold a series of hearings to more fully explore the nature of these problems and possible strategies for curbing them. In our hearings we have heard from varied segments of the educational community including superintendents, principals, parents, teachers, students, school security directors, as well as private educational research organizations and experts in the area of student rights and responsibilities. Our study shows that the dramatic increase in frequency and intensity of violence and vandalism in schools is a critical problem for the American education system.

Property damage and vandalism costs represent a staggering loss of precious educational funds for school districts already operating under stringent budgetary limitations. Last year, for example, Chicago and Los Angeles reported paying a total of $17 million for school vandalism and property damage. Testimony at our hearings places the yearly national cost of school vandalism in the hundreds of millions of dollars. In addition to these monetary losses, of course, vandalism has important social costs. These social costs are more difficult to quantify, but they are no less real to students and teachers confronted by them in schools every day.

Problems of school violence and vandalism require positive approaches by every segment of government from the Congress to the school board, and necessitate involving students, faculty, administrators and parents to develop solutions. The federal government has a part to play in this effort. Accordingly I recently introduced the Juvenile Delinquency In The Schools Act of 1975 (S. 1440) which will provide guidance and resources in this area. I believe, however, that there can be no "federal" solution to problems such as these. Essentially the role of the federal government is limited to assisting schools and school boards in a task which must, and should, remain theirs to complete.

John Zeisel's *Stopping School Property Damage* presents schools and school officials an opportunity to implement local strategies which can cut the cost of both intentional and accidental school property damage. This book provides practical guidelines to design future school buildings and to set up administrative programs for existing structures, which can be immensely helpful to a district confronted by these problems. The proposals contained in *Stopping School Property Damage* were developed through extensive interviews with experienced educators, architects, and students throughout the country and represent logical, straightforward approaches to the problems of school vandalism. Moreover many of them can be implemented with relatively little expense.

We cannot continue to absorb losses attributed to school vandalism as just another cost item in our educational budgets. We must do something to reduce school property damage costs. Zeisel's *Stopping School Property Damage* is a good place to begin.

The Honorable Birch Bayh
The United States Senate
Chairman, Subcommittee to
Investigate Juvenile Delinquency

Table
of
Contents

Foreword

As Senator Bayh has pointed out in the preface to this book, school property damage has become a major financial consideration for the schools of America. This is particularly true in 1976 when administrators throughout the nation are coping with tight school budgets, rapidly escalating energy costs and inflation in all aspects of operation.

Any survey of school officials today will show that the issue of vandalism in schools ranks near the top of the major concerns. It is also an issue which school administrators and other educators are determined to significantly reduce through concerted programs.

The American Association of School Administrators, in its official resolutions adopted at its annual convention in Atlantic City, N.J. in February, 1976, called upon school administrators to build a positive climate in the schools which "supports education and permits each student to learn in a safe environment." Said AASA, "These policies and procedures should be developed and implemented with appropriate involvement of school personnel, students, parents and other interested members of the community."

We believe the guidelines and recommendations contained in this book will provide school officials throughout the nation with a solid document to not only implement this resolution, but also to build positive programs to reduce vandalism.

We would also like to underscore that the joint publication of this book by EFL and AASA represents another cooperative endeavor to seek solutions in design and architecture for the benefit of education.

Paul B. Salmon
Executive Director
AASA

Alan C. Green
President
EFL

The City of Boston has found a fundamental, workable approach to curbing vandalism in our public buildings through the efforts of John Zeisel and the Harvard Graduate School of Design.

The findings and recommendations of this report are being instituted in the design of every new public school in Boston, The next series of schools will be more durable and less likely to be vandalized because of the innovative conclusions drawn from Zeisel's work.

We are proud to endorse publication of *Stopping School Property Damage,* and encourage its wide distribution. Hopefully, other municipalities will share the gains we are making to minimize the costs of public building vandalism.

Kevin H. White
Mayor
City of Boston

Introduction

The Architecture Research Office project — Stopping School Property Damage — began in 1973 under contract to the City of Boston, Public Facilities Department (PFD). Since then, continued support for different segments of the project has come from the Educational Facilities Laboratories (EFL) and from the Massachusetts Advisory Council on Education (MACE).

PFD is responsible for design and construction of all public buildings except housing in the City of Boston. In 1972, PFD architects Stuart Lesser, Ralph Clampitt, and Roger Roman decided that an understanding of the relationship between design and property damage could help them reduce costs of maintaining Boston school buildings. Under Robert Vey, PFD funded the first phase of this study. Results of this phase included redefinition of the problem of vandalism to include attractive nuisance design issues, design guidelines for school exterior, an in-depth annotated bibliography, and testing basic concepts through design review procedures on eight schools to be occupied in 1975-76.

In 1973, Educational Facilities Laboratories, New York, became interested in the project, focussing an issue of their newsletter, *Schoolhouse,* on design guidelines. EFL with PFD then funded development of materials and format to present design guidelines to reduce property damage in a way useful to school architects and their clients.

EFL also sponsored a new direction for the project: a study of administrative programs for reducing property damage problems. In this study, research team members visited schools where such programs were operating. The results of this phase included an understanding of the way in which several successful programs work.

In 1974, the Massachusetts Advisory Council on Education sponsored a major effort to make the property damage project relevant to the needs of the Commonwealth of Massachusetts. This study produced design guidelines for renovating and rehabilitating school building interiors, worksheets for establishing cost effectiveness of actions to reduce property damage, and a survey of Massachusetts School Superintendents. Under the leadership of MACE, all basic materials were compiled into one document. In conjunction with the publication and dissemination of this document, MACE sponsored a series of workshops for Massachusetts school personnel including custodians, superintendents, business officials and school committee people. These were conducted in the spring of 1975 with the help of the regional offices of the Massachusetts Department of Education.

The American Association of School Administrators (AASA) and Educational Facilities Laboratories are now publishing this revised and updated edition of the book for national distribution.

While the project — Stopping School Property Damage — has been directed by me, several other researchers have played vital roles in the development of ideas and the production of sections of reports.

Deana Rhodeside, psychologist and city planner, was involved during the project's first year and helped develop its initial directions with Boston's Public Facilities Department. The humane orientation we have tried to maintain throughout was due greatly to her. In addition, she is responsible for writing and organizing the annotated bibliography.

Andrew Seidel, policy planner and architect, was Project Manager during the Project's last year under its sponsorship by the Massachusetts Advisory Council on Education. He organized and carried out much of the Massachusetts based research, oversaw production of the final MACE document, and participated in the four workshops for Massachusetts school personnel. Mr. Seidel was responsible for the section on Cost-Benefit Guidelines which appears in the MACE workbook.

Mary Griffin, design researcher and future architect, worked primarily on the administrative program section of the project, observing ongoing projects and interviewing personnel throughout the country. Much of the content and presentation format for the administrative section was planned by her.

Others also helped to keep the project going over its three year life. These included Read McCarty, Daniel Cooper and Diane Klotz.

The true test of our work now lies in the hands of the most important participants: administrators, teachers, students, parents, planners and architects.

John Zeisel
Harvard University

Chapter I

Organization and Study

This book is designed for people concerned with problems of property damage and vandalism in planned and existing school buildings. Sections are meant to be useful separately, but to be used together if desired. These sections are:

I. Building Exterior Design Responses

Ways to reduce on-going cost of property damage by careful design of a school's physical plant. Exterior design considerations are especially essential in early design phases when the over-all concept of the building is being developed.

II. Building Interior Design Responses

Ways to minimize costs of property damage and maintenance through design and materials specification. Interior design considerations are crucial during design development and working drawing phases of the design process.

III. Administrative Responses

Ways to cut property damage costs through administrative programs aimed at involving students in the school, at using personnel effectively, and at keeping "eyes on the school." These detailed descriptions of model programs can be helpful to administrators, teachers, and students who want to develop their own program specially suited to their problems.

IV. Design Accountability Checklists

For every major design issue — both interior and exterior — this section presents one general question and then a series of specific "yes-no" questions to determine if the issue has been taken into account by the architect in his or her design. These checklists are helpful during design review between client, user, and architect as a focus for discussion.

V. Annotated Bibliography

This literature survey presents important literature on vandalism and property damage with in-depth summaries of important works. Thorough reading of this section gives an overview of available research and theory, and can help direct the reader to further information.

Redefinition of Vandalism

Early in one of the studies leading up to this book, it was realized that it is easy to respond defensively to "vandalism." Defensive physical responses include such things as prison-type schools, bars on windows, no windows at all if possible, and high fences around all school grounds. Defensive administrative responses include guard dogs, silent burglar alarms, stiff punishment for offenders, and cutting down free time for students generally. While such responses may sometimes be appropriate, they are by no means the only way to respond to the problem.

We began by looking at the implications of the term "vandalism." Its popular connotation implies that vandals are conscious aggressors. However, vandalism is more than just the actions of malicious persons. Vandalism popularly means breakage, defacement, and theft, as well as many types of property damage.

For the purpose of developing appropriate responses to "vandalism" we separated different types of property damage. First we distinguished between theft of materials and property damage itself. While this distinction is usually made in other types of facilities, it is seldom made in schools. We then grouped property damage into four categories — described in terms of the motive of the person being destructive and the indirect effect of the damage:

	Consequence	
	Instantaneous Damage Demanding Immediate Attention	Cumulative Damage Demanding Eventual Attention
Motive		
Conscious	Malicious Vandalism	Non-malicious Property Damage
Not Purposeful	Misnamed Vandalism	Hidden Maintenance Damage

These four types of property damage each have different implications for the design of school facilities. An example of each type will clarify its definition:

1. **Malicious Vandalism**

   In an attempt to hurt the principal who has given a student a stern lecture, the student breaks a window in the principal's office. The motive is conscious and the consequence is a broken window which needs immediate attention.

   Malicious acts like these are primarily social, educational, or legal problems and must be dealt with primarily through such mechanisms. In most cases the designer can do little to respond to malicious vandalism except provide more protective screening and stronger locks on doors.

2. **Misnamed Vandalism**

   A basketball court is planned next to a series of windows in a school hallway. In playing ball one afternoon, neighborhood teenagers break a window. There is no purposefulness in the act, but nevertheless the broken window must be repaired immediately to keep out intruders and bad weather.

   This type of damage is often called "vandalism" by those who must repair the window. But in actuality it is accidental damage which could be avoided by better predicting activity adjacent to the windows, and by planning walls and windows better able to withstand the legitimate rough use they get.

3. **Non-malicious Property Damage**

   Boys use a school building wall to play street hockey, but there is no built-in hockey net to use as a goal. So the boys spray-paint a hockey net onto the wall.

   They are providing something necessary to their game. People walking by, however, see the lines on the wall as graffiti and vandalism.

   While the boys are conscious that they are doing something which might be considered destructive of property, they paint their lines not out of maliciousness, not to damage, but rather to meet what they see as a legitimate need. The consequence of such actions do not demand immediate repair for the school to continue operating. Possible design responses to damage of this kind include painting lines on the wall in initial construction of helping the children paint their lines neatly. Of course, there are many other potential responses. It also helps if adults understand the needs of the street hockey players and therefore are more tolerant of spray painted hockey nets. The designer needs to better predict informal needs of school children.

4. **Hidden Maintenance Damage**

   To soften the edge between a pathway and the school building itself, a designer specifies a strip of low bushes. While the bushes look nice initially, over time they catch debris dropped by passers-by on the path or blown by the wind. The custodian, if he finds the time, has to make a special effort to wade among the bushes to clear away the highly visible litter.

   This type of subtle property defacement is neither done purposefully by people who use schools, nor does it require immediate attention. Such problems are seldom, if ever, called vandalism, and hardly ever included in calculation of damage costs. But these types of design specifications increase the cost of maintenance. Designing responses to such problems means avoiding surfaces and plantings which show up slight damage and increasing use of easily maintained surfaces. Some researchers have found that poorly maintained areas tend to be more frequently vandalized than those which appear to be more cared for.

Focus On Non-Malicious Vandalism

According to reports, malicious vandalism causes under fifty percent of school property damage, if we do not include theft of property. Designers and planners have primarily directed their attentions towards defending schools against breaking and entering and against malicious mischief. We are mainly concerned with the other half of the problem because this has, in the past, largely been ignored. We direct our attention primarily towards arriving at design responses to the problems of misnamed vandalism, non-malicious property damage, and hidden maintenance damage, although our administrative responses are directed at traditional malicious vandalism as well.

Research Methods Used in the Study

In carrying out this study we performed the following tasks:

- In depth focussed interviews with over 200 students, teachers, administrators, custodians, and school superintendents.
- Working sessions with architects designing schools for the City of Boston.
- Site visits to schools in Boston, New York, Washington, and in smaller towns throughout Massachusetts.
- Site visits and interviews with personnel involved in administrative programs in various states from Massachusetts to California.
- Questionnaires sent to all 286 Massachusetts School Superintendents, which received 156 responses.
- Literature search of available books and pamphlets on property damage and vandalism.
- Computerized literature search of the Educational Resources Information Center (ERIC) at the National Institute of Education.

Approaches and Values Underlying School Design

Three fundamental approaches have developed from and now underlie our study. The first is that schools, by their availability and familiarity to young people, and by the facilities they provide, attract and sometimes challenge young people. We feel that designers who want to limit property damage must take at least some responsibility for design decisions which challenge young people to damage schools and which make schools easy and inviting targets. This concept of the designer's responsibility for school design relates to the legal definition of facilities which potentially attract destructive or dangerous misuse — like swimming pools — as "attractive nuisances." The law assigns responsibility for both use and misuse of attractive nuisances to persons providing such facilities who do not predict and plan for their misuse.

Our second basic approach is that school designers must plan for the informal social and activity needs of young people as well as for their formal educational requirements. When normal rough play is overlooked — like that which takes place when students are on their own or when schools are not in session — a great deal of property damage occurs.

The third approach relates to a strategy for design responses. We have explored responses which provide bridges for people's needs as opposed to setting up fences which stand between them and their desires or needs. An analogy can best describe this distinction: if a child needs to cross a river but does not know how to swim, there are several ways to deal with the problem. The first is to build a high fence on the river's edge to keep the child away. Depending on the child's need to cross the river, and depending on how much he is challenged by the fence itself, he may

climb it, break it down or cut through it, and eventually drown anyway. On the other hand, if a bridge is built to the other side, the child can achieve his own goals safely and without doing harm to any property. We are concentrating our efforts to find solutions which act as bridges to meet the needs of school users, rather than those which act as challenging fences.

Since most schools have not been designed in this way, they often invite property damage. The following guidelines present specific problem areas which exist in most schools and which thoughtful design and small scale renovation and rehabilitation can correct. Each issue is accompanied by suggestions for possible design strategies a school district might take.

13

What's Wrong With This School?

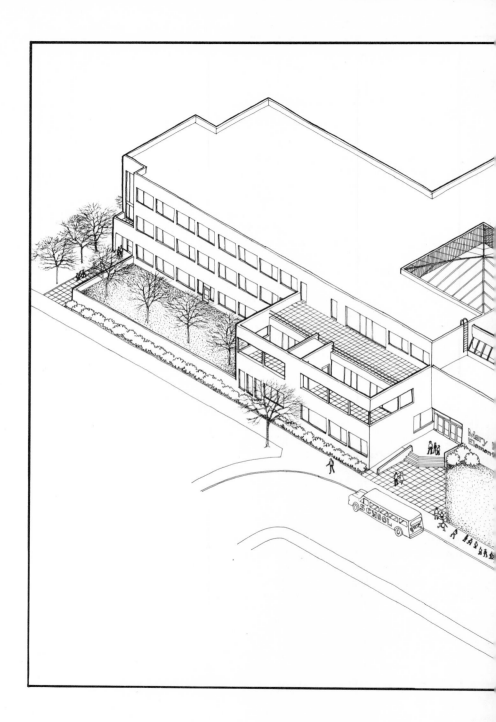

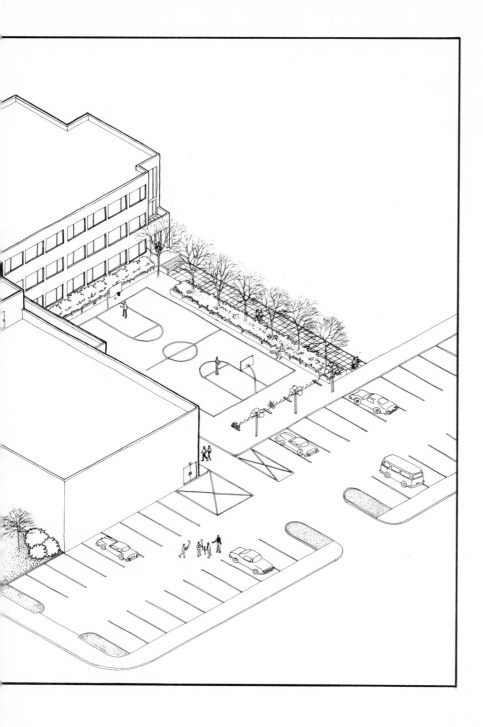

- Challenging Accessible Rooftops

- Hidden Doorway Niches

- Misplaced Decorative Planting

- Vulnerable Playground Windows

- Unnecessary Door Hardware

- Unclear Entry Statement

- Unplanned Graffiti

- Visible Panic Bars

- Misplaced Planned Pathways

- Reachable Wall Lettering

- Inviting Unplanned Hang-outs

CHAPTER 2
Exterior Design Responses

Design Issue

Ground-to-Roof Access: *Playing on rooftops is a problem if these are not consciously planned as recreation places. Problems of damage to rooftop equipment, hardware, windows, and skylights can be minimized if getting onto roofs from ground level is difficult, or if hardware on accessible rooftops is specified to accommodate rough play.*

Possible Design Responses

1. *Windows, Hardware, Fixtures:* On accessible roof areas, use ground floor type glazing, hardware, and fixtures. Avoid exterior hardware on roof doors and windows.

2. *Surfaces:* Plan exterior surfaces with no footholds.

3. *Fixtures:* Avoid unnecessary exterior fixtures on building wall that provide footholds for climbing. Place such hardware at another convenient location.

4. *Planting:* Near buildings use planting which cannot be climbed and which will not grow to a height or strength suitable for climbing.

5. *Planting:* Locate planting which can be climbed far from walls.

6. *Telephone Poles:* Remove built-in footholds from telephone poles adjacent to building.

7. *Wall Heights:* Design walls too high to be climbed with readily accessible ladder substitutes like standard 12-ft. 2x4's.

Design Issue

Roof-to-Roof Access: *Where access to one part of a roof is either unavoidable for reasons of landscaping and design or desirable because it is to be used as a play area, special care must be taken to avoid easy access to other more vulnerable roof areas.*

Possible Design Responses

1. *Incinerator:* Place incinerator and design incinerator housing so that it cannot be climbed upon.

2. *Gas Meter:* Place gas meter very low in an enclosure or very high so that it will not be climbed upon.

3. *Fixtures:* Avoid fixtures on walls which might be used as ladders, like unnecessary handles and lamps.

4. *Custodian Ladders:* Do not install permanent custodian ladders between roof levels, if local regulations allow. Provide convenient storage for portable roof ladders to be used by custodians.

5. *Roof Heights:* Plan the height of roofs so that they cannot be reached from other roofs by a 12-ft. 2x4.

6. *Railings:* Avoid roof guard rails and half walls which provide easy jumping off points for adjacent roofs.

7. *Wall Heights:* Design walls too high to be climbed with readily accessible ladder substitutes like standard 12-ft 2x4's.

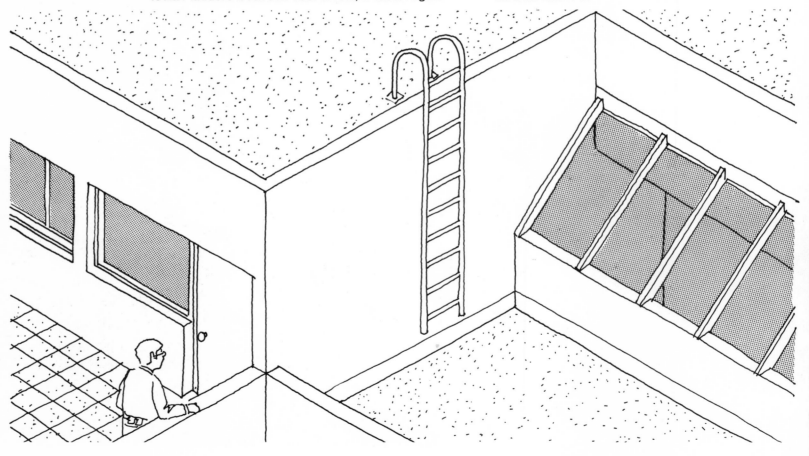

Design Issue

Formal Rough Play Places: *Some open spaces around schools are formally planned as basketball courts or baseball fields. Although it seems obvious to stress that walls around such areas must be specified to withstand stray balls, school planners often overlook this. Schools then end up having a series of breakable windows within easy reach of a home run.*

Possible Design Responses

1. *Surfaces:* Make play areas usable. Avoid hindrances to normal play, such as surface irregularities or inadequate space behind the backboard.

2. *Walls:* Install wall surfaces which bounce balls back to players.

3. *Fixtures:* Specify low lighting and other hardware out of the way of ball playing.

4. *Game Lines:* Paint lines on walls and on ground to accommodate all local street games. This can be done in cooperation with young people.

5. *Buffer Area:* Provide a buffer between formal play areas and school buildings, to clearly delineate the difference. This buffer might be ground sloped away from the school, a symbolic fence, or a sitting area for spectators.

6. *Glass:* Eliminate glass around rough play areas, or protect glass there in an attractive way.

7. *Planting:* Avoid planting immediately adjacent to formal play areas which might be damaged by children chasing stray balls.

Design Issue

Playground Equipment: *Playground equipment is designed to withstand specific amounts of use. What is durable enough for a small rural school might be useless in another more active location.*

Since playgrounds are one of the few acceptable areas where students can expend as much energy as they want, equipment there must permit them to use this energy without risk of damage.

Even strong play equipment is sometimes inadequate to handle "normal" rough play. For example, it is seldom realized that a series of poorly executed dunk shots will rip a basketball net and bend the hoop, even in "normal" rough play.

Possible Design Responses

1. *Equipment:* Choose playground equipment that will withstand the roughest use to which it might be put, even if this use is not "official," i.e., teenagers sitting on children's swings.

2. *Equipment:* Choose playground equipment that cannot be disassembled with simple hand tools readily available.

3. *Equipment:* Do not repair often damaged equipment that will only be broken again. Replace it with equipment that will withstand more rough use.

4. *Equipment:* Maintain play equipment so that it works properly, because improper installation invites damage. For example, a basketball hoop installed at an angle may get broken when players try to adjust it.

Design Issue

Pick-up Play: *Much recreation in school open spaces takes place during recess, after school, or on weekends. Children or teenagers gather around the school for informal games of street hockey, basketball, stick ball, soccer, or catch. These games generally require minimal equipment which participants bring from home, a hard ground surface large enough for throwing ball, and a wall to serve as an impromptu backstop.*

Formal play areas are sometimes used as pick-up play places — for instance basketball courts may be used to play a game of stick ball. At other times pick-up games take place on the plaza in front of a school, or in the children's play yard — if these provide a backstop and a hard surface. Different parts of the country and different areas of a city will have their own special pick-up games and most neighborhood groups do have some kind of pick-up games.

Possible Design Responses

1. *Location:* Consciously identify and develop places well suited to informal pick-up play.

2. *Lighting and Fixtures:* Move lighting and other fixtures out of the way of potential pick-up ball playing.

3. *Walls and Ground Surface:* Treat ground and wall surfaces in informal game areas as if they were formal play areas: install wall surfaces which bounce balls back to players; remove ground surface irregularities; paint lines on walls or ground for street games.

4. *Glass:* Eliminate glass around areas predicted to attract informal pick-up games, or protect glass there attractively.

Design Issue

Pick-up Play in Parking Lots: *Students often use parking lots to play street hockey or other pick-up games.*

If a few cars are parked haphazardly throughout a lot used for play, one or more cars are likely to be in the midst of a play area and therefore be likely to be damaged unintentionally.

Also, parking lots rarely have the fencing necessary to prevent a ball from travelling out of the lot and through a neighbor's or the school's window.

Possible Design Responses

1. *Location:* Plan parking lots as informal pick-up play areas.

2. *Closure:* Specify fixtures so that parking lots can be closed to automobiles on weekends and during evenings when there are no planned activities at the school.

3. *Fences:* Erect a fence in strategic locations around the parking lot to prevent balls, pucks, or other objects from breaking windows or entering adjacent private property; not to keep children out.

4. *Size:* Design larger parking lots so that parking will be concentrated in obviously more convenient spaces nearest the building entrance. This will leave area further from the building entrance free of parked cars and available for children's play.

Design Issue

Hang-out Areas: *Hang-out areas are places next to formal and informal play places and near active walkways, where people sit to watch games, to be seen by others passing by, and to talk to one another. These areas are distinguished by having walls, steps, benches, or tree stumps to sit upon; by being points from which to observe and comment on games nearby; and generally by being visible to adjacent public areas.*

Possible Design Responses

1. *Location:* Predict, identify, and prepare appropriate hang-out areas for inevitable informal use.
2. *Fixtures:* Avoid nearby fixtures which can be easily removed or damaged by kids sitting. Use tamper-proof screws in this location, and strengthen hardware and fixtures which must be there.
3. *Windows:* Remove or protect nearby windows.
4. *Planting:* Specify planting which bends easily and grows quickly. Avoid planting which will be easily damaged by being scratched, burned or broken.
5. *Benches:* Provide benches for sitting far away from breakable windows, hardware, or planting.
6. *Planters and Steps:* Specify extra durable materials for steps, low walls, and planters in hang-out areas, because they will probably be used to sit upon.

7. *Trash Containers:* Install heavy trash containers which will be emptied regularly and which make burning of rubbish difficult, i.e., not the open basket type.
8. *Trash Containers:* Use garbage cans which seem like targets for beer and soda cans, as an attraction for litter disposal.
9. *Planters:* Avoid planting containers which can be easily used as trash baskets in hang-out areas.
10. *Materials:* If bricks or other small-unit building materials are used in hang-out areas, maintain a stock of spares to allow quick and easy repair. This cuts down "epidemic" vandalism in which slight damage quickly leads to greater damage.

Design Issue

Watering Holes: *Partially hidden areas around schools which are large enough for small groups of children and teenagers to sit in together provide groups of local kids with informal clubhouses. These places are the least officially sanctioned play areas and are often considered trouble spots by custodians and school administrators. Property damage occurs in these places ranging from graffiti to broken bottles; from broken hardware to destroyed trees; from burnt and broken windows to breaking and entering.*

For urban teenagers, such places are the club's turf. "Watering holes" adjacent to schools are places for get-togethers. Kids do not have any place else. They can't have parties at home; formal social clubs are too structured.

People just sit and talk there; sometimes they drink beer (hence the name "watering hole") or smoke. They almost always rough-house and write their names on the walls.

Possible Design Responses

1. *Location:* Identify "watering holes" and design such areas to withstand sustained and often destructive use and abuse.

2. *Fixtures and Hardware:* Specify highly durable hardware and fixtures in these areas, and locate them out of reach.

3. *Windows:* Avoid fenestration in watering holes.

4. *Walls:* Install wall and ground surfaces here which can be written on, which can withstand abuse, and which can be easily maintained and painted.

5. *Planting:* Specify planting which cannot be easily damaged by being scratched, burned, or broken. Specify pliable fast growing shrubs, rather than trees in such areas.

6. *Planters:* Avoid planting containers which can be easily used as trash baskets.

7. *Trash Containers:* Install heavy trash containers which seem like targets for litter and which cannot be used for burning trash. Empty them regularly.

8. *Materials:* If small-unit building materials like bricks are used in watering holes, there is a good chance for "epidemic vandalism" in which slight damage attracts attention and leads to cumulative damage. Having a stock of bricks and mortar available for quick repair of small damage and getting custodians to do so can reduce "epidemic vandalism."

9. *Wall Panels:* Avoid modular wall panels in watering holes. These are often removed just to prove that the school is vulnerable, even if not used to enter the building.

Design Issue

Niches: *Small spaces just large enough for one or two people are called "niches." For example, they are created by fire stairs adjacent to walls, depressed entrances, or delivery docks. These places are used for, among other things, prying at windows or picking locks, smoking, or drinking secretly.*

Possible Design Responses

1. *Doorways:* Avoid useless doorway niches by extending existing doors to building perimeter.

2. *Fixtures and Hardware:* Specify as few reachable fixtures and as little hardware as possible in niches.

3. *Door glass:* Specify glass-free doors through which locks cannot be seen.

4. *Door Hardware:* When possible, avoid all exterior hardware on doors in niches.

Design Issue

Clarity of "Come In" and "Stay Out" Statements: *School architects sometimes feel that major building doorways represent the "face" of the school towards the community. Wanting to involve the community in the life of the school, these planners design doorways which are often seen as inviting when the school is closed, as well as when it is actually open. Easily broken glass panels are the only barriers to interior door locks. Because of their accessibility, some school entrances designed originally to be inviting are soon either covered with chain-link fencing, plywood, or locked with bicycle chains during the night. To avoid this, the building must be designed to be inviting when the school is open, and to express the fact that the school is tightly shut after school hours, evenings and weekends.*

Possible Design Responses

1. *Sliding Grills:* Install sliding grills or garage-door type gates which can be pulled down over transparent doorways when the building is closed.

2. *Gates:* If deep recesses are planned, at building entries, avoid their being accessible when school is not in use.

3. *Doorways:* Design doorways so that it is clear from a distance that the school is closed when it is closed, but that it is open whenever the school is in session or a program is being conducted inside.

Design Issue

School Bus Drop-Off at Entry: *When entrance areas are used for loading and unloading school buses, they become extra heavily used student hang-out areas. As such, they often receive more use and abuse than they were designed to withstand.*

Possible Design Responses

1. *Location:* Locate bus stop areas near entrances but in open and visible areas, away from windows.

2. *Waiting Areas:* Provide conveniently planned waiting areas as far as possible from hardware, windows, and other equipment at building entrances.

3. *Fixtures, Windows, Hardware:* Treat hardware and fenestration at entries according to recommendations for hang-out areas.

4. *Glass:* If possible, avoid large amounts of glazing in entrance doors and around entry areas.

Design Issue

Exterior Door Hardware: *One common problem in schools is that exterior hardware is uniformly specified for all doors, although many doors hardly ever need to be accessible from the outside. This is true for secondary exits in gyms, some doors to storage areas, and other doorways.*

Possible Design Responses

1. *Hardware:* Systematically identify all doors used primarily as exits, and remove locks and handles from these doors.
2. *Hardware:* Specify exterior door hardware on only one door in a series of connected doors. Seldom does the custodian need to unlock all four doors from the outside. He can just as easily unlock one with a key and open the rest inside.

Design Issue

Panic Hardware: *There is a conflict between the need for school users to get out in case of fire and the need for custodians to keep everyone out when school is closed. Panic hardware usually meets the first need, but dismally fails in meeting the second. A bent coat hanger often opens panic hardware from the outside.*

When this problem is not resolved, custodians in existing schools eventually buy bicycle chains, locks, and five foot long 2x4's to make fire exits impermeable at night. These may get left on during the day, creating a dangerous situation for fire safety.

Possible Design Responses

1. *Door Glass:* Avoid clear glass or acrylic panels on doors and near doors which may give a clear view of accessible panic hardware.

2. *Astrigals:* Specify astrigals on single doors with panic hardware, where regulations allow.

3. *Center Mullions:* Specify extra duty double doors with center mullion and astrigals.

4. *Panic Hardware:* Specify panic hardware which requires a minimum amount of mechanical movement to operate successfully.

5. *Panic Hardware:* Specify panic hardware which can be easily repaired if damaged.

Design Issue

Pathways: *Official pathways around school grounds often reflect the designer's wishful thinking, rather than the students' and teachers' needed circulation links. As a result, a route crossing the grass is often chosen as a path rather than the misplaced official paved walkway. In addition, soft surfaces and planting next to heavily used paved areas are readily trampled.*

Possible Design Responses

1. *Location:* Plan paved pathways so that they provide the shortest walk between the two points they connect.

2. *Location:* Accept as legitimate and predict location of naturally made shortcut paths.

3. *Paving:* Pave pathways where natural shortcuts have developed, after the building has been in use for six months.

4. *Barriers:* Install or landscape subtle but real barriers, like a change in level, between hard traveled pathways and adjacent soft areas, like grass. This will not prevent people from walking there, but it will decrease it.

5. *Grass:* Remove soft materials like grass or flowers which are immediately adjacent to narrow paths or parking lots.

Design Issue

Parking Lot Boundaries: *In many schools, automobiles will be parked on grassy areas adjacent to parking lots or driveways. Unpaved areas are often used to turn around on when leaving. If this is done continually, the result is an unintended dust or mud pond.*

Possible Design Responses

1. *Curbs:* Erect a curb, a change in level, or some other similar low barrier to keep cars on paved surfaces and off soft grassy areas.
2. *Turn-arounds:* If drivers need a place in which to turn around, design a paved, curbed turn-around area to meet the need.
3. *Grass:* Between parking lots and buildings, avoid small decorative patches of grass which will soon be destroyed by cars.

Design Issue

Planting: *Planting on school grounds is often specified with a direct but misguided logic: "Because damage may occur to plants, have stiff, unbreakable plants." Unfortunately, stiff also means brittle, and these plants break more easily than do more pliable ones.*

Another logic dictates: "Since kids mess up bushes by running through them, have thorny bushes which keep kids out." Unfortunately, thorns collect debris and also keep out custodians who might otherwise clean up around the plants.

Possible Design Responses

1. *Planting:* Near active areas, specify bendable, resilient planting and avoid stiff, breakable planting like unprotected young trees.
2. *Planting:* In decorative areas specify planting such as trees or bushes with no thorns, which does not readily collect litter, and is easy to rid of litter.
3. *Planting:* Avoid climbable planting near edge of building.
4. *Planting:* Avoid planting in predictable pick-up play and hang-out areas, and in watering holes.

Design Issue

Walls: *Walls are highly prone to the "epidemic effect" of vandalism. If one scratch is left for a long time, or one pane of glass broken, there is a high probability that further damage will occur around the same spot. Conversely, quickly repaired damage is less likely to re-occur.*

Possible Design Responses

1. *Wall Panel Size:* On large expanses of easily marred wall space, specify small wall sections so that rapid repair is possible. Keep replacement panels in stock, or paint for sections.

2. *Repairs:* As expensive surface materials are damaged, replace with easily and inexpensively repaired surface materials.

3. *Paint:* Paint walls with a color which is similar to the color of the material underneath. This minimizes the visibility of scratches.

4. *Paint:* In high damage areas, use specially resistant paints and glazes as high as kids can reach, to allow easy washing.

5. *Paint:* Specify quick-drying paint so that a touch-up stock can be kept for easy repair.

6. *Signs:* Plan permanent signs, building names, and decorative hardware to be out of reach from the ground.

Design Issue

Expressive Graffiti: *Self-expressive graffiti takes the form of names and street numbers, love declarations, or verbal attacks. While self-expressive graffiti is often meant to be offensive, some self-expressive graffiti is an attempt by teenagers and younger children to communicate with their friends, just as adults often do through more acceptable channels. New teachers see their name in the school paper, administrators talk over the loudspeaker, and custodians sometimes have their names on the door. When students advertise themselves, they are called vandals.*

Decorative Graffiti: *Decorative garffiti, though very similar to the self-expressive type, is usually more elaborate, more colorful, and often does not contain words. Graffiti on New York City subway cars is a combination of decorative and self-expressive graffiti.*

Possible Design Response

1. *Wall Color and Texture:* Allow some walls in appropriate places to attract graffiti. These walls may be formally labeled or they can just be informally made easier to write on than surrounding surfaces. Lighter surfaces with large blocks attract more graffiti than dark surfaces. Formally labeled graffiti walls may remove the challenge aspect of graffiti, and thus may not work in specific settings.

2. *Materials:* Develop informal "graffiti walls" around front and back entries and in "watering holes." It is important that these walls be easily painted or cleaned at long but regular intervals, like every six months.

3. *Tile and Paint:* Where graffiti is to be discouraged, specify certain walls with glazed tile or epoxy paint to reduce cost of washing.

4. *Materials:* Specify surfaces so that during daily maintenance, only abusive graffiti may be removed, allowing non-abusive messages to remain until the bi-yearly cleaning or repainting.

Design Issue

Legitimate Graffiti: *Legitimate graffiti is the simplest, yet most often overlooked type of marking. When there is no hockey net in the school yard and children paint one on the wall, this is considered graffiti and vandalism. Yet, lines on paving or on a wall are considered legitimate when they are drawn neatly and when they have a purpose such as basketball foul lines or stripes in a parking lot. If markings are missing in a parking lot and the school custodian paints a set of lines on the ground, these would be considered legitimate. In the same way, painted-on hockey nets are legitimate to the young people who paint them on walls.*

Possible Design Responses

1. *Location:* Acknowledge, predict, and accept "legitimate" graffiti painted by children.
2. *Game Lines:* Paint necessary game lines on appropriate walls and ground surfaces after consultations with game players.
3. *Game Lines:* Work together with street groups to provide them with stencils so that they themselves can neatly paint goals for hockey, strike zones for stickball, and other game lines on walls and ground.

Design Issue

Prime Graffiti Surfaces: *Light, smooth symmetrically blocked-out surfaces attract more graffiti than do dark, rough, jagged surfaces. Unfortunately, this does not mean that if all walls in a watering hole are dark and rough there will be no graffiti. What it does mean is that we can predict that if there is a convenient choice, gffiti artists will tend to choose lighter, smoother surfaces over darker, rougher surfaces. Realizing this, school officials may informally channel graffiti onto one wall or another, specially treated to with-stand such treatment.*

Prime Graffiti Locations: *Much self-expressive and decorative graffiti is written in areas with high visibility to one of two audiences: the general public and the neighborhood street group. For the general public, graffiti is written on walls near front and back entrances. These walls would be con-sidered prime advertising space. For the neighborhood street group, graffiti occurs on walls near gathering places: in pick-up game places, in hang-out areas, in watering holes, and in niches. Graffiti here serves both as territorial marking and as a means of identifying group members. "Legitimate graffiti" occurs primarily in pick-up game and formal play areas.*

Possible Design Responses

1. *Location:* Develop "legitimate graffiti" space in both formal and informal gathering areas.
2. *Walls:* Install some informal "graffiti walls" which can easily be painted by maintenance staff at regu-lar intervals.
3. *Surface Material:* In more public areas, where graf-fiti is mostly expressive, and where other more sanctioned messages might be placed, provide an easily cleaned exterior tile wall.

Design Issue

Hardware Fixtures: *Hardware, such as light fixtures, street lamps, walk lights, and guard rails, are often used for purposes other than those for which they were intended. In addition to being used as targets for stone throwing contests, they are swung on, leaned on, and climbed on. People rest heavy objects on hardware and generally play with them. This unintended use damages hardware and may cause safety hazards.*

Much hardware is reachable from the ground, easy to break, to unscrew, to open, to dismantle, to dent, and to damage. It is important to consider each piece of school hardware in terms of the unintended uses it is sure to get.

Possible Design Responses

1. *Fixtures:* If possible, do not place fixtures on an otherwise blank wall where they are likely to be used as targets. If for safety reasons they must be placed there, protect them by grille covers or other coverings from items that could be thrown at them, or have them recessed.

2. *Fixtures and Hardware:* Place as many fixtures and hardware items as possible high, out of reach of people stretching or holding sticks. While this may be a bit inconvenient for maintenance staff, in the long run it will reduce their work load.

3. *Fixtures and Hardware:* Remove all unnecessary exterior fixtures and hardware. For example, street lighting may be sufficient to light certain walkways and exit door areas, and some doors do not need locks because they are opened only from the inside.

4. *Fixtures and Hardware:* Avoid fixtures and hardware close to ground level. At this height it is very easy to stand on or to kick.

5. *Fixtures:* Recess as many fixtures as possible into the wall of the building and cover with a protective plate.

6. *Rain Pipes:* Avoid vulnerable rain water pipes which are below 6 ft. from the ground.

7. *Lighting Fixtures:* Specify armor plate glass for lighting fixtures near the ground. Avoid plastic covers.

8. *Equipment:* Kids play hard — provide sufficient durable official equipment to reduce overuse of hardware for play.

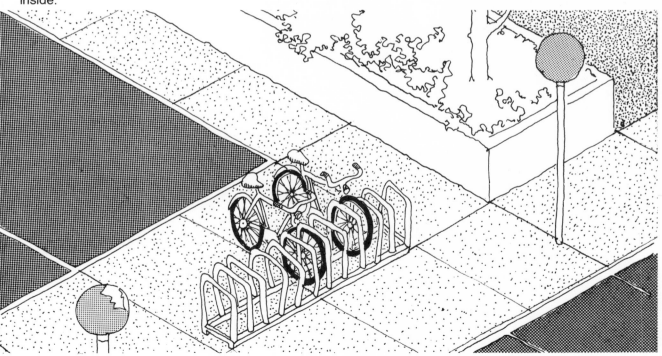

Design Issue

Windows: *Glass breakage in schools is the largest property damage problem and expense. While some glass breakage is malicious and related to theft, much glass breakage is not malicious vandalism. For example, a student sitting on a ledge may swing his legs, kicking and cracking vulnerably placed glass panels in an adjacent door. Or, during a fight, one student pushes another into a window, resulting in damage. While damage to the child is malicious, the damaged window is an unintentional consequence, non-malicious in character. Much of this damage could be avoided if those playing near glass had a different attitude; but as long as kids are kids, such dangerous play will take place, and fragile environments will be damaged.*

Possible Design Responses

1. *Window Location:* Identify and avoid windows which are vulnerably placed in formal or informal gathering and play areas.

2. *Window Size:* Specify small panes of glass so that one break can be inexpensively and easily repaired.

3. *Non-glass Panels:* Specify solid non-glass panels and avoid all glass up to three feet from the floor, as this area is most vulnerable to damage.

4. *Glass Substitutes:* Where acrylic or plexiglas is used instead of glass, avoid placing it in watering holes or hang-out areas within reach of people standing on the ground. Problems with these materials include: carving, burning, scratching, and fading. In addition, while a pane of plexiglass or acrylic may not break, it may be entirely knocked out of its frame.

5. *Glazing Material and Location:* Specify increasingly sturdy glass as windows are closer to ground. On the ground floor, specify thick tempered glass, possibly thick acrylic or plexiglass, and if necessary, screens or grills in non-visible areas. On floors two to four, specify thinner tempered, acrylic, or regular plate glass. On the fifth floor and above, specify plate glass. All these specifications vary by the nature of the interior use.

6. *Glazing Material and Location:* When interior areas are to be highly used, such as informal hang-out areas in hallways, then specify sturdier glazing, regardless of floor level.

7. *Window Thickness:* Use double-layer glass or extra thick tempered glass where plexiglass is inadvisable.

8. *Windowless Locations:* Avoid useless windows entirely in: student stores, administration storage offices, and industrial arts storage areas.

9. *Security Screens:* When all other possibilities have been tried and proved unsuccessful, install thin wire mesh security screens over ground floor windows.

CHAPTER 3

Interior Design Responses

Design Issue

Hang-Out Areas: *Many areas inside schools provide places for groups of students to sit together to be seen, and to watch others go by. These hang-out areas are places where students meet eeach other informally. When school is not in session, students might meet at the corner drug store. Teachers know they will meet other teachers in the administrative office during the day. But during school, students have neither the right to go to the corner store nor the formal office to serve as a visible social gathering place.*

Not much malicious property damage takes place in hang-out areas such as the main entrance lobby, the gym bleachers, or near the main student locker area. Rather, these places tend to be underdesigned for the great amount of sitting, jumping, roughhousing, graffiti, and other action they get. One result is that hang-out areas become marked up and marred faster than other areas.

Systematic planning for predictable activity in such places can appreciably reduce property damage.

Possible Design Responses

1. *Location:* Identify hang-out areas throughout the school and prepare them for the heavy use they will receive. Hang-out areas can be identified by their location near highly used traffic or recreation areas, by the availability of places to sit or lean, and by the number of students there.

2. *Fixtures and Hardware:* For fixtures and hardware in hang-out areas which can be reached, specify those which cannot be easily unscrewed, snapped off, poked into, or broken.

3. *Wall Fixtures:* Plan all wall fixtures and adjustments — thermostats, fire alarms, light switches — far from convenient and comfortable hang-out areas, or out of reach if they must be located there.

4. *Fixtures and Hardware:* For all fixtures attached to walls and ceilings which might be hung from or climbed upon, specify reinforced attachments.

5. *Equipment and Fixtures:* Identify equipment and fix-tures which will be used to sit on in such areas — radiators, window-sill, garbage cans. Specify specially sturdy equipment suitable for sitting. As this equipment is damaged, replace it with equipment which is still sturdier and which can be well attached to the wall or floor.

6. *Seating:* In hang-out areas, provide comfortable and durable seating far from any breakable windows and equipment.

7. *Trash Containers:* Provide convenient trash containers which are emptied regularly.

8. *Walls:* Plan for writing on some walls near hang-out sitting areas. Formal message boards in these highly visible places might help channel informal messages onto one wall.

9. *Agreement:* Make an agreement with students to formally acknowledge their right to use hang-out areas.

Design Issue

Watering Holes: *Few schools have authorized places where students can meet out of view of staff and faculty. However, most school building interiors provide partially out-of-the-way places which act as informal, unauthorized lounges for students more secluded than "hang-out" areas. Places used for informal gathering are usually located out of sight of office and classrooms, are usually among the least supervised places in the school, and are often considered trouble spots by custodians, teachers, and school administrators. For students, these lounges provide an important and necessary refuge from surveillance by those in positions of authority. The area may act as a place for uncensored discussion, as a smoking lounge, or as a place to show off to a small group of friends.*

Watering holes are established in out-of-the-way places large enough for groups of people: stairwells, ends of corridors, lavatories, back door entry lobbies.

Some watering holes become the territory or "turf" of a particular group, and are seen therefore as the group's clubhouse. Because clubhouses represent specific groups interests, they are often personalized by wall graffiti, in addition to receiving normal rough use.

Possible Design Responses

1. *Location:* Identify watering holes and plan specifically for the rough use they are sure to get. Do not "harden" these areas so that they are no longer comfortable for this purpose. If this is done, students will move to another area of the school, into a watering hole which has neither been hardened nor planned for.

2. *Walls:* Use epoxy paint or glazed tile on all surfaces which will be subject to graffiti so they can be easily washed.

3. *Wall Color and Texture:* On walls where graffiti predictably will occur, provide light blocked out surfaces for the graffiti. These should contrast sharply in color and texture with surrounding surfaces, and thus will attract and channel the graffiti.

4. *Fixtures and Hardware:* Specify that all fixtures and hardware like lamps and handrails be firmly attached. If the hardware is unnecessary, remove it altogether from the watering hole area.

5. *Glass:* Avoid glazing — especially below three feet from the floor — which will be easily damaged by being broken, burned, or scratched.

6. *Equipment:* Identify equipment which will most likely be used as a bench — radiator, window-sill, cabinet — and specify that it be reinforced to accept this use.

7. *Trash Containers:* Provide convenient trash containers which are emptied regularly and which do not make burning rubbish or papers attractive.

8. *Alternative Lounges:* Develop legitimate, i.e., authorized, lounge areas — non-visible from offices and classrooms and accessible to students without having to pass through offices and classrooms.

9. *Equipment:* Possibly provide legitimate ways for students to personalize watering holes, such as attaching unfinished wood planks to walls for carving initials; or large white painted panels for writing. These would have to be replaced regularly.

Design Issue

Lavatories: *Lavatories provide one of the few places in schools where students can find what they feel to be deserved privacy. Groups of students may use a particular lavatory as their "clubhouse" during school hours. This privacy is used not only for destructive activity. It also allows for personal chats and group discussions about common problems.*

When students hang around a place for non-destructive reasons, an attempt to have fun can lead to property damage. In lavatories, these include removing plumbing pipes, breaking porcelain fixtures and other accessories, dissembling partitions, burning paper, burning graffiti into ceilings and walls with cigarettes, and writing graffiti on all surfaces.

Possible Design Responses

1. *Pipes and Accessories:* Minimize exposed plumbing pipes and accessories.

2. *Fixtures:* Install bathroom fixtures which can be easily and inexpensively replaced if damaged.

3. *Fixtures:* Locate and specify airvents and waste paper baskets which will not attract use as ashtrays, yet will withstand such use if it occurs.

4. *Surfaces:* Specify walls and floors in lavatories with as durable material as possible all the way to the ceiling.

5. *Ceilings:* Specify solid ceilings in lavatories. If this is not possible, specify ceiling elements which can withstand poking. Avoid drop-in ceiling panels in lavatories.

6. *Screws:* Specify toilet partitions with tamperproof screws and hinges so that partitions cannot be dissembled with simple hand tools.

7. *Toilet Partitions:* Construct toilet partitions so that vertical elements are attached to structural members in floor and ceiling.

8. *Toilet Partitions:* Specify painted surfaces for interior walls of toilet partitions, since these can be expected to be written on. To reduce cumulative graffiti, these surfaces must be painted or washed at regular intervals. As partition surfaces are scratched or otherwise permanently marred, replace them with partitions which can be regularly painted or which are inexpensive to replace.

9. *Acceptance:* Develop an attitude of acceptance among custodial staff towards toilet stall graffiti. Otherwise, this relatively minor property damage can become a major source of confrontation between students and staff.

10. *Equipment:* Provide chalk boards or other erasable surfaces in the lavatory. Let students know they can write anything they want except obscenities and misspellings, and that it will only be erased by students. Make a formal agreement with students about this.

11. *Alternative Places:* Develop sufficient private social places elsewhere in the school building so the bathroom does not become the main one. These might be structured private lounges, or they might be dead-end school areas provided with places to sit.

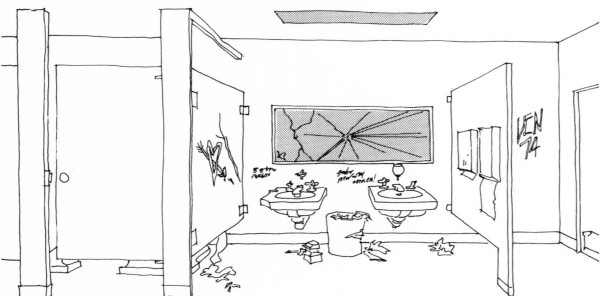

Design Issue

Niches: *Interiors of school buildings provide many small gathering places large enough for one or two people. These places are created by indented exit doors, stairwells, fire hose attachments, and corners of lockers.*

Niches like these tend to be used more for destructive than social purposes.

Possible Design Responses

1. *Location:* Wherever possible, design away niches.
2. *Hardware and Glazing:* If niches must be left, specify no damageable hardware, glazing, and wall materials.
3. *Ceilings:* Ceilings in necessary niches must be solid.

Design Issue

Auditoriums: *Auditoriums in schools are often overused, used by unsupervised groups, and used in ways for which they were not originally intended. In planning auditoriums, it is important to accurately predict the amount and type of use fixtures and furnishings will get. During study halls, for example, students remain seated for relatively long periods of time. Seats which are comfortable enough for this purpose also may provide diversion for students who, out of boredom, pull loose threads from cushions. This eventually can add up to major cumulative damage.*

When informal activities take place such as a senior play rehearsal, students sit on the edge of the stage, on backs of seats, or on the steps up to the stage. In such cases, seating, equipment and material on the stage skirt are vulnerable.

When auditoriums are used for less supervised activities such as lunch periods or informal meetings, greater damage may occur to fixtures. Seats can be disassembled; graffiti may appear on chair backs and walls; initials may be carved in wood or on painted metal.

Auditoriums may also be empty and unsupervised for long periods of time. During such times, electrical, lighting, and sound equipment must be specially protected.

These considerations do not belittle the fact that it is essential to design properly for activities which take place during normal use.

Possible Design Responses

1. *Durability:* Openly assess uses to which auditoriums might be put during the life of the building. Realistically predict and plan for both standard and potentially special uses.

2. *Seating:* When uses include such things as formal assemblies, dramatic presentations, or graduations, specify comfortable seating which is easy to clean and does not offer materials to play with like string or buttons.

3. *Seating Screws:* Specify seating with sunken bolts or tamperproof screws to prevent disassembling with common hand tools.

4. *Wall Material:* Specify epoxy paint or tiles as high as people can reach in auditoriums.

   If tiles are used, they should be small so that replacement is both easy and inexpensive.

5. *Fixtures:* Locate lights, loud-speakers, and other wall fixtures so they are out of reach of kids standing on seats.

6. *Fixtures:* Around the stage area, specify heavy duty ventilation grilles, floor lights, and other fixtures so that normal but rough informal use will not damage them.

7. *Equipment Covers:* Specify heavy duty lockable grilles to cover all control boxes — stage lighting, sound, electrical, and so on.

Design Issue

Cafeterias: *Cafeterias are like playgrounds in the freedom they offer students. Cafeterias tend to be noisy and generate a lot of trash. Many schools cope with these problems by assigning teachers to cafeteria supervisory duty. This may keep the room quieter and cleaner, but it requires an added burden on teachers.*

Possible Design Responses

1. *Trash Receptacles:* Place trash receptacles at the end of each row of tables and be sure there is a system to empty them before they overflow. This makes it easier for students to clean after themselves and gives the appearance that if students do their part in cleaning, so will the schools.

2. *Furniture:* Choose furniture for cafeterias which cannot be easily disassembled and which can withstand constant and hard use.

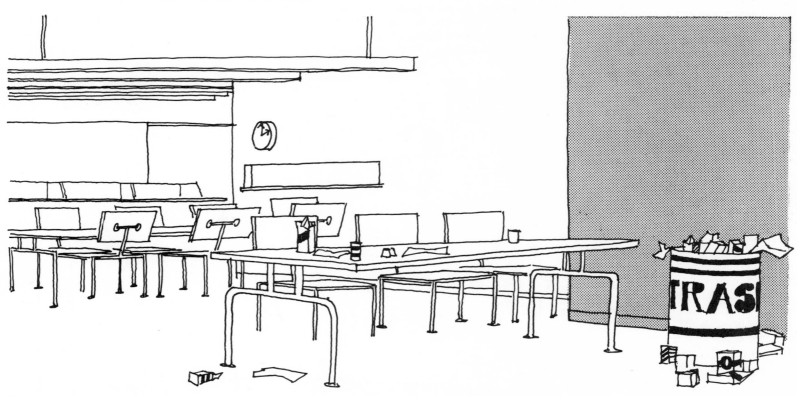

Design Issue

Gymnasiums: *Property damage in school gymnasiums often occurs because: first, wall fixtures are located in the way of flying objects like basketballs, bats, baseballs, and are within reach of spectators sitting in bleachers, serving as targets for playful mischief; second, heavy equipment provides opportunity for improvised rough play; third, floor surfaces are specified for single uses like basketball playing and require special cleaning methods. The varied uses they get and traditional all-purpose cleaning methods used cause damage to floors.*

Possible Design Responses

1. *Walls:* In the gymnasium, provide large uncluttered expanses of wall to be used for impromptu ball playing.

2. *Fixtures:* Locate all wall fixtures out of reach of spectators sitting on bleachers, people playing on the floor, and people climbing gymnastic equipment.

3. *Fixtures:* Locate fixtures like clocks and loudspeakers on side walls or in corners. Avoid placing them on end walls in back of basketball backboards where they may be accidentally hit by stray balls.

4. *Equipment Storage:* Locate equipment storage lockers so that they are visible to permanent staff offices.

5. *Rules:* Responsibility for use of play equipment must be clearly assigned, either to students using the gym or to a staff member.

6. *Gym Floor:* Gym floor surfaces should be multi-use, if possible, so that they stand up to being walked on, to have tables on them, and to other non-gym uses.

7. *Gym Floor:* Gym floor materials requiring special care should be specified only if a training program in maintenance techniques is conducted for custodians. It is essential that such a program be ongoing to reach new members of the staff hired later in the life of the school.

Design Issue

Shop Areas: *Shop classrooms have many potential targets for both malicious and non-malicious property damage. Students may jam machine tools because they do not know how to use it properly or because they do not want to work during that class. Students may also steal tools to damage other areas of the school, or just to be mischievous.*

Shop area damage must be dealt with through social means as well as through design.

Possible Design Responses

1. *Tool Storage:* Plan a central storage area large enough to keep all hand tools.
2. *Rules:* Students must demonstrate their ability to use each major piece of machine equipment properly, before being given unrestricted access.

Design Issue

Places and Types: *Teachers have their names on doors or walls and principals speak over loud speakers, but students often have no legitimate ways to establish their own identity in school. Some students write graffiti for this purpose.*

Those who do choose areas that are highly visible to persons in the school. It may be a wall facing a locker room, near an entrance, or in any other area where there is a large volume of traffic. In a sense, these walls become "advertising" space for students.

Popularly, graffiti is seen as anti-social, malicious behavior. This is only sometimes the case. While some interior wall writing is malicious, other is self-expressive or decorative. Self-expressive graffiti takes such forms as love declarations, nick-names, and group identification symbols. Decorative graffiti often is placed on personal property or lockers and takes forms ranging from flowers to cut-outs.

Administrators, teachers, and custodians often have formal places for such expression. When students take over a wall for these purposes, they are called "vandals."

In dealing with graffiti, it is important to distinguish between malicious wall-writing and self-expressive and decorative writing.

Possible Design Responses

1. *Location:* Systematically identify those areas of the school which have large volumes of traffic and which therefore have surfaces likely to receive graffiti. In such areas, be more accepting of graffiti.

2. *Walls:* Specify wall materials so that malicious graffiti can be removed rapidly, while other forms of non-malicious wall-writing can be left until a regular bi-monthly cleanup.

3. *Surface Color and Texture:* Channel graffiti onto certain surfaces by painting them light colors. Lighter areas tend to attract graffiti more than adjacent dark surfaces, especially if the light surfaces have some regular pattern on lines or boxes which people can write on. In this way, graffiti can be planned for and left up as long as desired.

4. *Graffiti Walls:* Another way to channel graffiti, which works only where the problem is not overwhelming, is to formally designate one wall as a graffiti wall. This wall may just be a light-painted wall with a sign on it, or it might be a specially erected piece of plywood, a chalk board, or a large sheet of butcher paper. The potential problem with this approach is that it takes away some of the challenge inherent in informal graffiti.

5. *Surface Material:* In areas prone to graffiti, specify glazed surfaces from floor to ceiling and epoxy paint. Wash such surfaces regularly, but only every month or two. Otherwise, the writing/washing cycle becomes a form of competition.

Design Issue

Walls: *Walls are highly prone to the "epidemic effect" of vandalism. If one scratch is left for a long time, or one pane of glass is broken, there is high probability that further damage will occur around the same spot. Conversely, quickly repaired damage is less likely to recur.*

Possible Design Responses

1. *Wall Panel Size:* Specify small wall panels instead of large expanses of wall space. Keep replacement panels in stock and replace damaged panels as soon as damage occurs.

2. *Surface Materials:* In potential problem areas, specify inexpensively and easily replaced or repaired surface materials.

3. *Paint Color:* Paint walls with colors similar to the substance of the wall material itself. Contrasting colors reveal scratches more easily.

4. *Surface Materials:* Specify harder surfaces in damage-prone areas. Avoid soft textures there.

5. *Surfaces:* Use epoxy paint or glazed tile whenever possible on walls in highly traveled or used areas.

6. *Paint:* Use quick drying paint so that custodians can keep quick-drying touch-up paint in stock.

Design Issue

Glazing: *Glass on interior walls and doors are prone to both misdirected as well as casual damage. This is true especially for glass near the floor which can be easily kicked and glass in hangout areas and watering holes, where it serves as a diversion. Exterior windows in heavily used areas are also particularly damage-prone.*

Possible Design Responses

1. *Solid Panels:* Specify solid panels in the lower half of doors and in walls along passageways. Avoid glass that can be easily kicked. This is especially true in areas where students tend to congregate.

2. *Glass Substitutes:* While acrylics and plastics may sometimes be suitable substitutes for glass, they are easily marred by scratching and burning. Thick glass or metal and enamel panels may be more appropriate for heavily used areas.

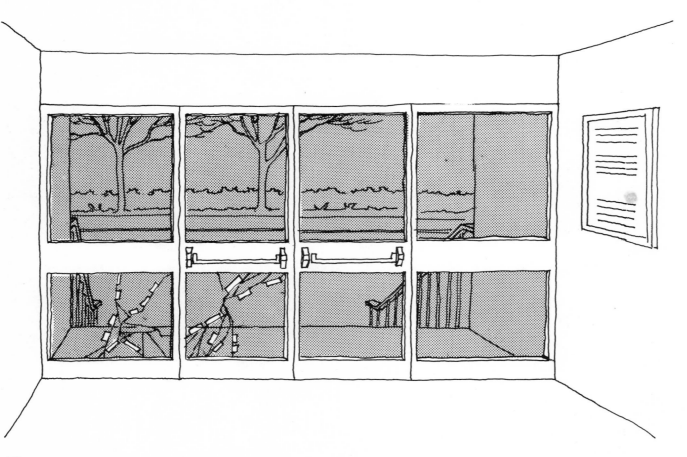

Design Issue

Ceilings: *Kids often find ceilings a challenge to jump up and touch and to hit with rulers or sticks. This is especially true for drop-in ceilings which offer the interest in finding out what is above the tile, and the chance of having a trophy to take home — a full tile. This is particularly true in hallways, informally used social areas, lavatories, and other heavily used places.*

Drop-in tiled ceilings are prone to the "epidemic effect" of vandalism. If one tile is left pushed in for a long time, there is a high probability that further damage will occur around the same spot. On the other hand, quickly repaired damage is less likely to recur.

Possible Design Responses

1. *Ceilings:* Specify hard surfaced ceilings in lavatories, watering holes, and hang-out areas. Avoid large expanses of drop-in ceiling tiles in such areas.

2. *Tiles:* When ceiling tiles are imperative in areas where students can reach the ceiling by jumping or using sticks, specify firmly attached, heavy ceiling tiles that give way only slightly under pressure.

3. *Surface Finish:* Resist damage from marking by using an easily cleaned surface material, like epoxy paint or glazed tile, even on the ceilings.

4. *Paint Color:* When painting, use a color that does not contrast with the sub-surface color. This is so that if ceiling paint is marred, the sub-surface color will not noticeably show through.

5. *Paint:* Use quick-drying paint so that custodians can keep touch-up paint in stock.

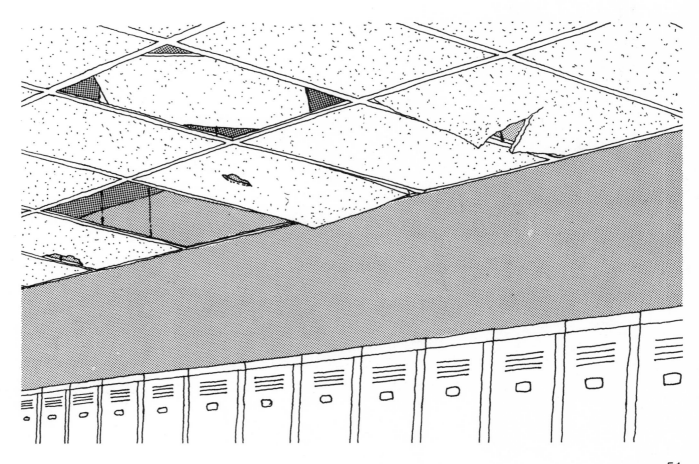

Design Issue

Floors: *Floors, like other surfaces, are prone to "epidemic vandalism." One loose board, a missing tile, or a rip in the rug readily leads to further damage. It is important to find materials which resist damage well, and which, when damaged, do not provide the culprit with a trophy or prize (e.g., a piece of tile.) Materials used must be easily replaced with minimal visible effect.*

A second problem with floor surfaces is that one material is often specified for large areas of a school and thus for many different uses. As a result, some floor surfaces are abused by activities for which they were not intended to withstand.

Possible Design Responses

1. *Carpet Size:* Where soft floor surfaces are necessary or desired, install squares or other units of carpeting which, though destroyed when removed, are easily and neatly replaced.

2. *Material:* Specify floors such that damage can be repaired quickly, so that "epidemic vandalism" does not set in.

3. *Surface Appropriateness:* Provide hard surfaces for areas where there will be hammering or painting. Provide soft surfaces where there will be reading, discussion, or music listening.

4. *Surface Appropriateness:* There are no carpets in arts and crafts areas, home economics areas, snack areas, and near sinks and easels in classrooms.

5. *Noise Barrier:* If carpets are desired to reduce noise in work areas, place carpets or acoustical tile on walls instead of on floors.

Design Issue

Fixtures Accessible to Play: *Students sit on anything which can be sat upon and climb on anything climbable. Students respond to fixtures and hardware which are challenging and intriguing. Systematically identifying and then strengthening, protecting, removing, or replacing such equipment can decrease property damage.*

Possible Design Responses

1. *Strength:* Specify specially sturdy performance for all equipment and fixtures which protrude from the surface of school buildings. Treat them as vulnerable items which will be climbed upon.

2. *Location:* In play and gathering areas, avoid hardware and fixtures which can be climbed upon and played with.

3. *Assembly:* Specify tamper-proof screws on all equipment.

4. *Lights:* Place light fixtures out of reach.

5. *Recessed Lights:* Recess light fixtures.

6. *Thermostats:* Place thermostats out of reach.

7. *Recessed Thermostats:* Recess thermostats.

8. *Challenging Fixtures:* In places where gathering and play is dangerous, avoid hardware which attracts students, e.g. things to hang on, things to chin themselves on.

9. *Air Conditioners:* Place air conditioners out of view in an inaccessible place on the roof.

10. *Trophy Equipment:* Avoid equipment and fixtures which reward students if hit, touched, or damaged. In other words, avoid equipment which makes a loud sound when hit or which remains in one piece when damaged.

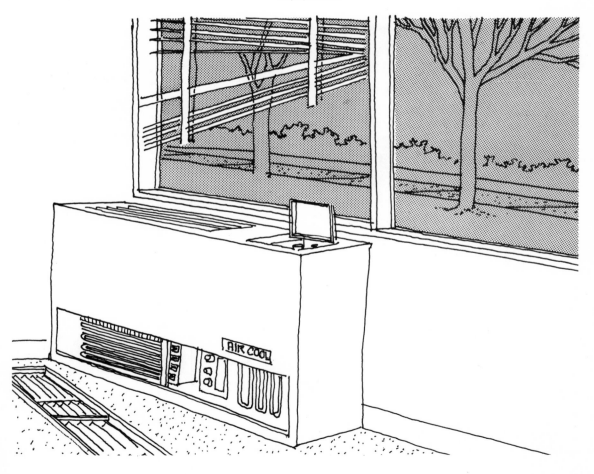

Design Issue

Thermostats: *Thermostats, like much other hardware, protrude from wall surfaces and become easy targets for mischief. Typically, they are located at a height that makes them easy to reach.*

Possible Design Responses

1. *Location:* Move thermostats high on wall and set them a few degrees higher than normal. In this way, the school will remain at the same temperature and the thermostats will be out of reach.

2. *Recesses:* Recess thermostats into wall. Cover the opening with a grill flush with the wall. The grill must allow for the free passage of air around the thermostat. Adjust thermostat so the school will remain at the same temperature as with the former setting.

Design Issue

Door Closures and Door Knobs:
While doors generally are problems for school custodians, closures and knobs are special damage problems. Often they are not used for their mechanical purpose. People hang heavy objects on them, lean on them, and use them as a foothold to climb somewhere.

Door knobs are also used as outlets for nervous behavior; continued turning, leaning, and fidgeting.

Finally, door locks and handles are the first target of thieves who might dissemble them in order to enter a room.

Possible Design Responses

1. *Durability:* Specify door knobs and door closures which can withstand especially rough types of use.

2. *Disassembly:* Choose door closures which cannot be disassembled with ordinary hand tools.

3. *Reparability:* If built-in door hardware is used, be certain that it is easy to repair if damaged. Otherwise, repair costs can be greater than potential costs of damage to exposed hardware.

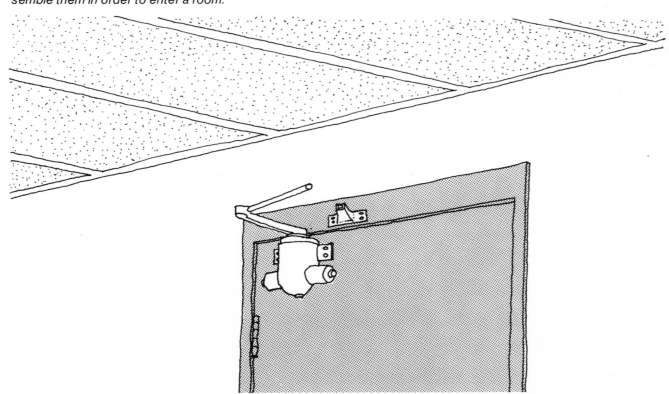

Design Issue

Alarms: *Alarm systems serve to warn against fire and to discourage and sometimes catch those seeking unauthorized access to a school building. Alarms have been successful in decreasing incidence of fire, of breaking and entering, and of theft. They have been less successful in preventing the occurrence of non-malicious property damage.*

Three kinds of alarms are prevalent in schools: audio alarms which pick up loud sounds; contact alarms which register the breaking of an electrical circuit; and sonar alarms which register movement within the building. The action of these alarms is of two types: either registering at an outside agency, e.g., police or fire department, while remaining silent within the school; or setting off a loud sound within the school, possibly also registering at an outside agency.

Criteria for choosing one or another system depends on many factors, among which is whether school administrators are interested more in catching intruders or in discouraging and scaring them away.

A common problem of alarm systems is the false alarm. Audio alarms may be triggered by passing planes or loud refrigeration systems. Contact alarms may be triggered by absent-minded superintendents on a late trip to the office. Sonar alarms may be disturbed by wind currents or by a stray piece of paper. Fire alarms are particularly prone to false alarms triggered by passing students.

No matter what system is chosen, it is important to place them selectively in the school. A blanketing of all school areas with alarms is wasteful and can cause more problems than they are worth. Questions of priority placement are therefore crucial.

Possible Design Responses

1. *Location Priorities:* High priority for installing theft alarm systems are: (a) administrative offices and record areas, (b) cafeteria and pantry, (c) teachers' lounge, (d) audio-visual equipment, data processing equipment, typewriters, P.A. system, instructional material resource center, and auto mechanic/industrial arts center, (e) library, (f) band-room, (g) storage areas, (h) student store, (i) portable classrooms.

2. *Fire Alarm Locations:* To minimize opportunity for false fire alarms, fire alarm boxes should, if regulations permit, be placed where they can be seen, for instance in classrooms and in offices.

3. *Fire Alarm Types:* Specify fire alarms which require several small steps to be set off: take hammer, break glass, pull lever. Avoid one step fast fire alarms which are easy and fun to set off.

4. *Fire Alarm Type:* Specify alarm boxes with a double bell system which rings first only in the box, and then several seconds later in the fire station. Do this where regulations permit. If the alarm is false, a supervisor can turn off the alarm with a special key before the alarm is spread or registered with the fire department.

Design Issue

Joint Community-School-Use Entries: *Programs in some schools encourage community members to use the gymnasium or swimming pool on weekends, to hold adult education classes at night, and to conduct community meetings in the auditorium. While such multiple use can result in cooperation, it can also cause conflicts. One way conflicts arise is when property damage occurs in community schools and each group blames the other. Careful planning and renovation can better accommodate multiple use and lessen conflict over property damage.*

Possible Design Responses

1. *Internal Gates:* Install built-in flexible internal gates to be able to selectively zone off specific corridors or parts of school while other parts, e.g., the auditorium or a set of classrooms, are open for use. Flimsy gates which are only symbolic barriers are not useful because they challenge young people to get by them.

2. *Separate Entries:* Provide separate exterior entries to the different school zones: community-use and school-use.

3. *Office Location:* Locate offices of supervisory personnel near multiple use entries so that these adults may serve as informal surveyors of people coming in and out of the school. This is especially useful around recreational facilities.

4. *People Locks:* People gathering at entrances serve as a "human lock" for the rest of the school. Therefore, provide places for informal meeting and activity near entrances and exits on the inside of school, e.g., benches or soft-drink machine.

CHAPTER 4

Administrative Responses to Property Damage and Vandalism

EDUCATIONAL OBJECTIVES

Three Types of Programs

Administrative programs to reduce property damage and vandalism are as important as design and renovation of buildings. In fact, while physical design can respond well to issues of unintended damage, misnamed vandalism, and hidden cost maintenance damage, physical design can respond to malicious vandalism mainly with alarms, bars on windows, and prison-like buildings. Administrative programs, on the other hand, respond well to malicious damage by (1) finding ways to control behavior around the school, (2) finding ways to increase parents' and students' feelings of responsibility for the school, and (3) finding ways to get different members of the school community to talk to one another.

1. Behavior Programs

Programs which maintain orderly behavior around school by supervision or punishment we are calling behavior programs. There are two types of behavior programs: (1) those organized to prevent damaging behavior by keeping "eyes-on-the-school" 24 hours a day; and (2) those aimed at setting an example by apprehending and punishing students and their parents for acts of vandalism which have already occurred.

An example of an "eyes-on-the-school" program is in Chattanooga, Tennessee, where custodians are scheduled on several shifts to keep the school building occupied 24 hours a day. Punishment programs include ones like Los Angeles' well publicized program to collect restitution from apprehended vandals.

2. Motivation Programs

Programs to reduce property damage by educating students, parents, teachers, and others to be involved with their school and to be more aware of the problems, we are calling motivation programs. There are at least two types of motivation programs: (1) those which involve different school groups in projects from which they benefit directly and which motivate them to feel the school is partly theirs; and (2) those which tey to make these groups more conscious of and knowledgeable about property damage.

An example of an involvement program is Louisville, Kentucky, where students in their School Beautification Program are given money to buy equipment and furnishings to make their school buildings more attractive. San Diego, California's "Handbook to Develop School Pride" is an example of an awareness type motivation program.

3. Dialogue Programs

Dialogue programs are those which bring together custodial staff, teachers, students, administrators, parents, neighbors, and others to discuss their different attitudes towards what to do about property damage. There are two kinds of dialogue programs: (1) those which are created as catalysts to make on-going behavior and motivation programs work better; and (2) those which are developed purely for the sake of opening continuing communication channels between interest groups.

An example of a dialogue program developed from a behavior program is in El Paso, Texas, where senior custodians live in apartments or houses on school grounds. While this program formally just keeps buildings policed most of the time, informally successful live-in custodians are parents of children in the school, have an office next to the principal's, organize student activities, and help teachers get in on the weekend. These custodians are actually the center of informal dialogue programs, which make the "eyes-on-the-school" program even more effective.

Examples of pure dialogue programs can be drawn from several Massachusetts schools where head custodians regularly take part in faculty meetings. Unfortunately, small scale pure dialogue programs are too few in number and not old enough to provide useful feedback. Nonetheless, the more comprehensive "community school" approach instituted in parts of Massachusetts, in Michigan, California, and in other states, can be seen as a type of large-scale dialogue program. Where successful, these programs involve a broad cross-section of the school and community in on-going dialogue about day-to-day issues.

One off-shoot of successful applications of the "community school" concept is lowered property damage and vandalism. Again, because the approach is so comprehensive, it is difficult to show what specific part might be usefully abstracted to cut property damage. Cause and effect in this case is unclear. However, isolated instances of this approach do allow us to see pure dialogue programs at work.

Summary of the Three Types of Administrative Programs

1. Behavior
   a. "Eyes-on-the-school" programs
   b. Punishment programs

2. Motivation
   a. Involvement programs
   b. Awareness programs

3. Dialogue
   a. Catalyst programs
   b. Pure dialogue programs

Two Goals of Schools

Educators have long contended that in American schools since the American Revolution there has always been tension between traditional schooling which emphasizes obedience to existing rules, the basic curriculum, and order in schools, and progressive schooling which emphasizes the growth of the child, his or her personal development, and the child's adjustment to a set of everchanging rules.

This tension is the tension between what we have been calling "behavior" and "motivation" goals:

1. BEHAVIOR GOALS: Training new citizens; conveying to these new citizens society's expectations of what is acceptable behavior; and transmitting to them the rules and regulations of the community;

2. MOTIVATION GOALS: Motivating individuals who are developing; presenting to them the conceptual world or older generations; and showing them how to use reason and individual judgment.

Schools are required to achieve both behavior goals and motivation goals, although each school usually emphasizes one more than the other in its day-to-day operations. Among the many operational decisions administrators make is what type of programs to institute to reduce property damage: administrators who emphasize behavior goals often choose behavior programs, while those who emphasize motivation goals tend to choose motivation programs. This is where conflict arises. No matter what the major goal orientation of a school is, the staff will include positions with both orientations: either towards behavior, e.g., custodians, superintendents of maintenance, guards, monitors, or towards motivation, e.g., counselors, teachers, and superintendents of curriculum.

Preliminary research indicates that people in jobs which include more behavior than motivation tasks often find it difficult to work with programs which concentrate on changing attitudes but which may not immediately change destructive behavior. Similarly, people in school positions made up more of motivation than behavior tasks understand and endorse motivation programs directed at adjusting motives, but find it difficult to accept behavior programs aimed primarily at property damage consequences through strong discipline.

Since the best method for reducing property damage in a given school probably includes both types of programs, it is important for all those involved in schooling to communicate their perspectives and concerns to each other, so that each understands the other's point of view. To carry out programs effectively for decreasing school property damage, it is essential that this division of goals and of staff be softened.

Dialogue programs serve this purpose.

Motivation and behavior objectives are at times in conflict. Programs for reducing property damage by attacking causes are at times incompatible with those that attack consequences. But, the fact that these programs are incompatible at a particular moment does not mean that, over time, they might not be reconciled. By having schools' different interest groups discuss and exchange their views, a comprehensive and flexible program which includes both motivation and behavior goals, dealing with both cause and consequence, can be developed to reduce property damage.

	Staff	
	Personnel oriented toward "motivation"	Personnel oriented toward "behavior"
Goals		
Motivation	Effective motivation programs	Need for dialogue programs
Behavior	Need for dialogue programs	Effective behavior programs

SPECIFIC PROGRAMS

Questions and Answers About Specific Administrative Programs to Reduce Property Damage and Vandalism

The following administrative programs to reduce property damage represent only a few of many such programs around the country. We have chosen the ones which best exemplify a type of program, so that each school district might use the questions and answers provided to develop an innovative program particularly suited to its own needs.

Each program is introduced by a short description and analysis. Then there follows for each program a series of questions and answers elaborating practical issues which will interest administrators who want to consider instituting such a program.

● School watchers are residents who live near a school and parents of school children who keep watch over the school by walking through and driving by school grounds on weekdays after school and evenings and on weekends. If they see any problems they call other school watchers, the principal, and the police. Cooperation of neighbors and parents with the school through a school watchers program is an inexpensive and effective way to keep eyes on the school. Such programs work best if they are organized, yet based on informal involvement rather than formal routine; if they are accompanied by comprehensive involvement with the school on the part of the parents and neighbors; and if the program offers some form of prestige to participants. One major limitation of the school watchers program is that it can respond to external property damage and to damage done when school is not in session, but not to internal and unintended damage.

1. **How Formal Should the Schedule of School Visits Be?**

   Maintaining a formal schedule can be difficult, especially when there are conflicts with family activities. More practical and equally effective is an informal schedule of surveillance: simply suggesting, for instance, that school-watcher parents drive a block out of the way to survey the school on the way back from a shopping trip or on the way home from work. An unpredictable "spot check" can be more of a deterrent than a familiar routine patrol.

2. **Do School Watchers Eliminate the Need for Guards?**

   School watchers are limited to the building's exterior, and thus are not as thorough as guards authorized to enter the building. Where breaking and entering is a major problem, guards may be needed; but where minor damage is the problem, school watchers may be enough.

3. **How Can Interest in the Program Be Sustained?**

   A newsletter can be distributed to parents informing them about program successes; and public news media reports reward participants with attention to their efforts while keeping the community aware of their activities.

4. **Where Can a School Watchers Program Be Most Successfully Established?**

   It is easiest to set up a school watchers program where there are already a number of ongoing school programs involving parents and community; and when "school watchers" themselves are actively involved in a variety of school affairs. The sense of responsibility school watchers feel is greatest among those already expressing concern for the school in such activities as PTA and parent-student projects.

   In a Houston school where this program has successfully been established, there are two programs involving parents: "block homes" where neighborhood parents have signs showing that their home is a place students may stop in case of emergencies; and parents running food concessions at school functions such as athletic games and fairs, and using the proceeds to buy equipment for the school.

● Custodians can be present in and keep an eye on school buildings 24 hours a day if they are scheduled on several shifts. This measure is relatively inexpensive because it covers some major security costs with minor maintenance expenses. School districts have found this system cuts down on some nighttime vandalism. Several problems arise with 24-hour custodian shifts, but proper planning can overcome them: Having three separate maintenance staffs can be inefficient; nighttime personnel has a higher turnover rate if not properly chosen; it is more difficult to supervise night shifts than day shifts. Proper choice of personnel and assignment of tasks can begin to overcome these problems. Clearly, the major criteria for instituting such a program is that the building be large enough to need the requisite number of custodians.

1. How Much Extra Does It Cost to Have Custodians 24 Hours a Day?

In one Tennessee School District, costs increased only 10%. Cost increase is kept down by the fact that 24-hour custodians are used only in schools where there were previously more than two custodians; so shifts merely had to be rearranged. In smaller schools where additional custodians must be hired, costs are greater. Nevertheless, if security costs are thereby avoided, the program still may be worth it.

2. Are There Any Problems With Unions When Custodians Work at Night?

This varies according to the particular locale. Where there are specific unions, union policies must be considered and negotiated before beginning a 24-hour plan.

3. Are There Any Problems With Supervision When Custodians Work at Night?

Sometimes there are problems of low productivity by custodians working at night when there is no consistent supervision. In order to overcome this problem, principals in the Tennessee school district are given a copy of the work schedule given to each shift of custodians. This helps to determine what has and has not been done when night custodians are checked in the morning by the head custodian. It is reported that these schools get much better cleaning and care, along with 24-hour security, making up for the increased cost of hiring another custodian in schools formerly having fewer than three custodians.

4. How Does the Custodian Deal With What He Suspects to be Either a Vandal or Someone Breaking and Entering?

He calls the police. Custodians must be asked not to try to apprehend anyone who breaks and enters a building. If they see anything out of the ordinary, like a parked car in the school vicinity, or someone lurking on the grounds, they must be asked to notify the police immediately.

5. Why Use Custodians on a 24-Hour Shift Instead of Hiring Guards?

Where property damage problems or breaking and entering are sporadic and not created by adult criminals, permanent guards may not be necessary, while roving guards may not be sufficient. 24-hour custodians provide enough of a deterrent for minor-criminal activities and are constantly keeping an eye on the school. Since their presence is enough to do the security job, the fact that they are cleaning up at the same time is an efficient use of school funds.

6. What Other Devices are Needed to Back Up 24-Hour Custodial Schedules?

In larger buildings, where a custodian cannot hear what is going on in one part while he is cleaning another area, noisy burglar alarms may be helpful. These must be placed carefully, so that pranksters do not use them to run custodians around the school.

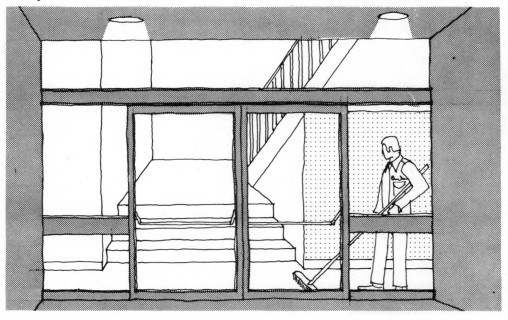

Live-in custodian programs have head custodians and their families living in a house or apartment built on school grounds. One benefit of the program is that it serves as an early warning system to prevent costly breakdown to equipment such as heating, ventilating, and air conditioning; kitchen freezers, and so on. In addition some property damage problems are averted or caught before too much damage occurs such as from fires and broken windows. The "human alarm" potential of a live-in custodian is greatest when the custodian becomes part of the school community and feels the school in part belongs to him. The live-in custodian program only works if the custodian feels it is a positive benefit to live in the community where the school is located, and feels he is getting a good deal as far as housing is concerned.

1. **What Does the Live-In Custodian Do That is Different from a Regular 9-5 Custodian?**

In total, the live-in custodian works a full 35-hour or a 40-hour week. Every weekday evening he makes a 1 hour round of the school and its mechanical equipment — a total of 2-1/2 hours a week. On weekends he makes two rounds each day — once in the morning and once in the evening, making

another two hours. The rest of his hours are scheduled normally throughout the week. When there is an extra-curricular activity at the school at night, the custodian gets paid time-and-a-half. In addition, he sometimes gets called on to let the principal or a teacher into the school at odd hours, if they forget important papers. This is a minor drawback to the program which cannot be avoided.

2. What Type of Person Should a Live-In Head Custodian Be?

Live-in custodians must be interested in and get along well with young people. It is important to look for persons with experience with children, such as having been a coach or scoutmaster. He must like to deal with people because he must be able to get along with teachers, administration, kids, and people in the neighborhood. Finally, since it is best if he becomes part of the school community, it is often good if the live-in custodian has a family with children. This allows him to get to know neighborhood people through taking part in PTA, Scouts, as well as through general public relations.

3. What Costs are Involved in Having a Live-In Custodian?

Since a live-in custodian still works a normal week, salary costs do not differ from that of usual custodial service. The cost of the residence is a factor because it includes utilities, maintenance of dwelling, and extension of school phone. The cost of housing varies slightly with the type of housing selected: whether it is possible to adapt existing structures to this purpose or whether it is necessary to construct a complete new dwelling. Clearly, all these costs are less in warmer climates and in schools where an apartment is built-in during initial construction.

4. Who Builds Homes on Existing School Grounds?

In older schools, small new homes can be built on the grounds, possibly with assistance from vocational classes. Materials can be provided by the central office while classes in electrical work, building trades, masonry, and plumbing provide labor. In El Paso, where much low-wage labor is available anyway nearby, the unions encourage such arrangements. A building there costs about $8,500.00 and takes a school year to complete, given the good Texas weather.

5. When Does the Custodian First Have Contact With the Dwelling In Which He Will Live?

In order to encourage a feeling of ownership in new schools or new houses, the custodian and his wife can fruitfully be brought into both the design and construction process as early as possible.

6. What Should the Designer Keep in Mind When Planning a Dwelling Unit Inside the School?

The apartment within the school building or the house on the school grounds must look like a home. It must be visually distinguishable from the school, and offer the resident custodian and his family a sense of "home." The dwelling should not be considered a live-in office. There must be adequate privacy, and minimum noise from the school. In other words, the apartment ought not be next to boiler room or noisy play or gathering places. There should be a view from the living room which serves to associate the dwelling with the neighborhood — a view away from the actual school building. A parking space for the custodian adjacent and separate from the regular school parking lot is helpful to create a feeling of "separateness" from the school and to protect the car from students hanging out there. Because it is important that the custodian and his family feel part of the community, it is desirable that the dwelling's appearance conform somewhat to neighboring homes, if possible.

● In mobile home programs, one or two mobile home sites are prepared on the grounds of each school, depending on the size of the school building. The site is offered rent-free to trailer-owners who wish to live there in exchange for their agreement to informally watch the school. Sewer, water, and electricity connections are included in the preparation of the site.

One California community reports this program has proved 95% effective. The cost of preparing the site was recovered after a period of only three years, and the monthly cost for electricity is less than $15.00. Mobile home programs are better suited to some communities than to others. They will work better in more rural or suburban towns with a tradition of mobile homes, than in the center of large urban areas. Nevertheless, some variation of the program might be well adapted to new types of school communities.

1. **In What Level of School Has This Program Been Successful?**

   It has been proved successful at all levels. But a community beginning such a program might well start off first at an elementary school then work up to higher level schools after some successes.

2. **What is Involved in Preparing the Site?**

   It is important that the sites be competitive with or better than commercial mobile home parks in the area. In addition to installing sewer, water, and electricity connection, it is good to provide gravel or blacktop for patios and automobile parking. Residents can be asked to pay for their own gas, telephone, and garbage service. A telephone extension from the school is essential for emergencies. Fences may be installed around the mobile home site where the school district or the mobile home occupant feels the need. Construc-

tion costs for a site can vary from about $2,500 to $3,000 depending on whether a fence is necessary, and on how costly utility connections are.

3. **What is the Best Type of Family to Occupy the Mobile Home?**

   There seem to be no set rules regarding the selection of families, except that there be no alcoholics or drug addicts. Some administrators feel that larger families or families with teenage children are best because they provide the highest level of visible activity. Retired people, singles, or couples without children might be away from home a lot; and unless they agreed to always have someone stay in their mobile home while they were away, they do not usually make very good mobile home school watchers. But experience

has shown that these generalizations cannot always be applied. Schools setting up such a program are best off accepting applications from residents based on their probability of providing visible activity, and the probability that they will feel at ease talking to adults and children on school property.

6. **Where Should the Trailers be Located?**

   They should be located as close as possible to the "action" spots without interfering with the school's normal activities. Proper landscaping and siting are necessary to help the mobile home site fit in near school properties.

7. **Is It Legal?**

   Regulations vary by state, county, city, or town, and should be investigated before setting up such a program.

● School security officers are private guards hired directly by school officials or supplied by private security agencies. Generally schools hire their own guards, seeming to prefer them to guards from an agency.

The most important thing for a school administration and school committee to do when they decide to hire school security officers, is to hire two types of officers: one nighttime guard to be responsible for after-school "adult-type" crimes; and another daytime guard to deal with student problems which are as much educational as they are criminal.

1. Why Is One Security Force Not Appropriate for All Shifts?

The night police force deals with illegal activities such as stealing, breaking and entering, and miscellaneous vandalism. During the school day, members of the school security force serve in human relations and counseling roles as well as looking after the welfare of students and teachers, and their possessive property.

2. Who Selects Security Officers?

Both school personnel and security officials must set up criteria and share responsibility for evaluating applicants.

3. What are the Best Kind of People to Hire?

Night time guards: The traditional police professional or guard is best.

Day time guards: Officers successful in working at the school during the day in the multiple roles of property guard, protector, peacemaker, and emergency aide are persons with experience in educational situations and school problems who are able to establish good rapport with kids. In Houston, a city with a large security force, one of the most successful day-time security officers is an ex-waiter who has had lots of experience with people.

4. What Special Training do Officers Receive After Hiring?

Night and day officers must receive different

training. Nightshift guards are trained in police work; dayshift security officers receive in-service human relations training. At regular intervals day-time guards should meet with school personnel to discuss specific situations experienced during the day.

5. What if a Mistake is Made in Assigning An Officer to Day or Night Shift?

If an officer originally assigned day-time duty proves unsuited to the special needs of the school day and more suited to the night-time guarding, he should be reassigned and vice versa. It is useful to have a 2-3 month probation period during which the appropriateness of shift-assignments can be determined and adjustments made if necessary.

6. What is a Day-Time and a Night-Time Shift?

Day-time guards normally work from before schools begin until schools let out, and also during school functions in the evenings or on weekends: in other words, they work whenever there are large gatherings of people. Night shifts begin after school and continue as late as necessary. Night-time guards work holidays and weekends as well, but are not assigned any duty for school activities in evenings.

7. When Might the Use of Dogs be Desirable?

In some cities night-time guards keep dogs with them — more as a deterring image than as an aid to catching vandals. Generally, the costs and potential community problems with dogs dissuade schools from using them.

8. How are Day-Time Officers Made Part of the Educational Process?

Students' attitudes toward security officers is important. Cooperation and personal rapport between guards and students is possible if guards are hired and trained correctly and if they are presented along with other school personnel as part of the school administration.

● Restitution programs are a set of administrative and legal procedures whereby school administrations try to get money from identified vandals for damage they incur. This means developing a procedure for identifying and prosecuting, and for enforcing the restitution claim. An important part of restitution programs is a mechanism for publicizing positive results of these efforts, so that the school department can maintain an image of forcefulness towards vandals.

Carrying out restitution programs exhaustively often entails more expense than is compensated by monetary restitution. On the other hand, occasional thorough investigation and prosecution which is well publicized, may reduce damage enough to compensate for the program's cost.

1. **How is a Restitution Program Conducted?**
   The school department administers such a program through a school security office staff, working closely with the courts.

2. **How is a Restitution Program Organized?**
   A series of steps must be established, employing at least the following staffs: investigative staff; accounting; notification of offender and family; receipting; enforcement; court officer preparing suits.

3. **How Can Restitution Programs Be Made Visible?**
   School newsletters, the press, and other normal news channels can be kept informed of

specific events. In Los Angeles, every case goes before the school board in a public meeting and is therefore reported in the newspapers.

4. **How Effective is the Enforcement of Restitution: How Much Damage Can be Repaired with Funds Obtained?**

Restitution does not seem to be cost effective. The majority of persons responsible for property damage cannot be caught. In Los Angeles only 30% of the offenders are even identified.

As can be seen in the diagram on the following page, most restitution from identified vandals is received at an early stage in the process: after writing several adamant letters to vandals and their families. This stage is the least expensive one, yet accounts for over 95% of the restitution. The expense of obtaining the rest through lengthy legal processes has a greater effect in establishing the image of uncompromising justice than in alleviating property repairs.

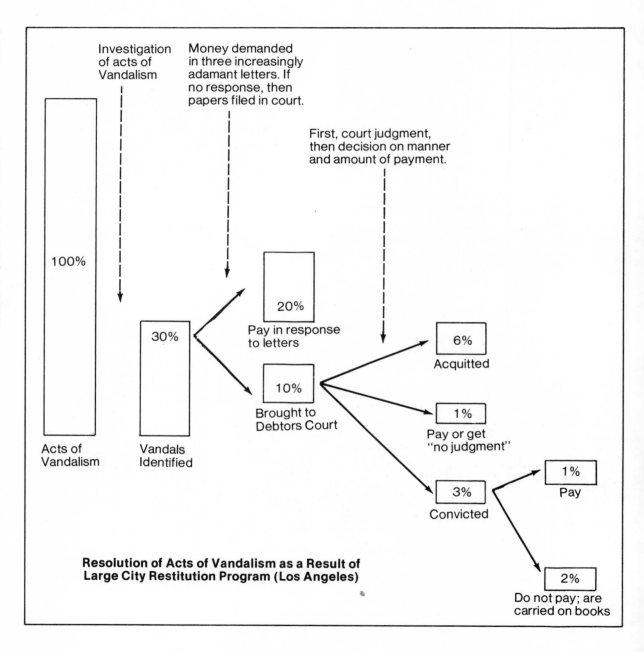

Investigation of acts of Vandalism

Money demanded in three increasingly adamant letters. If no response, then papers filed in court.

First, court judgment, then decision on manner and amount of payment.

100%

30%

20%
Pay in response to letters

10%
Brought to Debtors Court

6%
Acquitted

1%
Pay or get "no judgment"

3%
Convicted

1%
Pay

2%
Do not pay; are carried on books

Acts of Vandalism

Vandals Identified

Resolution of Acts of Vandalism as a Result of Large City Restitution Program (Los Angeles)

● A student vandalism account is a special student account established with funds from the regular maintenance or vandalism budget. Students are told that any money not spent to repair property damage during the year may be spent by students for anything they want at the end of the year. In San Francisco where this program originated, it was begun because school administrators and community members were frustrated with the results and implications of alarms systems, police surveillance, and roving guards. The community decided that vandalism should be approached by exerting more effort "in the area of parent and student attitude."

Programs such as these, involving rewards, tend to be more effective with younger grade-school age children than with high school students. Yet such a program may motivate high school students by giving them the status of sharing in administrative authority and responsibility for managing part of the repair budget. To maximize the attractiveness of defending the school from damage during school hours (the only period during which students might have preventive control) there must be no constraint on what students may spend their money. In addition, since the program has to motivate the entire student body, strong student leadership is essential as is involvement of well-liked teachers.

1. **What are the Objectives of a Student Vandalism Account?**

The goals of the student vandalism account program are:

(a) *To educate students as to the cost of vandalism.*
Students including those not involved in property damage have no idea of the costs involved in these losses. Twenty broken windows may not be very meaningful, but the price of these windows subtracted from a proposed project becomes very meaningful. The $900 avail-

able for a new projector may suddenly become $700 as the result of a smashed lavatory partition.

(b) *To allow students to see the positive results of non-damage.*
If funds are needed for repair, that is what they are used for; but if the student cooperation makes repair unnecessary, then the students enjoy the benefits.

(c) *To turn the responsibility for either the cost of vandalism or the positive results of non-damage over to the students themselves.*
In San Francisco, vandalism of student group projects was nil.

2. **Where do the Funds for the Program Come From?**

They come from the maintenance, repair, or vandalism budget. The idea behind this program is to take money already earmarked to be spent on repair, and give students a chance to rechannel it into projects they choose.

3. **How Much Money does the Program Take Per Pupil?**

Some school systems allocate one dollar per student per year. Others have a lump sum for each school which they divide into monthly allotments.

4. **When do the Students
Get to Spend the Money?**

If student interest is to be maintained, visible results are essential; so try to make the money available within the current school year. The program can be run on a January to January calendar year. This policy assures that at least some money saved during the on-going school year is spent that year (an important fact, since seniors or others leaving the school do not have interest in the promise of next year!). The money also can be divided up on a monthly basis available to spend each month, or left to accumulate for several months.

5. **For What Types of Damage is the
Account Held Responsible?**

Funds from the student vandalism account should be used only for in-school intentional building damage except that caused by major fires. In order to make the program fair to students, it is critical to define what is malicious property damage and what is normal wear and tear. If students are charged for damage they cannot prevent — such as white walls getting dirty — they will soon be frustrated with the program. In order to maintain incentive, cases of damage bordering between vandalism and wear and tear should be judged to give students the benefit of the doubt.

6. **Should the Student Vandalism Account
Be Held Responsible for Damage After
School, Over Vacations, and During
the Summer?**

If students are held accountable for damage which occurs while they are not at school, the student vandalism account may soon be depleted, and students will be punished for situations over which they have no control. Enthusiastic elementary school students can lose all interest in the program if they have to spend all their money to pay for windows broken by local teenagers over the weekend.

It makes sense to use this program to reduce in-school damage; deducting from the student vandalism account only the cost of acts of vandalism which occur while school is in session.

7. **What Limitations Should be Put on the Use
of the Funds Saved by Students?**

None!

8. **Who Decides How to Spend Money
Not Used by Repair Costs?**

Giving the students as much freedom and control as possible will probably attract the maximum cooperation and participation of students. In some cases it is good to have a student committee decide how to spend the money. In other cases students can run a survey to get student ideas on how to use the money.

The most important thing is for as many students as possible to participate in deciding how to spend and in actually spending the money. If only the student leaders choose a project, then many of the students who are potential vandals are left out. The program needs to be well publicized within the school, and the spending of the funds must be as democratic as possible.

9. **What Happens When a Student
Vandal is Identified?**

When vandals are identified, then restitution is made and the student vandalism account is not charged. One possibly controversial aspect of this program is that students in their eagerness to keep their funds have an incentive to tell on other students. Parts of the community may react to the program by wondering if the school is bribing informants. Hopefully, an incentive program aimed at a group of students changes attitudes towards damaging the school, and teaches students the cost of damage, and does not pay off students to get others in trouble.

10. **How Can a Student Vandalism Account
Program be Publicized to the Community?**

The community can become aware of the program through PTA meetings, community meetings, memos, and articles in the local paper. In order to avoid confusion and negative press, it is essential that the program, its goals, and procedures be carefully described to the community before it is established.

11. **How Do Students React to the Program?**

The more thoroughly the program is explained, publicized, and talked about in the school, the better is student participation. In some schools, charts are kept in the halls telling students how much money is in the account.

12. **How is the Cost of Vandalism
Damage Determined?**

It is determined by either estimating or using the exact contract cost for making repairs, including labor and materials.

The better the records of prices for repairing damage, the easier it is to set fair prices. The involvement of students on the Student Vandalism Account Committee in price setting can further give students a sense that it is actually their money and their responsibility to determine its use.

13. **What is the First Step in Establishing a
Student Vandalism Account Program?**

Set up a committee including students, teachers, principal, and maintenance staff to discuss program details and tailor it to your school. To ensure interest later, get students involved from the start in setting up and running the program.

● Programs to increase pride in school buildings and awareness of the condition of schools include events geared at "selling" students pride and involvement in their school facilities. Pride programs are inexpensive to run. But while they may strengthen student respect for property, they will do it most for socially-oriented students. Pride programs miss the real vandals who tend to shun such general social programs. Thus, malicious property damage might be reduced slightly during school hours because of increased watchfulness of more property-conscious classmates; but the greatest effect of the program will be in increasing school morale and reducing nonmalicious maintenance problems.

1. How Can Pride be Made a Visible and Tangible Goal to Students?

In San Bruno Park, California, where a Project Pride is ongoing, schools are inspected by a school team each month, and if they receive an "outstanding" or a "satisfactory" rating, the school is allowed to fly a Project Pride flag. Schools that receive a "needs improvement" rating cannot fly the flag until their rating improves. The project also awards plaques to individuals or groups showing special pride in the school through "worthy projects or deeds."

2. Who are Members of the Inspection Team?

The team inspecting each school represents most members of a school community — teachers, PTA representatives, day custodian, principal, and others. Most importantly, it includes two students.

3. Who Receives the Special Awards and Plaques?

Awards are given to students, teachers, or community members who show extra care for the school. Special efforts by students are rewarded with small Smiling Face buttons, such as a kindergarten student picking up paper without being asked to. Sew-on patches are given to class members who carry out projects expressing their pride in the school. Plaques are given to parents, students, or teachers for special efforts, such as two parents who watered the flowers at one school all summer, or a student who helped secure the return of some stolen audio-visual equipment.

4. How is Student Interest in the Program Maintained?

It is important to continually change and update the program. A potential problem with any program such as this is that students lose interest in whether their school is allowed to fly a flag or not. The program needs to be a base for continually trying new ideas to interest students in caring for the school environment. Also, since different age groups are motivated in different ways, thought must be given to the kinds of rewards appropriate to various groups. Flying a school flag or getting sew-on patches may work better with elementary students than with high school students.

5. What Role Does the Appearance of the Building Itself Play in the Development of Pride?

San Bruno Park school administrators decided that if students were to have pride in

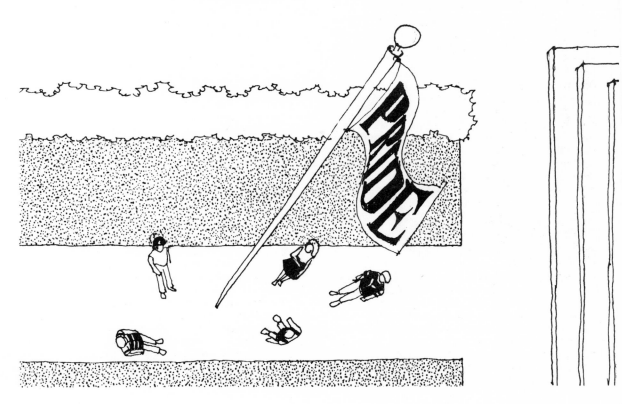

their building, the building needed to be worthy of pride. Therefore, they refurbished ten schools in the district. This included painting the interior and the exterior, and revamping the landscape of each school.

In some cases investment in the appearance of the school pays off. The San Bruno district superintendent reports that the investment made in the appearance of the school buildings and grounds has paid off over three years, since the amount of money spent on vandalism repair has decreased considerably.

6. **How Can Students be Given Information so They can Start Their Own Programs?**

Schools can distribute handbooks to students graphically describing vandalism costs and outlining types of activities they can organize in their schools to increase awareness of the problem. This can serve as a source book for students, but the choice of activities and responsibility for carrying them out must be left up to the students.

7. **What Types of Activities Does a Handbook Describe?**

In San Diego, California, where a handbook is distributed, it described activities including special days for activities; suggested projects such as clean-up campaigns and talks by student leaders; suggested speakers for assemblies such as attorneys, baseball players, and the head custodian; films and other audiovisual presentations to help build attitudes and teach responsibility; a sample student survey to assess student attitudes; evaluation guides; and tips on how to outline a speech or conduct an assembly.

8. **At Whom is Such a Handbook Aimed?**

The booklet must be written to appeal to and be understood by elementary and junior high school students, although high school students should also be able to use it. The more copies available the better, since service clubs and other groups may want to sponsor one of the activities described.

9. **How Much Does a Handbook Cost?**

Very little. The main cost is reproduction and perhaps paying someone to prepare it.

● School Beautification projects make money available for projects to improve the school's appearance and thus aim indirectly at reducing property damage and maintenance costs. These projects involve students in the care of the school facility and grounds in an attempt to increase their pride in and responsibility towards "their" school.

Advantages of freeing personnel from maintenance duties and saving operating funds must be counted as benefits from beautification programs in addition to any reduction of vandalism in areas where student awareness has been strengthened.

1. How Effective Are School Beautification Projects at Reducing Vandalism?

Such projects tend to reduce non-malicious damage, and some malicious damage in areas where students have some control and where they are involved. Also, the program can save maintenance money.

2. How is the Project Organized and Funded?

In Louisville, one of the first cities to initiate such a program, $10,000 is available each year to be distributed equally to participating schools on a per pupil basis (averaging 20 cents per pupil). The principal or project sponsor submits a written proposal to the district task force which oversees the project. Money is allocated to the school, after the project is approved.

The Office of Business Affairs is responsible

for figuring out the amount of money each school is eligible for, and also responsible for furnishing guidelines on how the money can be spent. At the end of the school year, all participating schools submit a written evaluation of the past year's project. Schools who want to participate in the project for the following year present plans at this time.

3. **At What Level School is the School Beautification Project Most Successful?**

Student involvement in elementary school projects is higher than in junior or senior highs.

4. **What Attitudes Do School Principals and Teachers Hold Toward Beautification Projects?**

Some of the principals may be worried that the program will become competitive. They rightfully do not want to be judged on the basis of who reduces vandalism the most.

The Louisville decision to divide available money equally on a per pupil basis was made to allay such worries. To further cut competitiveness, the program turns back to the school Beautification Project half of any money cut from the annual vandalism bill. But instead of returning it to individual schools based on their success in reducing costs, the money goes into a district-wide pool. The whole school district is thus competing against its own record, instead of schools competing against each other.

5. **What Types of Projects Are Most Successful?**

Effective projects involve students in continuous activity throughout the year and focus on motivating marginal students rather than school leaders.

6. **Which Projects Are Less Successful?**

Less successful programs are those where funds are used to put a new tree or something else on the grounds. The tree is planted and forgotten, without even engaging the students in the project.

7. **What Other Measures Complement the Effects of School Beautification Programs?**

Many other programs aimed at reducing vandalism support beautification programs: police-school liaison officers, electronic systems, flood lights, and maintenance programs. School beautification is not a total solution to the problem of vandalism, especially since much vandalism may be caused by other than school age kids. Other measures are used to prevent breaking and entering and theft, while beautification projects try to increase student awareness for caring for the school — especially at the elementary level.

CHAPTER 5

Design Checklists

What have you done to minimize breakage of objects around playgrounds and basketball courts?

What have you done to be sure that objects will not be broken around pick-up play areas — areas near buildings like entry ways and pathways with hard ground surfaces, a wall, and enough room to throw or hit a ball?

	YES	NO
There is sufficient space around formal play areas for normal play	[ ]	[ ]
Ground surfaces in and around formal play areas have no major irregularities or hindrances to play.	[ ]	[ ]
Wall surfaces around formal play areas can be used to bounce balls back to players.	[ ]	[ ]
Low lighting fixtures and other hardware are out of the way of ball playing.	[ ]	[ ]
Lines on walls and on ground accommodate local street games.	[ ]	[ ]
There is a buffer between formal play areas and the school building.	[ ]	[ ]
There are no windows or glass doors around formal play areas.	[ ]	[ ]
Glass around formal play areas is specially protected.	[ ]	[ ]
There is no damageable planting immediately adjacent to formal play areas.	[ ]	[ ]

	YES	NO
There are consciously designed areas for pick-up play.	[ ]	[ ]
There is no low lighting or other fixtures which can be hit by balls in pick-up play areas.	[ ]	[ ]
Walls and ground surfaces in pick-up play areas are the same as in formal play areas.	[ ]	[ ]
There are no windows in pick-up play areas.	[ ]	[ ]
Any windows near pick-up play areas are protected from balls and sticks.	[ ]	[ ]

GATHERING: Hang-out Areas

What provision have you made to ·minimize damage when students sit on — hang-out on — convenient walls, steps, planters, ledges, and so on near play areas, pick-up play places, entries, and pathways?

	YES	NO
There are consciously designed and located areas for hanging out.	[ ]	[ ]
There are no fixtures in or near hang-out areas.	[ ]	[ ]
All fixtures in hang-out areas have tamper-proof screws.	[ ]	[ ]
All hardware and fixtures in hang-out areas are extra durable.	[ ]	[ ]
There are no windows in or nearby hang-out areas.	[ ]	[ ]
Windows in hang-out areas are specially protected.	[ ]	[ ]
Planting in hang-out areas bends easily and grows quickly.	[ ]	[ ]
There is no stiff and breakable planting in hang-out areas.	[ ]	[ ]

	YES	NO
There are benches or steps or ledges for sitting in hang-out areas.	[ ]	[ ]
All predicted sitting places in hang-out areas are far from breakable windows and fixtures.	[ ]	[ ]
Low walls, ledges, and steps in hang-out areas are made of extra durable material.	[ ]	[ ]
There are heavy trash containers in hang-out areas.	[ ]	[ ]
Trash containers in hang-out areas are designed to seem like targets for litter.	[ ]	[ ]
There are no planters in hang-out areas which can be used as trash baskets.	[ ]	[ ]
Replacements for small unit building materials used in hang-out areas, like bricks or panels, can be easily stored.	[ ]	[ ]

GATHERING: Watering Holes

What have you done to minimize damage in areas around schools which students use after hours as club-houses — partially hidden places adjacent to buildings and large enough for small groups?

	YES	NO
There are consciously and appropriately de-signed watering holes.	[ ]	[ ]
All fixtures in watering holes are located out of reach of teenagers standing on one another's shoulders.	[ ]	[ ]
Fixtures in watering holes which are within reach are extra durable.	[ ]	[ ]
There are no windows in watering holes.	[ ]	[ ]
Wall surfaces in watering holes are extra durable.	[ ]	[ ]
Walls in watering holes can be easily cleaned.	[ ]	[ ]
Walls in watering holes can be painted.	[ ]	[ ]
Plants in watering holes are flexible and pliable.	[ ]	[ ]
There are no stiff breakable plants.	[ ]	[ ]
There are no planting containers in or near watering holes to be used as trash baskets.	[ ]	[ ]
There are heavy trash containers.	[ ]	[ ]
Trash containers in watering holes are de-signed as targets.	[ ]	[ ]
Small unit building materials used in watering holes can be easily replaced and stored.	[ ]	[ ]
There are no modular wall panels used in watering holes.	[ ]	[ ]

GATHERING: Niches

What have you done to eliminate or minimize damage in small niches created by recessed doorways, loading docks, fire stairs, and so on?

	YES	NO
All niches around building are essential for pur-poses of safety when doors are open.	[ ]	[ ]
There are no non-essential niches.	[ ]	[ ]
There are no fixtures in niches.	[ ]	[ ]
There is no reachable hardware in niches.	[ ]	[ ]
Doors in niches are glass-free.	[ ]	[ ]
There is no exterior door hardware on doors in niches.	[ ]	[ ]

ENTRY: Main Entry

What have you done so that people can see from a distance that the school is closed when it is closed but open when it is open?

	YES	NO
There are large sliding grills or garage type doors to cover over-transparent doorways in the main entrance, visible from a distance when school is closed.	[ ]	[ ]
Deep recesses at entries are inaccessible when school is closed.	[ ]	[ ]
The entry way looks open when school is open, but closed when school is closed.	[ ]	[ ]

ENTRY: School Bus Drop-off

What have you done to accommodate the rough behavior which will take place around school bus drop-off areas?

	YES	NO
Bus stop is visible to school offices or other interior areas.	[ ]	[ ]
Bus stop is located near entrance.	[ ]	[ ]
Bus stop is located away from windows.	[ ]	[ ]
There are waiting areas near bus stops.	[ ]	[ ]
There are durable benches in waiting areas.	[ ]	[ ]
There are no fixtures or hardware items in the bus stop waiting area.	[ ]	[ ]
School entry areas are planned as hang-out areas with limited hardware, glass, and fixtures.	[ ]	[ ]

ROOFTOPS

What have you done to be sure that rooftops accessible from the ground are able to withstand rough play?

What have you done to be sure that people cannot climb onto vulnerable rooftops from the ground or from accessible parts of the roof.

	YES	NO
Glass on accessible rooftops is ground floor type.	[ ]	[ ]
Fixtures on accessible rooftops are ground floor type.	[ ]	[ ]
Hardware on accessible rooftops is ground floor type.	[ ]	[ ]
Doors on accessible rooftops have minimum exterior hardware.	[ ]	[ ]
Windows on accessible rooftops have no exterior hardware.	[ ]	[ ]
There is no climbable planting or planting which will grow to be climbable located near building walls.	[ ]	[ ]
There are no built-in footholds on telephone poles adjacent to the building.	[ ]	[ ]

	YES	NO
Walls are too high to be climbed with 12 ft. 2x4 or other ladder substitute, i.e., wall is over 14 ft. high.	[ ]	[ ]
Fixtures on buildings do not provide footholds for getting onto roofs.	[ ]	[ ]
Incinerator and incinerator housing on roof cannot be climbed upon or used to get from one roof to another.	[ ]	[ ]
Gas meter cannot be climbed upon.	[ ]	[ ]
Fixtures on rooftop walls cannot be used as footholds for climbing to other parts of roof.	[ ]	[ ]
Permanent custodian ladders are replaced by convenient storage for portable ladders.	[ ]	[ ]
Heights of roofs adjacent to rooftops accessible from the ground are too high to be climbed with use of a 12 ft. 2x4.	[ ]	[ ]

MOVEMENT: Parking Lots

What provisions have you made to accommodate informal pick-up play in parking lots?

What have you done to be sure that there will be no damage to grass and other soft materials next to formal parking areas caused by extra cars and cars turning around?

	YES	NO
Parking lots are planned to accommodate pick-up play games.	[ ]	[ ]
There is a way to close the parking lot to cars when school is closed.	[ ]	[ ]
There are fences in selected spots around parking lot to protect nearby windows.	[ ]	[ ]
Parking lots are big enough for both partial parking and pick-up play.	[ ]	[ ]
There are low barriers between car parking areas and adjacent grass or other soft material.	[ ]	[ ]
There is a paved turn-around in the parking area.	[ ]	[ ]
There are no small grassed patches between parking lot and buildings.	[ ]	[ ]

MOVEMENT: Pathways

What have you done to minimize trampling of grass adjacent to paved pathways and along natural shortcuts?

	YES	NO
Paved pathways are located so that they provide the shortest walk between the two points they connect.	[ ]	[ ]
Naturally made shortcut paths have been predicted.	[ ]	[ ]
Escrow funds have been set aside to pave formal pathways after six months, when natural paths have developed.	[ ]	[ ]
There are subtle barriers between hard paved pathways and adjacent soft grass or dirt areas.	[ ]	[ ]
There is no grass or other soft material immediately adjacent to narrow pathways.	[ ]	[ ]

What have you done to minimize potential damage to vulnerable windows?

	YES	NO
There are no windows in formal play areas.	[ ]	[ ]
There are no windows in informal gathering areas.	[ ]	[ ]
In vulnerable areas windows are made of several small panes, rather than one large pane.	[ ]	[ ]
There are no windows lower than three feet from the ground.	[ ]	[ ]
There is no acrylic or plexiglass in windows in watering holes and hang-out areas.	[ ]	[ ]
Ground floor windows are made of extra thick tempered glass.	[ ]	[ ]
Ground floor windows are made of thick acrylic or plexiglass.	[ ]	[ ]
Ground floor windows are covered with protective screens.	[ ]	[ ]

	YES	NO
Windows on higher floors are of decreasing strength.	[ ]	[ ]
Windows adjacent to interior watering holes or hang-out areas on upper floors, as well as on the ground, are especially durable.	[ ]	[ ]
There is extra thick tempered glass or double layer glass where acrylic or plexiglass is not advisable.	[ ]	[ ]
There are no windows at all in student stores.	[ ]	[ ]
There are no windows at all in administration storage offices.	[ ]	[ ]
There are no windows at all in industrial arts storage areas.	[ ]	[ ]
There are thin wire mesh screens over specially vulnerable ground floor windows.	[ ]	[ ]

DOORS

What have you done to minimize unnecessary damage to exterior door hardware, especially potential problems caused by highly visible and easily accessible panic hardware?

	YES	NO
All doors which are primarily exit doors have no locks or door handles.	[ ]	[ ]
Where there is a series of connected doors, only one of these doors has exterior door hardware.	[ ]	[ ]
There are no glass or other transparent panels on doors which give a clear view of panic hardware.	[ ]	[ ]
There are astrigals on all single doors.	[ ]	[ ]
Double doors are extra duty strength.	[ ]	[ ]
Double doors have sturdy center mullions.	[ ]	[ ]
Double doors have astrigals.	[ ]	[ ]
Panic hardware requires minimum amount of mechanical movement.	[ ]	[ ]
Panic hardware is easily repaired.	[ ]	[ ]

WALLS: Graffiti Walls

What have you done to minimize the possibility of damage to exterior walls and to fixtures and signs attached to exterior walls?

	YES	NO
Large expanses of easily marred wall space are composed of small sections easily replaced.	[ ]	[ ]
Wall surface materials in vulnerable areas are inexpensively and easily repaired.	[ ]	[ ]
Paint on walls is the same color as the material underneath.	[ ]	[ ]
Epoxy paint, glazed tile, or another highly durable easily cleaned material is used as high as kids can reach in high-damage areas.	[ ]	[ ]
Quick drying paint is used in high-damage areas.	[ ]	[ ]
Signs and other decorative wall hardware are out of reach from the ground.	[ ]	[ ]

GRAFFITI

What have you done to plan for expressive and decorative graffiti and to minimize the negative consequence of such forms of self-expression?

	YES	NO
There are some walls for possible graffiti which are lighter than other walls and have blocked out sections in watering holes, hang-out areas, and entry ways.	[ ]	[ ]
There are some formally labeled "graffiti boards" in high-use public areas.	[ ]	[ ]
There are some consciously designed informal graffiti walls which have easily and inexpensively cleaned or painted surfaces.	[ ]	[ ]
Walls on which graffiti is to be discouraged have inexpensively and easily cleaned or painted surfaces.	[ ]	[ ]
Informal and formal graffiti walls have surfaces on which sections can be selectively cleaned.	[ ]	[ ]

FIXTURES

What have you done to accommodate the rough use given to fixtures and hardware reachable from the ground — both on walls and scattered around the site like lamp-posts, bike racks, and guard rails?

	YES	NO
There are no fixtures on otherwise blank walls.	[ ]	[ ]
Highly visible fixtures on otherwise blank walls are covered by extra heavy grills.	[ ]	[ ]
Highly visible fixtures on otherwise blank walls are recessed.	[ ]	[ ]
All fixtures are out of reach of kids on each others' shoulders or holding sticks.	[ ]	[ ]
All fixtures are higher than ground level where they can be kicked or stood on.	[ ]	[ ]
There are no unnecessary fixtures on building exterior.	[ ]	[ ]
All fixtures are recessed.	[ ]	[ ]
All fixtures are covered with heavy duty protective plate.	[ ]	[ ]
There are no vulnerable rainwater pipes below 6 ft. from the ground.	[ ]	[ ]
There are no lighting fixtures with plastic covers.	[ ]	[ ]
Lighting fixtures are covered with armor-place glass.	[ ]	[ ]
Site fixtures are able to be climbed on and used as targets.	[ ]	[ ]
Site fixtures do not challenge students to damage them.	[ ]	[ ]

PLAYGROUND EQUIPMENT

What have you done to be sure that playground equipment can withstand the especially rough treatment it receives?

	YES	NO
Playground equipment needs special tools to be disassembled.	[ ]	[ ]
Official play equipment can accommodate extra rough play by groups sometimes older than those for whom equipment is officially specified.	[ ]	[ ]

GAME GRAPHICS

What have you done to predict, avoid, or accommodate legitimate graffiti: the lines students paint on walls to be able to play informal pick-up games?

	YES	NO
Some walls in pick-up play areas such as parking lots, formal playgrounds, and entryways have been planned to accommodate "legitimate" graffiti in the form of game lines.	[ ]	[ ]
Local teenagers and children have been consulted to determine needed pick-up game lines.	[ ]	[ ]
Game lines for local pick-up play games, like street hockey and stick-ball, have been painted on walls.	[ ]	[ ]
Stencils have been prepared so that local street groups can apply their own pick-up game lines to walls where they are appropriate.	[ ]	[ ]

PLANTING

What have you done to minimize damage to shrubs, bushes, and trees?

_____

	YES	NO
Near active areas, all planting is flexible, resilient, and pliable.	[ ]	[ ]
There is no thorny planting to collect litter and prevent cleaning.	[ ]	[ ]
There is no thick planting which will be difficult to clean around.	[ ]	[ ]
There is no climbable planting near edge of buildings.	[ ]	[ ]
There is no planting in predictable pick-up play and hang-out areas, nor in watering holes.	[ ]	[ ]

INTERIOR DESIGN CHECKLIST

What have you done to be sure that students have places to meet in public, and to be sure that damage will be minimized in informal active hang-out areas?

	YES	NO		YES	NO
Hang-out areas are consciously identified and prepared for heavy use.	[ ]	[ ]	Fixtures and ledges in hang-out areas which might be sat upon by groups of students are durable enough for this use.	[ ]	[ ]
There are no wall fixtures and adjustments located in hang-out areas.	[ ]	[ ]	Fixtures and hardware on hang-out area walls and ceilings which might be hung upon or climbed upon have reinforced attachments.	[ ]	[ ]
There are some wall fixtures in hang-out areas, but these are out of reach of two teenagers, one on the other's shoulders or one with a stick.	[ ]	[ ]	Both formal and informal sitting places in hang-out areas are far from breakable windows and equipment.	[ ]	[ ]
Fixtures within reach in hang-out areas are extra durable.	[ ]	[ ]	There are some walls in hang-out areas which are lighter and more evenly scored than other walls, and which can be predicted to attract graffiti.	[ ]	[ ]
There are convenient and durable trash containers in hang-out areas.	[ ]	[ ]			
There are consciously planned places to sit in hang-out areas.	[ ]	[ ]	There is a formally identified graffiti board in hang-out areas.	[ ]	[ ]

What have you done to minimize potential damage to
lavatory fixtures, walls, and ceilings?

	YES	NO
There are no exposed plumbing pipes.	[ ]	[ ]
There are no exposed bathroom accessories.	[ ]	[ ]
Bathroom fixtures can be easily and inexpensively repaired if damaged.	[ ]	[ ]
Air vents are located so they cannot easily be used as ashtrays.	[ ]	[ ]
Wastepaper baskets are of a type which will not be permanently damaged if used as ashtrays.	[ ]	[ ]
Walls, up to the ceiling, are covered with heavy duty material.	[ ]	[ ]
Floors in lavatories are extra durable.	[ ]	[ ]
Ceilings in lavatories are solid.	[ ]	[ ]

	YES	NO
Ceiling elements in lavatories are specially specified to withstand poking with a stick.	[ ]	[ ]
Vertical elements holding up toilet partitions are attached to structural members in floor and ceiling.	[ ]	[ ]
Toilet partitions have tamper-proof screws.	[ ]	[ ]
Toilet partitions can be easily painted without looking shoddy.	[ ]	[ ]
There is some formally identified place in lavatories on which students can legitimately write — wood plank, painted wall, chalkboard.	[ ]	[ ]
There are consciously designed private social places for students, other than the lavatory.	[ ]	[ ]
There are durable benches in alternative social places for students.	[ ]	[ ]

GATHERING: Watering Holes

What have you done to accommodate behavior in and minimize damage to watering holes — somewhat out-of-the-way places where students gather for more private discussions?

	YES	NO		YES	NO
There are some consciously planned watering holes in the school, and these are durable enough to take rough use.	[ ]	[ ]	Equipment in watering holes likely to be used as a bench is reinforced and made extra durable.	[ ]	[ ]
Walls in watering holes are painted with epoxy paint.	[ ]	[ ]	There are no glass and no windows in potential watering holes.	[ ]	[ ]
Walls in watering holes are covered with glazed tile.	[ ]	[ ]	There is no glass in watering holes which is lower than three feet from the floor.	[ ]	[ ]
Some walls in watering holes are lighter than other walls and have blocked out surfaces in order to attract and thereby channel graffiti.	[ ]	[ ]	There are trash containers in potential watering holes.	[ ]	[ ]
There are no fixtures or hardware in watering holes.	[ ]	[ ]	There are alternative legitimate lounges for students to use as an alternative to watering holes.	[ ]	[ ]
Fixtures and hardware in watering holes are out of reach of students.	[ ]	[ ]	Legitimate student lounges are not visible from offices or classrooms and are accessible without having to pass through such places.	[ ]	[ ]
Fixtures within reach of students in watering holes are extra durable.	[ ]	[ ]	There are legitimate ways for students to personalize watering holes, for example, on graffiti-receptive wood or painted walls.	[ ]	[ ]

GATHERING: Niches

What have you done to minimize the probability of damage in niches: small hidden doorways and corners?

_____

	YES	NO
There are no niches around doorways, under stairways, or other places within the school.	[ ]	[ ]
Where there are niches within the school, these are necessary for reasons of safety.	[ ]	[ ]
There are no fixtures, windows, or door glass in necessary niches.	[ ]	[ ]
Walls in necessary niches are tiled or painted with epoxy paint.	[ ]	[ ]
Ceilings in necessary niches are solid.	[ ]	[ ]

GATHERING: Cafeteria

What have you done to maximize the probability that cafeterias will be able to be kept clean, and that furniture there will be maintained?

_____

	YES	NO
There are trash receptacles at the ends of each row of tables in the cafeteria.	[ ]	[ ]
Cafeteria furniture cannot be disassembled with conventional hand tools.	[ ]	[ ]

ASSEMBLY: Auditorium

What have you done to minimize damage to seats, walls, stage, and equipment during informal and formal use of auditoriums?

	YES	NO
Design of auditorium takes into account special informal uses as well as standard activities.	[ ]	[ ]
Auditorium seating is comfortable but does not offer materials to play with like string, buttons, knobs, or leather.	[ ]	[ ]
Auditorium seating is assembled with tamper-proof screws or sunken bolts.	[ ]	[ ]
Walls as high as can be reached in auditorium are painted with epoxy paint or tiled.	[ ]	[ ]
Fixtures around the stage, especially at foot level or along the stage skirt are especially durable.	[ ]	[ ]
All control boxes are covered with heavy duty lockable grilles.	[ ]	[ ]
Fixtures in auditorium are located out of reach of kids standing on seats or armrests.	[ ]	[ ]

ASSEMBLY: Gymnasium

What have you done to be sure that wall hardware and floors in gymnasiums will be damaged as little as possible?

	YES	NO
There are large uncluttered walls in the gymnasium for impromptu ball playing.	[ ]	[ ]
There are no wall fixtures within reach of people sitting on the bleachers.	[ ]	[ ]
Wall fixtures in the gymnasium are located in corners or on side walls out of the way of stray balls.	[ ]	[ ]
There are no clocks behind the basketball backboard.	[ ]	[ ]
Equipment storage lockers are visible to permanent staff offices.	[ ]	[ ]
Gymnasium floor surface can stand up to non-sport uses involving contact with tables, chairs, and walking shoes.	[ ]	[ ]
If gym floors requiring special maintenance are installed, commitments have been secured for ongoing maintenance training programs.	[ ]	[ ]

ASSEMBLY: Shop

What have you done to minimize potential damage to shop equipment?

_____

	YES	NO
There is a central locked storage area large enough for all hand tools.	[ ]	[ ]

WALLS

What have you done to be sure that walls can be easily repaired and cleaned, minimizing the possible "epidemic" effect of wall damage?

_____

	YES	NO
Large expanses of walls are made of small wall sections which can be individually repaired or replaced inexpensively.	[ ]	[ ]
Paint on walls is of a similar color to the substrate of the wall material itself.	[ ]	[ ]
In damage-prone areas, walls are made of harder materials.	[ ]	[ ]
Walls in highly traveled areas are covered with epoxy paint or glazed tile.	[ ]	[ ]
Paint used is quick drying.	[ ]	[ ]

WALLS: Graffiti Walls

What have you done to accommodate students' need to personalize their surroundings and to have some public recognition of what is theirs in a school — thus avoiding some random self-expressive graffiti?

	YES	NO
Walls on which graffiti is to be channeled are lighter colored than other nearby walls and have regular lines or squares as patterns to minimize chaotic appearance.	[ ]	[ ]
Walls on which graffiti is to be discouraged are easily painted or washed.	[ ]	[ ]
There are some strategically placed formal graffiti boards for students to write on.	[ ]	[ ]
Walls in areas prone to graffiti are painted with epoxy paint or are tiled from floor to ceiling.	[ ]	[ ]

CEILINGS

What have you done to minimize damage to ceilings, especially active passageways, informal gathering places, and lavatories?

	YES	NO
There are hard surfaced ceilings in lavatories, watering holes, and hang-out areas.	[ ]	[ ]
There are no drop-in ceilings in lavatories, watering holes, or hang-out areas.	[ ]	[ ]
When drop-in ceilings are used, these are firmly attached, heavy ceiling tiles that give way only slightly under pressure.	[ ]	[ ]
Ceilings are painted with epoxy paint.	[ ]	[ ]
Paint on ceilings is the same color as the subsurface.	[ ]	[ ]
Paint on ceilings is quick-drying.	[ ]	[ ]

FLOORS

What have you done to minimize damage to floors in wet, dirty, and particularly rough places?

_____

	YES	NO
Carpeting is installed in small squares or other easily replaced units.	[ ]	[ ]
All floor material can be repaired easily and quickly if damage occurs.	[ ]	[ ]
There are hard surface floors where rough or dirty activity will be taking place.	[ ]	[ ]
In quiet areas, there are soft surface floors.	[ ]	[ ]
There are no carpets in arts and crafts areas, in snack areas, or near sinks or easels in classrooms.	[ ]	[ ]
Carpets specified for noise reduction in work areas are attached to walls instead of floors, or acoustical tile is used.	[ ]	[ ]

DOORS

What have you done to minimize the probability of damage to doors and to door hardware, and to maximize ease of maintenance to these items?

_____

	YES	NO
Door knobs and door closures are specified to withstand especially rough use.	[ ]	[ ]
Door closures cannot be disassembled with ordinary hand tools.	[ ]	[ ]
Built-in door hardware can be easily repaired if damaged.	[ ]	[ ]

GLASS

What have you done to minimize damage to glass on interior walls and doors, and to windows in informal gathering places?

	YES	NO
There is no glass in the lower half of doors.	[ ]	[ ]
There is no glass below three feet from the floor in passageways and other highly used areas.	[ ]	[ ]
There is no acrylic or plastic used as glass substitutes in heavily used areas.	[ ]	[ ]
Extra thick tempered glass or metal panels are specified in heavily used areas where thin glass is inappropriate.	[ ]	[ ]
Windows adjacent to interior watering holes or hang-out areas on upper floors, as well as on the ground, are especially durable.	[ ]	[ ]
There is extra thick tempered glass or double layer glass where acrylic or plexiglass is not advisable.	[ ]	[ ]
There are no windows at all in student stores.	[ ]	[ ]
There are no windows at all in administration storage offices.	[ ]	[ ]
There are no windows at all in industrial arts storage areas.	[ ]	[ ]
There are thin wire mesh screens over specially vulnerable ground floor windows.	[ ]	[ ]

FIXTURES ACCESSIBLE TO PLAY

What have you done to accommodate predictable sitting, climbing, and rough use of attached wall fixtures?

	YES	NO
All fixtures or equipment which protrude from walls are extra heavy duty.	[ ]	[ ]
There are no hardware or fixtures which can be climbed upon or played with in informal gathering or formal play areas.	[ ]	[ ]
All equipment has tamper-proof screws.	[ ]	[ ]
Light fixtures are located out of reach of kids on each other's shoulders or carrying sticks.	[ ]	[ ]
Light fixtures are recessed.	[ ]	[ ]
Thermostats are located out of reach of passing students.	[ ]	[ ]
Thermostats are recessed.	[ ]	[ ]
Air conditioners are placed out of view on an inaccessible part of the roof.	[ ]	[ ]
Fixtures and hardware do not make loud sounds when hit, touched, or damaged.	[ ]	[ ]
When damaged, fixtures and hardware do not remain in one piece providing students with a trophy.	[ ]	[ ]

ALARMS

What have you done with fire and theft alarms to minimize the chance of false alarms; to maximize effectiveness of alarms; and to maximize safety and security?

	YES	NO
Theft alarms have been installed in the following places:		
administrative offices	[ ]	[ ]
administration records area	[ ]	[ ]
cafeteria	[ ]	[ ]
kitchen pantry	[ ]	[ ]
teachers' lounge	[ ]	[ ]
audio visual equipment room	[ ]	[ ]
data processing equipment room	[ ]	[ ]
P.A. system control room	[ ]	[ ]
auto mechanics center	[ ]	[ ]
industrial arts center	[ ]	[ ]
library	[ ]	[ ]
band room	[ ]	[ ]
supply storage areas	[ ]	[ ]
student store	[ ]	[ ]
student store	[ ]	[ ]
portable classrooms	[ ]	[ ]
All fire alarm boxes are placed where they can be seen by adults at their daily work place.	[ ]	[ ]
Fire alarm boxes are placed in classrooms or offices.	[ ]	[ ]
Fire alarms require several small steps to be set off, not just one brief procedure.	[ ]	[ ]
Fire alarm boxes are connected to the central fire station, but there is a short time delay between sounding in the school and sounding in the station.	[ ]	[ ]

ZONING: Community Use

What have you done to be sure that community programs can be run effectively and with least probability of conflict with the rest of the school?

	YES	NO
The school is zoned for different evening and weekend community uses as well as for alternative daytime school uses.	[ ]	[ ]
Different zones are separated by gates strategically placed at corridor entrances.	[ ]	[ ]
Zones, when separated, have separate entries from the outside.	[ ]	[ ]
Offices of school and community supervisory personnel are located near multiple-use entries to school building.	[ ]	[ ]
Some supervisory offices are located near entry to recreational facilities.	[ ]	[ ]
There are places for people to gather comfortably near entrances and exits, where groups can serve as potential "people locks."	[ ]	[ ]

CHAPTER 6

Annotated Literature Search on Vandalism

Literature on Vandalism: An Overview

Experts on vandalism differ radically as to the causes and meaning of destructive acts, what to do to persons who destroy property, and how to prevent destructive acts from occurring. There is, in fact, basic disagreement about how to define vandalism. In this overview of literature on vandalism we will try to clarify some of the apparent confusion resulting from these differences of opinion.

Acts of Property Damage

People who deal with vandalism on a day to day basis seem to define "vandalism" very narrowly. This leads to a distorted picture of the problem. For example, many public school districts list as results of vandalism only property damage for which a claim is made to an insurance company or for which a special order is processed. This list actually represents only a small percent of the true cost of property damage; it does not include damaged items of far greater cost such as doors, locks, paint, roofs, grounds and equipment which are often repaired by school custodians. Thus, items such as glass breakage, breaking and entering, and equipment damage are often discussed as the major instances of vandalism, while they frequently do not constitute the largest proportion of vandalism losses. To illustrate this, Bradley (1967) breaks down losses for 232 California school districts from various types of damage into the following six categories:

	% of Total Loss	Budget Cost/Pupil
1. **Operations** 80% of this loss involved lavatory mischief, graffiti and other interior and exterior markings on doors and walls, furniture defacement, grounds littering.	36%	$2.66
2. **Textbooks** 90% due to careless use, misuse and defacement.	21%	$1.64
3. **Maintenance** 70% due to theft, breaking and entering, equipment damage, exterior defacement, glass breakage.	19%	$1.21
4. **Instructional Supplies** 80% due to deliberate or careless waste, misuse or pilfering.	14%	$1.04
5. **Library and Supplemental Books**	7%	$ .69
6. **Miscellaneous**	3%	$.065

Dr. Harvey Schribner, former Chancellor of the New York City schools, corroborated the fact that malicious damage may not be the greatest property damage cost by reporting that although the recorded vandalism cost for New York in 1970 was just over $2 million, the real cost could probably be estimated at more than $5 million, if one included such difficult to account for items as wall and desk defacement and breakage of furniture and fixtures (New York Times, 1971).

This definitional problem is further complicated by the fact that it is difficult to judge if an act of destruction was actually the result of vandalism or of some other cause (e.g. over-use or misuse). In fact, several school districts have estimated that about 50% of the repair cost for instructional equipment is due to misuse, not vandalism (Wells, 1971).

The importance of clearly defining and measuring property damage is evident when one considers the effect the definition of vandalism has on preventive techniques. Preventive responses have most often been aimed at easily quantifiable items encompassed in the usual narrow definition. This means that major areas of damage are more or less passed over. Also, an apparent decrease in the costs of normally defined vandalism in a school (perhaps brought on by some preventive efforts) does not necessarily mean a real decrease in the cost of property damage.

Other forms of unaccounted for damage might, in fact, have been increasing, thereby counteracting the reported savings. For this reason, several people have argued against treating vandalism, in terms of symptoms, and for treating it diagnostically — delving into the nature and causes of the destructive act (Greenbert, 1969). A diagnostic approach is also recommended by authors who generally agree that one preventive method cannot be expected to have the same degree of success in a variety of situations and settings. Therefore, it is argued that diagnostic study is necessary to determine the appropriate deterrent or preventive technique to be used for each given situation.

Causes of Vandalism

Although often considered one manifestation of juvenile delinquency, "the cost to the American public for vandalism is greater than for any other form of juvenile property offense" (Wade, 1967). For this reason, much speculation has been made about the reasons for this costly form of behavior. Some authors have merely developed labels for individuals who commit these acts (e.g. "vindictive," "bored," "frustrated," "angry"), while others have gone beyond this to discuss (1) *how* an individual gets this label and (2) *why* he/she commits acts of property damage:

(1) **How:** The most interesting view of how someone gets labeled a vandal is one held by Stanley Cohen (1968) who argues that all deviant behavior (including vandalism) is relative and that it is often a political decision as to who is labeled "deviant" (i.e. someone with power acts to label someone else as deviant). To label someone a "vandal" is to conjure up images of "barbarous, reckless, ruthless" conduct, while this is sometimes not the case (as in ideological vandalism). Moreover, to describe property destruction as merely "reckless, ignorant vandalism" is a political judgement because it denies any rational motives behind the behavior, thus justifying certain punitive measures: "Conventional vandalism is not as meaningless or wanton as these labels imply. The acts both make sense to the actor . . . and possess a distinguishable pattern (e.g. the property damaged has certain physical and social characteristics)." The usual terms used to describe vandalism obscure what may be real explanations for it. "The only problems that these labels solve are the teachers' problems in trying to preserve the image that they are blameless."

(2) **Why:** In the literature, there are primarily two approaches taken in answering the question "Why does a person vandalize?": one deals with problems within the individual (psychological factors such as "the urge to destroy," or mental disturbances); the other deals with problems of society and how these affect the individual. The first approach is not of particular interest to us here for while it may account for the behavior of a small percentage of vandals, it does little more than this — short of recommending psychotherapy. The societal approach, on the other hand, is divided into two ways of looking at the problem. These are: (a) the general problems of society on the whole and (b) more finite problems of specific societal institutions.

(a) **Society in General:** Several writers have accounted for vandalism as a reaction to the "general ills" of our society (e.g. as a protest by adolescents against their ill-defined role in our social structure or as a response to the violence which surrounds us daily). Philip Zimbardo's study of aggression and vandalism among middle class white citizens based on laboratory and field work is an example of this. Zimbardo holds that destructive behavior is brought on by the "deindividuation" of people, caused by the "dissolution of many of the old restraints which normally control and expression of our drives, impulses and emotions. Factors such as the size of our cities, the widespread renting of apartments rather than owning one's home, and the immense mobility of Americans are cited as elements which seen to lead to a "weakening of controls" (Burnham, 1969).

While this type of approach can lead to greater understanding of the problem, its acceptance as a basis for social action among those trying to do something to alleviate the problem of vandalism can only lead to an increase in frustration.

(b) **Specific Institutions:** Although a 1960 *Nation's Schools* survey found that a large majority of school administrators blame parents for juvenile acts of vandalism, a substantial number of articles and reports have placed the blame on schools themselves.

Several have viewed the act as a type of communication:

"The most serious aspect of vandalism is the set of messages it conveys: that students see school as alien territory, hostile to their ambitions and hopes; that the student feels no pride in his school."

(HEW Report: *Urban School Crisis,* quoted in Sullivan, 1972)

Similarly, Bower (1954) argues that children finding no satisfaction in school, come to perceive the school as a punishing, hostile place and its objects (desks, chairs, teachers, windows, books) as objects of hatred.

The problem of why students come to view schools in a hostile way has been approached from the standpoint of the school's relationship to those outside of the institution and its relationship to those within. In the first case, it is felt that both the public and students have been alienated from schools because schools have become "overly professionalized," with the administration and faculty becoming merely another large bureaucracy (Sullivan, 1972).

Within the school itself, Nathan Goldman (1961) in a study comparing the interpersonal relationships of administration/faculty/students/parents in high- and low-damage schools, found that low-damage schools teacher-teacher and teacher-principal interactions were less formal and that the principal often had an "open-door" policy. In high-damage schools, teachers focused on faults in the administration and in the building itself as causes of vandalism. On the other hand, low-damage school teachers emphasized the role of the entire staff and student factors of age and interest as important in preventing vandalism. Moreover, "teachers in high damage schools identified damage as mainly occurring in classroom areas, while teachers in [low damage] schools seemed to have an acquaintance with student conduct in all areas of the building and outside the building" (p. 106). On the community level, parents in low-damage schools expressed more favorable attitudes toward the school than did those from high-damage ones. Finally, Goldman found that vandalism occurred when communication channels with the principal were poor, when he/she did not define policy clearly and when policy-making decisions were unilateral. Goldman concludes that: "Insecurity and dissatisfaction in a school are conducive to violation by children of some conduct norms applicable to property and education." Of course the correlation between vandalism and school attributes does not necessarily mean a causal relationship between the two.

Finally, several writers fault the physical facility of schools for creating atmospheres that result in build-ups in levels of tension and frustration which often seem to have outlets in destruction and school disruption. For example, Wells (1971) cites a finding of the Syracuse University report on *Disruption In Urban Public Secondary Schools* that "obsolete, overcrowded, repressive, noisy facilities, particularly in large urban schools, with attendant noise and fatigue provide 'a ripe climate for disruption'."

Preventive Measures

Reports, studies and articles dealing with vandalism prevention and reduction techniques chiefly emphasize only 20% of the problem (i.e. those problems involving breaking and entering, equipment damage, exterior defacement, glass breakage, etc. (see earlier table). This, in turn, seems to be where most money allocated for solving the problem is going. This is not surprising because monetary losses in this area are generally the most obvious and easiest to measure, and acts like breaking and entering, theft, equipment dam-

age and glass breakage are the most dramatic and publicly visible. Moreover, given this usual way of perceiving the nature and scope of the problem, it is also not surprising that people with the responsibility for vandalism prevention are often referred to as "Security Officers," and that techniques most often applied are of a police nature. A study of a large number of reports on prevention reveals that only 38%* discuss methods other than using ideas like bigger and better electronic alarm systems, patrol guards, dogs, tamperproof locks, window grills, or I.D. cards.

Some of the "softer" methods suggested for dealing with these same "security problems" were:

a. Techniques dealing with school **policy:**

1. Teachers carry their own keys (to prevent keys from being taken easily from a central location) and must pay to have the lock replaced if they lose them.

2. Neighbors are asked to report any suspicious actions occurring near schools. (In some cities, however, this technique has been countered by public apathy.)

3. Flyers are sent to residents within a one-mile radius of schools informing them of how the cost of vandalism affects them and asking for their help in preventing it.

4. Custodians are rescheduled to provide round-the-clock service. Sometimes this involves having the custodian live on the school premises. This would involve design as well as policy.

_____
*Given the nature of our own study, we felt that while it was necessary to familiarize ourselves with all of these techniques, it was not necessary to become experts on, say, alarm systems as well. We have not reviewed all articles that were obviously of this nature. The 38%, therefore, probably overestimates the proportion of articles dealing with "softer" techniques.

5. Deterrent signs are placed in schools (e.g. "This School Contains No Money") in combination with policies that back up these signs. Moreover, when signs are used, they are placed in areas where they are *relevant* (where the destruction occurs) and will be *noticed* (i.e. it does no good to place all signs "en masse" in one location where they frequently will not be read).

b. Techniques suggested for dealing with school *design:*

1. A great emphasis on window specification, with opinion ranging from the exclusive use of polycarbonate glazing (e.g. lexan), to the use of no windows or a few small windows, to a compromise of no exterior windows with interior windowed courtyard spaces.

2. Providing clear visibility of all areas; this would necessitate the avoidance of solid walls or solid gates around the school area. In addition, several writers recommend that schools be floodlit at night (*American School & University,* 1971), and that administrative offices and cafeterias be placed in the front of buildings where they can be seen from the street (Colmey & Valentine, 1961).

3. Avoiding areas which are not supervisable in either a formal administrative sense or visually and/or audibly in a more informal way.

4. Avoiding "add-on installations," e.g. air conditioners, light fixtures, bells and sirens.

5. Several writers have stressed the use of cheap finishes on walls which are easy to restore if damaged (e.g. paint).

6. Consulting in the design and construction phases with (a) the police as to the types of hazards prevalent in the area and (b) the school custodian for the "hazards" prevalent in a school.

Target Hardening

Some of these administrative and design suggestions are considered by a variety of authors as "target hardening" approaches — those which systematically toughen a school to withstand the onslaught of abuse and destructiveness and make it as impenetrable as possible. While some of these approaches might be useful several reports express concern that the impact of such measures might be more negative than constructive:

"The system's response to the message left by the vandals only serves to cause further frustration among students which is expressed by more serious forms of violence." [They accomplish this] "by doing those things which will further reduce pupil, parent, and teacher morale" [e.g. installing electronic alarms, employing armed guards, dogs, police, etc.] "and further destroy any feelings of mutual respect and openness so essential to good learning."

HEW Report: *Urban School Crisis* (cited in Sullivan, 1972)

Authors point out three major faults with target hardening approaches:

1. Several don't really work in preventing vandalism and, at times, cost more than the crimes they attempt to deter. For example, Cohen (1968) criticizes alarms for being themselves often a challenge or a target for vandalistic acts, attracting the opposite kind of attention than had been intended. Greenberg (1969), in his survey of school districts, found that the success rate for curbing vandalism in schools with alarms and/or security patrols was poor. In addition, he found that the false alarm rate was so high for these devices, that it became impractical to answer every warning (e.g. he found that for small businesses on a typical week in Los Angeles, the police reported from 91-100% of all alarms as false, with a 95% average for all companies).

2. The police-type approach which treats vandalism as a crime and the vandal as a criminal is criticized in a major study which concluded that:

"The fact that the vandals [all well-dressed, clean cut, white] did not feel they were committing a crime raises an important question about theories of deterring crime in a big city through the presence of large numbers of people, improved night lighting and aggressive police patrols."

Zimbardo Study on Vandalism (quoted in Burnham, 1969)

What good do crime deterrent tactics do if the offender does not consider himself a criminal?

3. Some reports criticize target hardening methods for being "Band-aid treatments"; that is, dealing symptomatically with a small part of the problem, thereby detracting much money and effort from larger aspects. By treating the symptoms of vandalism — not the "disease epidemic" itself — these measures operate on a trial and error basis. Unfortunately, the criticism continues, little can be learned or applied from such an approach because one method often cannot be used with the same degree of success in other situations — other schools, other times.

Causal Factors

Several authors have made suggestions for solving the vandalism problem by taking causal factors into account. In these instances, policy and design cannot be treated separately: design must closely follow policy in order for both to be successful. Therefore, reports suggesting policy action indicate that the designer should consider physical alternatives for implementing these policies. Such suggestions include:

(1) **Meeting students' needs:** In response to the charge that schools are not meeting the needs of students particularly on the high school level, two remedies have been offered. Both aim at the problem of promoting a greater sense of identity and achievement in students.

a. Critics of the traditional 4-year high school which offers only a limited variety of programs and schedules and often keeps students attending for the sole purpose of getting a diploma, have suggested the establishment of *alternative schools* which offer a more varied curriculum and more flexible time schedule. On the issue of diplomas, Bachman suggests that a diploma be given after 10th grade in order to eliminate 12th grade graduation as the sole achievement for high school attendance. He also criticizes negative anti-dropout campaigns which, he fears, unnecessarily injure the self-esteem of the dropout and may unintentionally persuade employers to hire only those with high school diplomas (cited in Sullivan, 1972).

b. One concept rapidly gaining in popularity as a technique for increasing school-student "identity" and for giving the student more individual attention so that his/her needs can be more easily met, is that of the mini-school: i.e. smaller schools which offer the students as many opportunities for "fulfilling" themselves as do larger ones, but increase the probability of this occurring because of their greatly reduced size. Gump strongly recommends that this approach be taken; as Sullivan concludes: "Gump's prescription is for high schools small enough so that individual students feel themselves to be significant." (Sullivan, 1972).

In connection with the mini-school concept, several larger schools are currently functioning on a "house" basis. Here the school is divided programmatically into several smaller groups called "houses" (often with a guidance counselor at the head) so that although in reality the students are all contained in one facility, they actually function in a smaller setting with which it is hoped they can more easily identify.

(2) **Community involvement:** The most direct and frequent technique used to cope with the problem of so-called community alienation has been the *community school.* Although in name many programs are labeled "community schools," in practice approaches differ greatly. Community involvement ranges from merely offering a school's facilities for community use after school hours to involving the community in the design of the school itself and giving them sole use and control of part of it.

In some community programs, residents of a school area are brought into the school in a paraprofessional student advisory capacity, becoming involved in school programs as well.

In Flint, Michigan, where the community school concept was pioneered, the director of the program reports that vandalism is being prevented.

"Teenagers think of the schools as they place they play basketball — their place — and they don't throw rocks at it . . . and most of the visitors are astonished at the good condition of schools that are 30 to 40 years old. There's nothing written on the walls, for example . . . We've found it impossible to wear out a school" (Wells, 1971).

It seems obvious that some community school programs will have been more successful than others in reducing and preventing vandalism. However, to our knowledge, no analysis of which approaches have been successful, which have not, and why, has been done. Before any specific recommendations regarding this approach can be made, such an analysis must be done.

(3) **Good maintenance:** Several writers have observed that deterioration breeds more deterioration; that is, a building that is poorly maintained seems to invite destruction.

"Deterioration in appearance can arise from causes other than vandalism, such as accidental damage, misuse or ordinary wear and tear, or weathering, decay, corrosion and other forms of failure; if these are allowed to develop, conditions favouring vandalism can become established in an estate previously free from it, or re-established in one from which it has been eliminated. Comparatively minor faults or incipient failure can provide temptation even to well-suppressed vandalistic tendencies" (Building Research Station, 1971).

It is not clear whether this relationship works by example (e.g. one unrepaired broken window leading to many window breakings in the same building) or by "tone" (i.e. a poorly maintained school sets a tone of no one caring about its condition, therefore there's no harm in damaging it some more). However, several steps are suggested to alleviate the problem: the first step is obviously to maintain good standards of maintenance — both by design (this might again harken back to consultation with the custodian during design phases) and operation. In the latter case, it has been suggested that the custodian's job might be made easier if a "good" (cooperative) custodial-student relationship is established. Moreover, students themselves can be enlisted in part of the maintenance program.

On the topic of designing for maintenance, however, the British Building Research Station warns that a happy medium must be found between those who emphasize maintenance to the exclusion of appearance and those who emphasize apperance alone. Neither prisons nor glass houses are recommended.

(4) **Avoiding Boredom, Challenge and "Nothing-to-do" Mischief:** The problem of filling up an adolescent's time with meaningful, constructive activities as a way of diverting his/her interest from the more destructive kinds, is a policy issue for the school, the community, the family — really for society in general. Several articles point out that it involves giving adolescents more meaningful roles and status positions in our society.

Few authors have suggested ways of accomplishing this. Some schools do report involving their students in anti-vandalism projects or in maintenance activities, but none delve any more deeply than this into changing the adolescent's status. Such techniques must be tailored to the needs of a specific group of students: programs for constructive activity in rural Michigan might only have limited applicability for students in Roxbury, Massachusetts.

Suggested design responses deal with such things as making school buildings "less satisfying" targets to damage by providing fewer tempting targets (e.g. smooth, light walls which encourage graffiti), and fewer places where a vandal can avoid being caught (e.g. areas invisible from the street). For example, one British study suggests avoiding features which "attract adventure" — like areas hidden from view, flat or low pitched roofs, posts, signs, special lighting fixtures. "Their design should either be kept simple and unattractive for adventure play or they should be strong enough to withstand it" (B.R.S., 1971).

Finally, the Fulton County School District, Atlanta, Georgia, reports trying to remove the challenge from breaking into a school by providing a relatively lockless one. Only three locks are found in the entire school: one for the storage of expensive equipment, another for the cafeteria, and a third for administrative offices (*Nation's Schools,* July, 1965).

Conclusions

This overview illustrates disagreement, opinion differences and divergent approaches among people concerned with vandalism. If any useful information is to be gained from all of this literature, this confusion must be sorted out. Some approaches must have greater likelihood of success than others, but as yet no recommendations can be made with a high degree of certainty. To be able to do this several approaches must first be tested to determine if, how and in what setting they work and when they do not work. After becoming familiar with what has been written one cannot help but agree with Greenberg (1969) who concludes:

"The most effective method for obtaining valid data for sound policy development is by conducting a series of controlled experiments in selected school districts."

Many other reports conclude finally that "more work must be done in this area." To our knowledge, few tests have been carried out. Such conclusions without the necessary followup are no more than cop-outs. They present much information, but can offer few of the tools for its use. As a result, our aim is not merely to add to the bulk of available information, but to add to its usefulness as well.

REFERENCES

Academy for Educational Development. "The Need for Immediate Action," Academy for Educational Development, New York, June 30, 1972. This is an interim report on school security measures emphasizing community involvement in solving the security problem, with emphasis placed on understanding and forewarning of problems rather than on punitive action against perpetrators.

American School and University. "Basic Electronic Security Devices," *American School and University,* July 1970, pp. 25-26. Review of different types of electronic security systems available, costs and manufacturers.

American School and University. "Lowering the Toll of Vandalism," *American School and University,* Vol. 38, August 1966, pp. 26-27. Administrators are attempting to make schools less vulnerable to vandalism through design.

American School and University. "Security Systems for Maximum Protection." *American School and University,* August 1966, Vol. 38, No. 12. Review of various fire detection systems and alarm devices.

American School and University. "Vandals Don't Like the Spotlight," *American School and University,* January 1971, pp. 26-28. A report on the spotlighting of schools in Syracuse, N.Y., where in 1968-69 vandalism cost the school system $100,000.

American School Board Journal. "The Anatomy of a School Vandal and How One District Catches Him," *American School Board Journal,* 159(7), January, 1972, p. 31. Gives a typology of vandals based on motivational factors, and FBI statistics. Describes noise-detection alarm system in use in Washington, D.C.

American School Board Journal. "Protection and Safety," *American School Board Journal,* December, 1964. 38 pages. Several aspects of school safety and protection are presented for school administrators and architects, including vandalism contrough proper design.

Armstrong, Ronald. "Student Involvement," ERIC Clearinghouse on Educational Management, (No. 14) Oregon, 1972. A list of suggestions for school administrators to involve students in educational decision-making as an alternative to school disruption.

Bailey, Stephen K. *Disruption in Urban Public Secondary Schools,* National Association of Secondary School Principals, Washington, D.C., 1970. A study of school disruption, (e.g. boycotts, strikes, property damage, etc.) related to disciplinary rules and racial issues.

Bates, William. "Caste, Class and Vandalism." *Social Problems,* 9(4), Spring 1962, pp. 348-353. Results indicate that vandalism is not something related to the socio-economic status of a census tract.

Beckman, Ron. "The Human Factor in Design . . . More Than Just a Pretty Chair." *American School and University,* April 1971. An interview with the Director of the Research and Design Institute to discuss how to bring human factors into consideration in the design of schools.

Bradley, C.E. "Vandalism and Protective Devices: Studies, Conclusions, Recommendations," *Association of School Business Officials, United States and Canada.* 53, 1967, pp. 236-45. A summary of survey of vandalism problems in 232 school districts in California reveals that many costs of vandalism are often hidden, with losses highest in categories where labor is the largest factor.

Brady, Edward D. "Ten Trends in School Security." *Nation's Schools,* 89(6), June 1972, p. 49. A review of steps which are generally being taken to make schools more secure.

Bried, Raymond. "Design Your Plant to Avoid Maintenance Sore Spots." *Nation's Schools,* Vol. 83(4), April 1969. Suggestions for preventing vandalism to glass areas, lavatories, etc. and maintenance trouble spots.

Building Research Station. "Security," *Building Research Station Digest,* 122, October 1970. A review of recommendations made to reduce crime and increase security on housing estates, schools, shops and building sites.

Caudill, William. "What Works and What Fails in School Design," *Nation's Schools,* 79(3), March 1967, pp. 85-116. An architect discusses 110 design ideas which have been used in school construction over the past thirty years. Each is evaluated to see which worked, which backfired, and why.

Chasnoff, R.E. "Structure of Delinquency," *National Elementary Principal,* 47, November 1967, p. 54. Account of a case of vandalism where the vandals had apparently done damage in an effort to "mock" the teacher.

Dauw, Betty. "The High Cost of Vandalism," *Safety Education,* 44, March 1965, pp. 3-7. A review of the findings of the Boston Study on School Vandalism, done in 1963 by the Department of Safety of the Boston School Committee.

Delacoma, Wynne. "Vandalism — Out of Control?" *Journal of Insurance Information;* Volume XXXI (2), March-April 1970. A report of the increasing problem of school vandalism for insurance companies.

Educational Facilities Laboratory, "Schoolhouse: Open Plan School for the Inner City," *Educational Facilities Laboratory Newsletter,* 2, May 1971. Over 55% of the schools now being built in the United States are open-plan or contain open-plan areas. This article discusses open plan as it applies to the Steuart Hill School in Baltimore.

Educational Research Service. "Protecting Schools Against Vandalism," *E.R.S. Reporter,* August 1968. A review of current practices being used to protect schools against vandalism.

Emory, V. "Vandalism and Protective Devices." Association of School Business Officials, United States and Canada Proceedings, 52, 1966, pp. 233-237. The article gives examples of types of design elements to avoid (large windowed walls, anything that serves as a ladder to the roof, "add-ons" which provide attractive targets), as well as four steps in the prevention of vandalism (alarms, activity in the school, fencing and lighting, instruction about respect for property).

Foreman, Enid Gittens. "Vandalism! Maintaining and Protecting the School Plant," *Catholic Schools,* September 1967, pp. 70-72. A prevention plan must include an analysis of times when destructive acts occur, areas where they occur, patterns of action and needs of the offenders.

Furno, Orlando F. and Lester B. Wallace. "Can You Reduce Your District's Vandalism Costs?" Division of Research and Development, Baltimore City Public Schools, April 26, 1972. From the group that gives us the annual reports on vandalism, comes this short compilation of that information.

Furno, O.F. and L.B. Wallace. "Vandalism! Recovery and Prevention," *American School and University.* July 1972. A report of how several school districts are attempting to cope with the problem of vandalism.

Greenberg, Bernard. *School Vandalism: A National Dilemma. Final Report.* Stanford Research Institute,

Menlo Park, Calif. October 1969. Description of a research program on school vandalism which discusses problems and attempts to identify solutions.

Greenstein, R. "Can We Lessen Vandalism?" *The Instructor,* 79, January 1970, pp. 90-91. Emphasis here is on instructional ways we can reduce vandalism.

Greider, C. "Vandalism Symptomatic of Our Societal Sickness," *Nation's Schools,* 85, April 1970, p. 10. In order to cope with vandalism, one must work on improved student, teacher and parent morale.

Hathaway, J.A., and L.F. Edwards, Jr. "How to (Just About) Vandal-Proof Every School in Your District," *American School Board Journal,* 159(7), January 1972, pp. 27-28. A discussion of immediate steps one can take to vandal-proof a school, as well as a description of various electronic detection devices.

H.E.W. "Urban School Criris: The Problem and Solutions." Proposed by the H.E.W. Urban Education Task Force, January 1970.

Jacob, Stanley. "Let's Do Something About Vandalism," *American County Government,* October 1967. A freelance writer who was prompted to find out more about the problem of vandalism after his own house was damaged finds that often vandals are acting out hostility that they are afraid to display to parents and teachers.

Juillerat, Ernest E., Jr. "Fires and Vandals: How to make them both unwelcome in your school," *American School Board Journal,* 159, January 1972, pp. 23-26. The best ways to prevent fires in schools involve good alarm systems for windows as well as doors, and adequate sprinkler systems.

L'Hote, John D. "Detroit Fights Theft and Arson," *American School and University,* 42(11), July 1970, pp. 19-21. Unrest and disorder during school hours correlates strongly with malicious damage outside of school hours.

Martin, John. *Juvenile Vandalism — A Study of its Nature and Prevention.* Springfield, Illinois. Charles C. Thomas, 1961. A study of characteristics of vandalism and vandal types, distinguishing between predatory, vindictive and wanton vandalism.

Moffitt, F.J. "Vandals' Rocks Can't Reach Flying Schoolhouse," *Nation's Schools,* 74, July 1964, p. 22. A humorous look at the problem, which con-

cludes that the ultimate solution to vandalism is a school airplane which flies over a territory telecasting educational material.

Nation's Schools. "Curbing Vandalism Costs," *Nation's Schools,* 89(6), June 1972, pp. 46-49. Four examples of steps being taken to curb vandalism include: electronic detection system in the library, mailers to residents of area construction site, hidden cameras in school corridors, teacher-responsibility for their own sets of keys.

Nation's Schools. "How Schools Combat Vandalism," *Nation's Schools,* 81, April 1968, pp. 58-67. A review of solutions to vandalism in several schools in America.

National School Public Relations Association. *Violence and Vandalism.* National School Public Relations Association, December 1975, 80 pages. A summary of practices to prevent school damage in use by school systems throughout the nation.

Nielsen, Margaret. "Vandalism in Schools: A $200 Million Problem," *Bulletin:* Bureau of Educational Research and Service, Vol. 15(4), Dec. 1971. A report of "strategies and preventive devices that have been tested by experienced school administrators and found to be effective," including hard-to-damage materials and maintenance.

O'Grince, Sylvester, and Hodgins, Harry S., "Public School Vandalism," *American School and University,* 40, July 1968, pp. 30-32. Review of different types of window protection devices — what works and what doesn't.

Olson, Carl. "Developing School Pride Reducing Vandalism: A Guide for Student Leaders," San Diego City Schools, California, 1970. A guide for beginning an anti-vandalism program in schools for student leaders.

Platzker, Joseph. "How Much Do We Know About Windowless Schools?" *Better Light Better Sight News,* July-August 1966. Report investigating whether states should build schools without windows and what standards would be necessary.

Redmond, James F. "Personnel Security Officer's Manual," Board of Education, Chicago, September 1968. Chicago employs off-duty policemen in its schools as school security officers.

Redmond, James F. "School Security Manual," Board of Education, Chicago, June 1969. A guide to school administrators containing legal proscrip-

tions for school security and procedural information on what to do if security rules are violated.

Reeves, David E. "Protecting Against Fire and Vandalism," *American School and University,* 44(9), May 1972, pp. 62-66. A review of the security system used in Ravenswood City School District, East Palo Alto, California.

Roye, Wendell J. "Law and Order in Classroom and Corridor," *National Center for Research and Information on Equal Educational Opportunity,* Tipsheet #6, November 1971. A plea against the use of police and guards in schools, and an emphasis on the role the teacher can play in the classroom, in promoting an understanding of behavior problems and their solutions.

Severino, Michael. "Who pays — or should pay — when vandals smash things in your school," *American School Board Journal,* 159(12), June 1972, pp. 33-34. Reviews the sides of an issue on parent liability for damage.

Sharp, J.S. "Proper Design Limits Vandalism," *American School Board Journal,* 149, December 1964, pp. 22-23. An architect involved in the "problem of building-damage control" gives some examples of the way his firm approaches the issue, by creating attractive and sturdy environments, as the most effective means of reducing school vandalism.

Slaybaugh, David J., and Koneval, Virginia L. "The High Cost of Vandalism," *School Products News:* Cleveland, Ohio, 1970. Results of a poll of 629 public school districts with enrollments ranging from 6,000 to 25,000+ students.

Slaybaugh, David, and Konevdal, Virginia. "Schools in Crisis: The Cost of Security," *School Products News:* Cleveland, Ohio, 1971. A report from the 1971 survey, which asked those administrators who responded to the 1970 survey what specific preventive measures they were using, what the cost of these is and whether their school districts were urban, suburban or rural.

Sommer, Robert. "People's Art," *AIA Journal,* Dec. 1972. Excerpt from his book, *Design Awareness,* discusses the characteristics of people's art, as distinguished from vandalism, and its useful purpose which should be controlled properly, not prohibited.

Today's Education, "Ways of Fighting Vandalism: Opinions Differ," *Today's Education (National Educa-*

tion Association Journal), 57, December 1968. pp. 28-32. Review of different prevention methods tried across the nation.

Totin, J. "School Vandalism: An Overview," *Association of School Business Officials, in the U.S. and Canada,* 52, 1966, 237-239. None of us can design a vandal-proof school. The best we can do is minimize temptation.

Training Key. "Juvenile Vandalism," *Training Key* (professional Standard Division of the International Association of Chiefs of Police), 117, 1969. Discussion of vandal-personality-types and types of vandalism acts.

Weinmayr, V. Michael. "Vandalism by Design: A Criotique," *Landscape Architecture,* July 1969, p. 286. Ninety percent of vandalism can be prevented through design; the remaining 10% is malicious and unaccountable.

Wells, Elmer. *Vandalism and Violence: Innovative Strategies Reduce Cost to Schools, Education U.S.A.* National School Public Relations Association, 1971. A report of the findings of various surveys, studies and experimental programs to reduce the cost and other effects of vandalism and violence in schools.

Won, George Y., Yamamura, Douglas S., and Ikeda, Kiyoshi. "The Relation of Communication with Parents and Peere to Deviant Behavior of Youths," *Journal of Marriage and the Family,* 31, 1969, pp. 43-47. Research on the effects of parental and peer influence on degrees of conformity to administration norms in educational setting and legal norms in police and court actions.

Young, George P., and Soldatis, Steven. "School Vandalism Can be Stopped," *American School and University,* July 1970, pp. 22-23. Methods of reducing and preventing vandalism.